Dying for Time

Dying for Time

PROUST, WOOLF, NABOKOV

Martin Hägglund

Harvard University Press

Cambridge, Massachusetts

London, England

2012

Library of Congress Cataloging-in-Publication Data

Hägglund, Martin.
Dying for time : Proust, Woolf, Nabokov / Martin Hägglund.
p.   cm.
Includes bibliographical references and index.
ISBN 978-0-674-06632-8 — ISBN 0-674-06632-4
1. Proust, Marcel, 1871–1922. À la recherche du temps perdu.   2. Woolf, Virginia, 1882–1941.
Mrs. Dalloway.   3. Nabokov, Vladimir Vladimirovich, 1899-1977. Ada.
4. Time in literature.   5. Desire in literature.   6. Psychoanalysis and literature. I. Title.
PQ2631.R63A8195 2012
843'.912—dc23   2012011489

For my beloved parents,
Hans-Lennart and Margareta Hägglund

Contents

Dying for Time

Introduction

Of Chronolibido

THE DEBATE BETWEEN philosophy and literature begins over the question of desire. In Plato's *Republic,* Socrates' main charge against Homer is that his poetry leaves us in the grip of the desire for mortal life.[1] The dramatic pathos in the *Iliad* is generated when the heroes cling to what they will lose and cannot accept the death that awaits them. Even the bravest heroes, such as Hector and Achilles, lament the fact that their lives will have been so short. When this pathos is transferred to the audience, it opens a channel that allows the spectators to come into contact with their own grief. "You know," says Socrates, "that even when the very best of us hear Homer imitating one of the heroes who is in grief, and is delivering a long tirade in his lamentations, that we then feel pleasure and abandon ourselves and accompany the representation with sympathy and eagerness."[2] A few lines further on, Socrates specifies that this fascination with tragedy stems from the part of our soul that "in our own misfortunes was forcibly restrained and that has hungered for tears" (606a). To be taken in by poetry is thus to be overtaken by the vulnerability and the desire for mortal life that the philosopher should overcome. Indeed, Socrates argues that the problem with poetry is that "it waters and fosters these feelings when what we ought to do is to dry them up" (606d). The philosopher should not let himself be "disturbed" by the loss of mortal beings; he should rather turn his desire toward the immutable presence of the eternal.

The issue of desire is the deepest motivation for Socrates' demarcation of poetry from philosophy. Poetry engages the desire for a mortal life that can always be lost. In contrast, the task of philosophy is to convert the desire for the mortal into a desire for the immortal that can never be lost. To be sure, Plato's denigration of poetry has been subjected to centuries of critique. Yet defenders of poetry have traditionally not pursued Plato's insight into the link between the affective power of aesthetic representation and the investment in mortal life. Rather, epiphanies of aesthetic experience tend to be explained in terms of an intimation of eternity and we will see how even modernist literature continues to be read in accordance with a desire for immortality. My aim, however, is not to provide an historical account of the persistence of Platonism in aesthetics. Rather, I want to call attention to a Platonic axiom that is still operative in our understanding of desire, namely, that the aim of desire is to repose in a state of being where nothing can be lost. This logic of desire is succinctly formulated by Socrates in the *Symposium*. Socrates argues that temporal objects do not answer to what we really desire. The proper destination of desire is rather an eternity that "neither comes into being nor passes away" and thus transcends temporal finitude.[3]

Two major consequences follow from Socrates' premise. First, desire is understood as the desire for what *is* in itself. Second, everything that is not in itself is understood as the *lack* of fullness. It would be hard to overestimate the influence of this notion of lack. In contemporary literary studies, it comes to the fore in what is arguably the most influential model for reading the problem of desire: the psychoanalytic theory formulated by Jacques Lacan. While Lacan clearly recognizes that there is no fullness of being, he holds that we *desire* to reach such fullness and that our temporal being is a lack of being. For Lacan, the lack of being is not derived from an object we once had and subsequently lost. As he explains in *Seminar II:* "It is not the lack of this or that, but the lack of being whereby being exists."[4] Even though Lacan often describes the absent fullness in terms that may seem to invoke a lost object (such as "the Thing"), it is important to understand that it cannot be equated with any object whatsoever. What is desired under the heading of "the Thing" is a state of absolute fullness to which no object can ever be adequate. The lack of such fullness is for Lacan the *cause* of desire, since it is precisely because desire cannot be fulfilled that there is desire.

If the notion of lack seems persuasive, it is because it apparently adheres to an impeccable logic. As Socrates argues, the movement of desire is predicated on a constitutive difference, since one can only desire to be what one is not. The one who really *is* wise or happy cannot desire to be wise or happy, since there is no reason to desire to be what one already is. The decisive question, then, is how to read the constitutive difference of desire. Traditionally, the constitutive difference of desire has supported the inference that desire testifies to an ontological lack. Because desire cannot be fulfilled—because it cannot repose in itself or in what it desires—it answers to a lack of being in itself. Consequently, to challenge the logic of lack one must provide another account of the constitutive difference of desire. It is such an account that I seek to develop as the notion of *chronolibido.*

The notion of chronolibido traces the constitutive difference of desire to the condition of time. For one moment to be succeeded by another, it cannot *first* be present in itself and *then* cease to be. A self-present, indivisible moment could never give way to another moment, since what is indivisible cannot be altered. The passage of time requires not only that every moment be superseded by another moment, but also that this alteration be at work from the beginning. Every moment must negate itself and pass away *in its very event.* If the moment did not negate itself there would be no time, only a presence forever remaining the same.

The condition of time thus allows one to account for the constitutive difference of desire without interpreting it as an ontological lack. It is indeed true that desire cannot coincide with its object, but not because the object of desire is a timeless being. On the contrary, both the subject *and* the object of desire are from the very beginning temporal. They can thus never be in themselves, but not because they have lost or aspire to reach a being-in-itself. Rather, they can only be themselves by not coinciding with themselves. This constitutive difference is what makes it possible to desire anything in the first place. Without a temporal delay there would be no desire, since there would be no time to reach out toward or aspire to anything whatsoever. Even if I only desire myself, auto-affection presupposes that I do not coincide with myself—otherwise I could never affect or be affected by myself. The point is thus not that the fulfillment of desire is impossible to attain. Rather, what is at stake is to rethink fulfillment as essentially temporal. Even the most ideal fulfillment is necessarily inhabited by non-fulfillment—not because fulfillment is lacking but because the state of fulfillment itself is temporal and thus altered from within. Even at the moment one *is* fulfilled, the moment is ceasing to be and opens the experience to loss.

Returning to the *Symposium,* we can trace the logic of chronolibido in Socrates' own account of desire. The key to such a reading is a logical conundrum to which Socrates calls attention. Why do we desire to be happy even when we are happy, if we cannot desire to be what we already are? The classical answer is that we continue to desire happiness because we *lack* the ideal state of full happiness. The constitutive difference of desire is thus interpreted as the difference between the imperfect and the perfect. The happiness we experience is *actually* imperfect, but we continue to desire happiness because we strive toward its perfection, which is *potential* in us. Remarkably, however, Socrates also provides a quite different explanation of why we desire to be what we already are. This explanation occurs at the beginning of Socrates' dialogue with Agathon. It is inserted to make sure that they are on the right track, but in fact it derails Socrates' entire trajectory:

> If, Socrates continued, the strong were to long for strength, and the swift for swiftness, and the healthy for health—for I suppose it *might* be suggested that in such cases as these people long for the very things they have, or are, already, and so I'm trying to imagine such a case, to make quite sure we are on the right track—people in their position, Agathon, if you stop to think about them, are bound here and now to have those very qualities, whether they want them or not; so why should they trouble to want them? And so, if we heard someone saying, 'I'm healthy, and I want to be healthy; I'm rich, and I want to be rich; and in fact, I want just what I've got,' I think we should be justified in saying, 'But, my dear sir, you've *got* wealth and health and strength already, and what you want is to go on having them, for at the moment you've got them whether you want them or not. Doesn't it

> look as if, when you say you want these things here and now, you really mean, what you've got now, you want to go on keeping?' Don't you think, my dear Agathon, that he'd be bound to agree? (200b–d)

Even though Socrates does not acknowledge it, the logic of his argument is incompatible with a metaphysical logic of lack. The man in Socrates' example is healthy and wants to be healthy, but not because he is lacking a perfect health. Rather, in his very experience of health there is an apprehension that his health will not last; otherwise there would be no need to "keep" it for the future. This temporal sense of keeping or persisting is even more evident in the Greek text. What Michael Joyce translates as the desire to "go on" having or being something is literally the desire to have or to be something "also in the time that follows *[kai eis ton epeita chronon]*."[5] In and through the very experience of being healthy, the man is seized by the desire to go on being healthy, precipitated by the sense that his health may cease to be in the time that follows. This anticipation of loss and the concomitant desire to persist are unthinkable unless the experience of health is always already divided within itself. If the man were simply reposing in perfect health, he would never have the sense that his state of being could be followed by another and that his health may be lost. Indeed, if the man were reposing in perfect health he would not care about his health in the first place. The condition for desiring health, then, is that health is threatened from within itself.

The point to underline here is that Socrates does not say that the man wants to transcend his condition of mortal health. On the contrary, he wants to *go on* being what he is. And since he is mortal, he wants to *live on* as mortal. As we will see, this desire for survival is incompatible with the desire for immortality, since it wants to hold on to a life that is essentially mortal and inherently divided by time. The reason why the movement of survival never reaches the consummation of eternity is not because the latter is unattainable, but because the movement of survival is not oriented toward such consummation in the first place.

Following the logic of survival, we can read the discourse on immortality in the *Symposium* against itself. Socrates presents his argument in favor of immortality by recounting a speech by Diotima of Mantineia. This speech is the canonical source for the conception of desire as a desire for immortality. Yet when Diotima sets out to prove her thesis that all creatures are driven by the "passion for immortality" (208b), she in fact shows that all creatures are driven by the passion for survival:

> Mortal nature *(physis)* does all it can to live forever and to be immortal. It can only do this by reproduction *(génesis);* it always leaves behind another, new generation to replace the old. This point applies even in the period in which each living creature is described as alive and the same—for instance, someone is said to be the same person from childhood till old age. Yet, for all we call him the same, every bit of him is different, and every day he is becoming a new man, while the old man is ceasing to exist, as you can see from his hair, his flesh, his bones, his blood, and all the rest of his body. And not only his body, for the same thing happens to his soul. And neither his manners, nor his disposition, nor his thoughts, nor his desires, nor his pleasures, nor his sufferings, nor his fears are the same throughout his life, for some of them grow, while others disappear. . . . This is how every mortal creature perpetuates itself. It cannot, like the divine, always be the same in every respect; it can only leave behind new life to fill the vacancy that is left behind in its species by obsolescence. Through this device *(mêchanê),* Socrates, the mortal partakes of immortality, both in its body and in all other respects; there is no other way. And so it is no wonder that every creature prizes its own offspring, since the whole creation is inspired by this zeal, this passion for immortality. (207d–208b, trans. mod.)

Diotima here demonstrates that the movement of survival is operative not only in the passage from one generation to another but also in the passage from one moment to another in the life of the same temporal being. A temporal being is constantly ceasing to be and can only perpetuate itself by leaving traces of the past for the future. This tracing of time is the movement of survival that transcends a particular moment of finitude and yet is bound to finitude as a general condition. If something survives it is never present in itself; it is already marked by the destruction of a past that is no longer while remaining for a future that is not yet. Indeed, the "offspring" that allows a temporal being to live on despite its own passing away is no less subjected to temporal finitude than its predecessor, since it has to give way to a successor that may erase the trace of what has come before.

The survival of a mortal being is thus quite different from the immortality of an eternal being. If a mortal being "partakes of immortality" through the movement of survival it is only by temporalizing the notion of immortality. This is why the supposed "passion for immortality" turns out to be a passion for survival. According to Diotima, the desire to have children, to be famous, or to be commemorated, is an expression of the desire for immortality. Yet, following her own description, we find that none of these achievements have immortality as their aim. To live on thanks to one's children or one's reputation is not to be exempt from death; it is to live on through others who themselves are exposed to death. The children that resemble one or the admirers that remember one are themselves mortal and offer no safe haven from oblivion. The desire to live on that is expressed through them is thus not a desire for immortality. Rather, one who desires to have children or to be remembered is seeking to *survive* as a mortal being for oneself and/or for others.

To be sure, Diotima holds that the desire to survive ultimately is driven by the desire to be immortal. According to her own analysis, however, proper immortality would require a state of being that is "always the same in every respect" (208a) and "neither comes into being nor passes away, neither flowers nor fades" (211a). As is clear from this definition, the timeless state of immortality would eliminate the condition of survival. In a state where nothing comes into being or passes away *nothing survives*. Thus, we will see that the desire for survival—which Diotima analyzes in terms of a desire for reproduction *(génesis)* that animates and sustains our temporal being—cannot be driven by the desire for immortality. The desire to perpetuate a temporal being is incompatible with the desire to be immortal, since immortality would not allow anything to live on in time.

One may nevertheless ask why the temporality of survival cannot—at least on the level of the imaginary—be reconciled with immortality. The Greek gods, for example, are said to be immortal but nevertheless live on in time. My claim, however, is that Diotima has good reasons not to align the life of the gods with a proper state of immortality. Even if one removes organic deterioration and death, the temporal finitude of living on is still operative in anyone who is susceptible to a change in his or her disposition, since such change minimally entails that a thought, feeling, or desire comes into being while another passes away. This is exactly what Diotima demonstrates in the speech quoted above. With remarkable precision she defines a "mortal creature" not primarily in terms of organic death but in terms of the temporality of survival, which entails a structural relation to loss even in the persistence of the "same" being across time.[6] Every moment of living on necessarily involves a relation to what does *not* live on, and this negativity already constitutes a minimal relation to death. If one survived wholly intact—unscathed by the alteration of time—one would not be surviving; one would "always be the same in every respect." By the same token one would not be susceptible to any form of change, since nothing could happen to one. Insofar as the gods are subject to change— insofar as they have thoughts, feelings, and desires that respond to what happens—they are therefore "mortal," even if they do not organically cease to be.

Diotima's discourse thus allows us to articulate the distinction between survival and immortality, which is central to the notion of chronolibido. To survive is to live on in a temporal process of alteration, where one is always becoming other than oneself. In contrast, to be immortal is to repose in a state of being that is eternally the same. While Diotima maintains that the latter state is the desired end of the former, her own account allows us to call into question this teleology. The desire to live on through reproduction cannot aim at transcending time, since temporality is intrinsic to the state of being that is desired. What I want to emphasize, then, is not only that the temporal finitude of survival is an inescapable condition but also that the investment in survival animates and inspires all the forms of care that Diotima analyzes. Without the sense of the beloved passing away there would be no desire to reproduce it or to care for its sustenance. Indeed, the notion of chronolibido seeks to elucidate that it is *because* of temporal finitude that one cares about life in the first place. If life were fully present in itself—if it were not haunted by past and future, by what has been and what may be—there would be no reason to care about life, since nothing could happen to it. Even a being free from organic death would have to remain susceptible to loss—

the affective "death" of what he or she wants to keep—in order to care. Inversely, a being exempt from such death could not sense the value of preserving anything at all.

The desire for survival, then, should not be understood exclusively or primarily in terms of a biological drive for self-preservation but includes all "spiritual" commitments to living on in time. It is because one is invested in the survival of temporal life that one seeks to save anything from death, since only temporal life can be threatened by death. Yet the state of immortality cannot answer to the survival that is desired. Rather than allowing a temporal being to live on, it would put an end to the time of life in favor of a state of eternity where nothing comes into being or passes away. Being in a state of eternity would therefore require that one renounce all care and become completely indifferent to the fate of survival. That is why it is consistent to emphasize (as many religious sages do) that detachment is the ultimate condition for attaining the state of eternity. Only by detaching oneself from the care for temporal life can one embrace the timelessness of immortality.

The chronolibidinal argument I will develop is that such an ideal of detachment dissimulates a preceding attachment to temporal life. The latter is the source of both what one desires and what one fears, both the desirable and the undesirable. As an *effect* of this double bind, one can come to embrace the desire for absolute fullness/absolute emptiness. The point, however, is precisely that this desire is an effect and not an originary cause. The desire for absolute fullness/emptiness is not the truth of desire but rather a self-defeating attempt to deny the attachment to temporal life that is the source of all care. Far from being an external refutation, the logic of chronolibido thereby seeks to read the desire for immortality against itself from within.

The key argument here concerns the co-implication of *chronophobia* and *chronophilia*. The fear of time and death does not stem from a metaphysical desire to transcend temporal life. On the contrary, it is generated by the investment in a life that can be lost. It is because one is attached to a temporal being (chronophilia) that one fears losing it (chronophobia). Care in general, I argue, depends on such a double bind. On the one hand, care is necessarily chronophilic, since only something that is subject to the possibility of loss—and hence temporal—can give one a reason to care. On the other hand, care is necessarily chronophobic, since one cannot care about something without fearing what may happen to it.

The philosophical tradition offers two different prescriptions for curing the chronolibidinal condition of care, one deriving from Plato and the other from Epicurus. The Platonic prescription seeks to eliminate chronophilia: to detach one from the care for mortal life in favor of an immortal state of being. Accordingly, Socrates argues that if one desires immortality, one has no reason to fear death, since death will bring about the end of mortal life. As he maintains in Plato's *Phaedo,* if you see a man who is afraid of dying, you can be sure that he is not a philosopher (that is, a lover of wisdom) but a lover of the mortal body.[7] The Platonic diagnosis, then, is that we will overcome the fear of death if we overcome the desire for mortal life and learn to desire immortality in a proper philosophical fashion.

In contrast, the Epicurean diagnosis is that we fear death *because* we desire immortality. Rather than eliminating chronophilia, the Epicurean prescription seeks to eliminate chronophobia: to convince one to accept death as the natural end of mortal life and not entertain vain hopes of living on. Through this operation, Epicurus aims to cure the chronophobic fear of death and stimulate the chronophilic enjoyment of mortal life. As he argues, "the correct recognition that death is nothing to us makes the mortality of life enjoyable, not by adding a limitless time but by removing the longing for immortality. For nothing is fearful in life to the person who is genuinely convinced that there is nothing fearful in not living."[8] If we remove the desire for immortality, we should therefore be able to remove the fear of death and learn to savor "not the longest time but the most pleasant."[9] As we have seen, however, the fear of death does not stem from a desire for immortality but from a desire for survival. If one fears death, it is not because one wants to be immortal but because one wants to live on as a mortal being. Consequently, when Epicurus argues that there is no reason to fear death because *death is nothing to us*—it is not something we can experience because our death excludes our existence— he misconstrues what is at stake in the fear of death. To fear death is not to fear the state of being dead (which indeed will be nothing at all to the living being who is afraid of dying) but to fear the loss of what one wants to keep. The fear of death is thus not limited to the care for one's own life or to the fear of actual physical death. Rather, the fear of death is operative in relation to everything one cares about, including "the most pleasant time" that one is savoring.[10]

For the same reason, being invulnerable to the fear of death (whether by virtue of Platonic immortality or Epicurean *ataraxia*) would amount to being completely indifferent. Both Socrates and Epicurus seek to cure the condition of chronolibido by eliminating the care for survival. What I analyze as the *constitutive* care for survival, however, makes clear that the condition of chronolibido is incurable. Contra Epicurus, chronophilia cannot cure chronophobia but is rather the cause of it. Inversely, contra Socrates, chronophobia cannot be cured by the promise of a deliverance from time. The promise of an eternal state of being cannot even hypothetically appease the chronophobic fear of death or satisfy the chronophilic desire to live on. Rather than redeeming death, the state of immortality would *bring about* death, since it would terminate the time of mortal life.

Accordingly, we can distinguish between the two propositions concerning death and the afterlife that Socrates makes toward the end of the *Apology*. On the one hand, Socrates appeals to the desire for survival by appealing to our desire for mortal life to continue beyond death (e.g., the hope that we will be able to spend time with Homer, Hesiod, and others who have passed away). On the other hand, Socrates appeals to the desire for death itself, which is incompatible with the desire for survival. As he argues, if death is a total annihilation that entails "no consciousness but only a dreamless sleep," then "death must be a marvelous gain."[11] My point here is that Socrates promotes death *for the same reason that he promotes immortality,* namely, that it cancels out the condition of temporality. Indeed, the dreamless sleep of total extinction is claimed to be desirable "because the whole of time *[ho pâs chronos],* if you look at it in this way, can be regarded as no more than one single night" (40e). That immortality is the same as death can thus be discerned in the Platonic text itself. If mortal life were oriented toward immortality, it would be oriented toward its own end, toward destroying the condition of its own survival.[12]

The above argument is not a paradox but follows from the logic of lack, which assumes that we desire to be consummated in a being that *is* completely in itself. Our most profound desire would then be a *desire not to*

desire. The very fact that we desire at all presupposes that we are not reposing in ourselves. If one postulates that we desire to transcend this condition, it can only mean that the goal of desire is to extinguish itself. The
same apparent paradox recurs in Freud and Lacan's writings, where the
drive for absolute fullness turns out to be a death drive. Although Freud
and Lacan recognize that absolute life would be absolute death, they do
not call into question that we desire such an absolute. Rather, they repeat
an assumption that is operative in the entire tradition and that ultimately
postulates that we desire to be dead.

The details of my critical engagement with Freud and Lacan are
worked out in the final chapter of this book, where I offer a systematic
articulation of the logic of chronolibido. Let me here emphasize that, in
challenging the notion of the death drive, I am not postulating a constitutive *drive* or *desire* for survival. The latter move would simply replace one
teleological principle with another, positing "survival" rather than "death"
as the desired end. In contrast, I seek to show—through an immanent
critique of Freud—why the account of libido should begin from the *bond*
to temporal life, which is not preceded by any principle or purpose. As
Freud himself makes clear, there is no libidinal life without the excitation
(Erregung) that is generated by internal and external stimuli, which have
to be "bound" in order for experience to be possible. All forms of experience thus answer to different forms of libidinal bonds, since they qualita-
tively synthesize and "bind" excitation. Even in relation to myself, I cannot
have any experience without binding excitation, and this bond is necessarily a double bind. While the bond makes it possible to negotiate what
happens—to transform internal and external stimuli into experiences that
can be assimilated—it is bound to an existence that may always break the
bond and exceeds what one can comprehend at any given moment. The
necessity of this double bind calls into question the death drive—as well
as any other teleological principle for the libidinal economy—since it precedes any possible purpose for psychic life. For the affective self who
comes into being through the bond, the binding of excitation is therefore
undecidable: it is the source of both pleasure and unpleasure, chance and
threat, love and hate. As an *effect* of this double bind, one can come to
experience the exigencies of survival as unbearable and be driven to terminate survival. The latter effect, however, presupposes an investment in

survival that has no given aim. While the *response* to external or internal stimuli may always be destructive, I cannot have any relation to it at all without binding it, without being bound to it, and thereby minimally invested in it.

I propose, then, to rethink the constitution of the libidinal economy on the basis of an *investment* in survival.[13] It is worth pausing to define this term, since it is of central importance for the entire book. By "investment" I mean "the impossibility of being indifferent to." Thus, what I call the constitutive investment in survival designates the impossibility of being indifferent to survival. Such a constitutive investment, I argue, follows from the necessity of binding. Because one is always already bound (as a condition for experiencing anything at all), one is always already invested. And because the bond is temporal—because it is never given once and for all—one cannot be indifferent to the survival of the bond, whether one seeks to maintain or to terminate it. That is why I argue that the investment in survival is a *necessary but not sufficient condition* for affectivity. If one is not invested in survival (whether one's own or another's), one does not care about what happens. And if one does not care about what happens, one is neither affected nor susceptible to any affective response. The investment in survival is therefore a condition for affectivity in general. Nevertheless, it cannot be aligned with a teleological principle. The investment in survival does not itself have *any* given aim or direction—it does not predispose one to seek preservation rather than destruction—since it is the condition for every positive *and* every negative affective response. Moreover, since life and death are co-implicated in survival, one is always divided against oneself in being bound to it. To be invested in survival is to be invested in life *and* death, which means that even the most active preservation of life or the most positive affective response is invested in its own destruction.

The argument about a constitutive investment thus allows me to locate the fundamental drama of libidinal being *in the very bond to temporal life*. As we will see, the latter move marks the most important difference between chronolibidinal reading and Lacanian psychoanalysis. While Lacan emphasizes that the fullness of timeless being is an illusion, he maintains that we are driven toward and desire such fullness. A striking example can be found in *Seminar XI,* where Lacan asserts that all objects of desire are representatives of an "immortal life" that is lost at birth.[14] One may certainly argue that Lacan does not actually believe that an immortal life has been lost, but only analyzes it as the fundamental fantasy of the subject. On this reading, Lacan grants that the lost immortality is only a retrospective projection—that there never was a state of fullness—but nevertheless insists on our mourning of a Thing we never had. Such a reading, then, holds that the *truth* of desire is the lack of immortality. The fundamental drama of desire is seen as the conflict between the mortal being that we are and the immortal being that we desire to be.

In contrast, chronolibidinal reading derives the drama of desire from the bond to temporal life and the investment in living on. I am not claiming that the temporal finitude of survival is desirable as such but that it is the condition for both the desirable *and* the undesirable. Without the investment in survival there would be no compassion and love (since one would not be committed to anything), but there would also be no resentment and hate (since one would not be threatened by anything). The only way to be truly indifferent to survival is to be dead, which is to say that it is impossible for a living being to be indifferent to survival.

The chapters that follow develop the chronolibidinal notion of living on and its implications for the practice of reading the dramas of desire as they are staged in the works of three canonical modern writers. Marcel Proust, Virginia Woolf, and Vladimir Nabokov transformed the art of the novel to convey the complexities of temporal experience and the desire for mortal life. Nevertheless, their works have persistently been read in accordance with a desire to transcend mortal life—whether through an epiphany of memory, an immanent moment of being, or a transcendent afterlife. Although psychoanalysis provides important resources for criticizing the assumed success of this desire, it still maintains that the ambivalence of desire stems from the lack of immortality. In contrast, chronolibidinal reading seeks to show that the ambivalence of desire stems from the double bind of temporal finitude. Desire is *chronophobic* since whatever we are bound to or aspire for can be lost: it can be taken away from or be rejected by us. Yet, by the same token, desire is *chronophilic,* since it is because we are bound to or aspire for something that can be lost that we care about it, that we care about what happens.

Given my focus on the problem of temporality, the question of the relation to Henri Bergson inevitably arises. Bergson's standing in the study of the modernist novel has followed the same fate as his general philosophical standing. After having been hailed as deeply important for Proust, Woolf, and other modernist writers, his influence was subsequently criticized or dismissed and only recently has he become a significant reference point again, especially due to Gilles Deleuze's influential revival of Bergsonism. By emphasizing the irreducibility of time, the legacy of Bergsonism may seem to have an important affinity with my argument. Yet, as I will seek to demonstrate, Bergson in fact fails to think the problem of time. While he emphasizes that nothing is exempt from temporality, his conception of the true reality of time does not involve negation or negativity. The temporal passes away, but it does not disappear or cease to be. On the contrary, it immediately belongs to the continuous movement of duration *(la durée)*, which preserves all of the past in a virtual coexistence that is not susceptible to loss or destruction. By thus denying negativity, Bergson effectively denies time. The duration of the past is not temporal at all but an eternal substance, since it exists absolutely in itself and does not depend on any spatial, material support in order to remain. In contrast, I argue that *time is nothing in itself;* it is nothing but the negativity that is intrinsic to succession. It follows that time cannot be a virtual coexistence, since it does not have the power to *be* anything or *do* anything on its own. Indeed, time cannot be anything or do anything without a spatialization that constrains the power of the virtual in making it dependent on material conditions.

It is precisely such a co-implication of time and space that I articulate in terms of the structure of "the trace." Derrida defines the trace as the becoming-space of time and the becoming-time of space, which he abbreviates as spacing *(espacement)*. This structure should not itself be understood as a *temporal* process, where time becomes space and space becomes time, but rather designates a *logical* co-implication of time and space. This logical co-implication is already implicit in the basic formulation of the problem of succession, namely, that the moment comes into being *at the same time* as it ceases to be.[15] Given that every temporal moment immediately ceases to be, it must be inscribed as a trace in order to be at all. The trace is necessarily spatial, since spatiality is characterized by the ability to remain in spite of temporal succession. The spatiality of the trace is thus the condition for the duration of time, since it enables the past to be retained for the future. The very concept of duration presupposes that something remains across time and only that which is spatial can remain. The spatiality of the trace, however, is itself temporal. Without temporalization it would be impossible for a trace to remain across time and retain the past for the future. Accordingly, the duration of the trace cannot be exempt from the negativity of time. The trace enables the past to survive, but it can do so only through the exposure to a future that gives it both the chance to remain and to be effaced. The tracing of time that makes it *possible* for life to survive makes it *impossible* for life to be given or protected in itself.[16]

Chapter 1 pursues the temporality of living on through a reassessment of Proust's modernist masterpiece *À la recherche du temps perdu*. The critical attention devoted to Proust's work has few equals in twentieth-century literature. His most influential readers include prominent philosophers (Paul Ricoeur and Gilles Deleuze), groundbreaking literary theorists (Georges Poulet and Gerard Genette), and outstanding contemporary critics (Malcolm Bowie and Leo Bersani). Across all the developments in Proust scholarship, however, the account of his ontological commitments has remained remarkably constant. In different variations, all the major interpretations of Proust maintain that the *Recherche* culminates in the revelation of a timeless being. The trend in recent Proust criticism has thus been to assume that the basic question of Proust's aesthetic and metaphysical vision is settled. Instead, attention has been directed to elements that are seemingly marginal or run counter to the established view of the novel, such as the vicissitudes of sexuality or the impact of technology on literary form.[17] While this strand of Proust criticism has produced excellent work, it has left the traditional interpretation of Proustian metaphysics untouched. In contrast, I recall the discussion of Proust to the fundamental question of temporality to challenge the canonical reading of his aesthetics and his metaphysics. In particular, I seek to demonstrate how the chronolibidinal conception of desire enables a new reading of both the aesthetic that is presented in the last volume of the *Recherche* and the perennial Proustian themes of time, self, and memory.

Chapter 2 takes on two other modernist masterpieces, namely, Woolf's *Mrs. Dalloway* and *To the Lighthouse.* I here pursue a chronolibidinal conception of trauma and mourning to give a new account of the experience of temporality in Woolf's writing. My point of departure is Woolf's "aesthetics of the moment." Woolf is renowned for her ability to depict moments of time in their unique texture. As in the case of Proust, however, her aesthetics has been read as aspiring to a state of being that is exempt from the condition of temporality. The influential accounts of her aesthetics proposed by Ann Banfield, J. Hillis Miller, and Karl Heinz Bohrer, among others, all converge on this point. I challenge their readings by arguing that Woolf's aesthetics of the moment does not reveal a timeless being but rather underlines the radical temporality of life. The moment can only be given *as* a moment by passing away, and it is the passing away of the moment that induces the passion for it. Accordingly, the affective experience of being alive—which Woolf explicitly seeks to call forth through her aesthetic practice—depends for its effect on a chronolibidinal investment. If we are moved by how Woolf records singular moments, it is because we care about the fate of a mortal life that may be lost. The mortality of life is both the reason why anything is precious and why everything can become traumatic. The exposure to trauma is thus not merely a negative determination; it is rather inseparable from the possibility of living on in the first place. A temporal being is by definition vulnerable to trauma, since it is exposed to an unpredictable future. I argue that it is precisely by rendering this temporal condition that Woolf's engagement with the problems of trauma and mourning acquire their depth. If Woolf has an exceptional ability to render the condition of trauma and the complexities of mourning, it is because she conveys how the threat of trauma and the possibility of mourning are inscribed at the core of life and resonate even in the most affirmative experience of happiness.

Chapter 3 analyzes Nabokov's aesthetics of time and memory, particularly as it is staged in his most comprehensive novel, *Ada or Ardor: A Family Chronicle.* The co-implication of time and space that I trace in Proust's notion of involuntary memory and Woolf's aesthetics of the moment is brought to the fore in Nabokov's persistent dramatization of the act of writing. On the one hand, writing is an inscription of memory, a trace of the past that spatializes time. On the other hand, writing is by definition left for the future and thereby marks a movement that temporalizes space. In Nabokov's work, we can see how such writing does not supervene on a given consciousness but is at work in the experience of presence itself. The necessity of writing—of inscribing the present as a memory for the future—follows from the negativity of time. Without the inscription of memory nothing would survive, since nothing would remain from the passage of time. The passion for writing that is displayed by Nabokov and his protagonists is thus a passion for living on. Writing is here not limited to the physical act of writing but is a figure for the chronolibidinal investment in living on that resists the negativity of time while being bound to it. Nevertheless, the dominant reading of Nabokov (articulated in different variations by Brian Boyd, Vladimir Alexandrov, Robert Alter, and others) maintains that his writing is driven by a desire to transcend time. Following the logic of survival, I take issue with this reading and demonstrate that Nabokov's writing is animated by a desire to live on in time. The drama of desire in Nabokov does not stem from the longing for an immortal being; rather, it stems from how the threat of negation is internal to the very being that is affirmed.

Chapter 4 articulates the double bind in a general theory of chronolibido. If one is bound to mortal life, the positive can never be released from the negative. Contesting Freud and Lacan's theories of the death drive, I argue that the chronolibidinal notion of binding allows for a better account of the trauma, violence, and repetition compulsion of psychic life. Through an in-depth engagement with Freud's metapsychology, I also articulate a chronolibidinal understanding of mourning and melancholia, pleasure and pain, attachment and loss. Finally, I pursue the implications of Derrida's engagement with psychoanalysis. Analyzing the love letters collected in Derrida's *Envois,* I show not only *that* he offers theoretical resources to think the double bind of survival but also *how* he stages this double bind in his own text and thereby pursues a version of the literary writing of chronolibido that is at the center of the preceding chapters.

Throughout the book, then, I am concerned with the ability of literary writing to address fundamental questions of life and death, time and space, memory and forgetting. The thinking of chronolibido is not simply an extrinsic theory that I apply to the novels in question, but a set of insights that I derive from the texts themselves. One may nevertheless wonder why I have chosen to study Proust, Woolf, and Nabokov in particular and what motivates bringing them together. In response, I want to offer two main reasons. First, few authors have elucidated in such depth the intricate connection between time and desire. Indeed, I have learned as much about chronolibido from Proust, Woolf, and Nabokov as I have from Plato, Freud, and Derrida. Second, the fact that these writers—despite their manifest chronolibidinal insights—continue to be read in terms of a desire to transcend temporal finitude testifies to the persistent influence of the latter conception of desire. As we will see, epiphany and aesthetic revelation in modernist literature still tends to be aligned with a supposed experience of timelessness. In contrast, I argue that it is rather the logic of chronolibido that is expressive of what is at stake in these literary works, even and especially in their moments of greatest significance and affective intensity. My ambition is thus not only to elucidate theoretical insights in the writings of Proust, Woolf, and Nabokov; it is also to show how they practice a chronolibidinal aesthetics, which depends on the attachment to mortal life and engages the pathos of survival in the experience of the reader.

Such a chronolibidinal aesthetics was already identified by Socrates in his analysis of Homer. According to Socrates, the affective power of aesthetic representation depends on a libidinal investment in the fate of mortal life. The investment in mortal life leads one to hold "contrary opinions at the same time about the same things" so that there is "division and strife of the man with himself" (*Republic,* 603c–d). This internal division—which generates the dramatic pathos of Homer's poetry—articulates the double bind of chronolibido. It is because one wants to hold on to a mortal life that one is devastated by its extinction and cannot come to terms with death. The source of what one desires, then, is also the source of what one fears. My argument is that the aesthetics of Proust, Woolf, and Nabokov are devoted to staging this double bind of mortal being; they do not aspire to transcend time but to render the radical temporality of life.

CHAPTER 1

Memory

Proust

MORE THAN A year after her funeral, he understands that she is dead. During the past year, he has often spoken and thought of her; he has even supposedly mourned her. But he has not understood that she is dead. Then, one evening as he bends down to take off his boots, he is seized by the visceral memory of how she once assisted him in the same task. The repetition of the physical sensation not only recalls the past event but also resuscitates the self he was at the time—the one who sought refuge in her and who now comes back with his intense desire to be in her arms. This past self does not yet know of her death and still adheres to the time when they were together in all its concretion. For this very reason, he comes to experience the fact of her extinction all the more forcefully. On the one hand, the return of his past self makes him remember the impact of her "living reality" (4:155/3:153); the sense of her "being alive, real, swelling my heart to bursting" (4:156/3:155).[1] On the other hand, it is precisely the proximity of her living being that makes him understand that she is dead: "it was only at this instant—more than a year after her funeral, on account of the anachronism which so often prevents the calendar of facts from coinciding with that of our feelings—that I had just learned she was dead" (4:155/3:153).

This scene from Proust's *À la recherche du temps perdu* will reverberate throughout my reading of his work. The protagonist and narrator Marcel recalls an evening at a hotel room in the seaside resort Balbec, when he was overwhelmed by the memory of his dead grandmother.[2] The scene belongs to a section called *Les intermittences du coeur,* a title that Proust first planned to use for the novel as a whole. While the novel title changed, the experience of involuntary memory—and the intermittences of the heart that it records—remains central to the *Recherche.* Indeed, the notion of involuntary memory is generally held to be the hermeneutic key to the novel and the search for an aesthetic vocation that pervades it. From early childhood, Marcel wants to become a writer, but he is plagued by doubts about his talent. Not until the end of the *Recherche* does he discover what the subject of his book should be, namely, his own life as he comes to understand it through the experience of involuntary memory.

The decisive aesthetic revelation is glossed at length in the last volume of the *Recherche,* but it is far from clear how it should be understood. The power of involuntary memory hinges on how it transforms the relation between the current self that remembers and the former self that is being remembered. In a voluntary memory, the current self is the active agent that ascribes meaning *to* the former self. Thus, when Marcel's voluntary memory recalls his grandmother, he remembers *that* he loved her but not *how* it felt, since he has become a different self who does not need her in the same way. In contrast, the experience of involuntary memory allows his former self to become active once again. Rather than being passively subjected to the perspective of the current self, the former self emerges with its singular experience as it was given in the past: "The self that I was then and which had vanished all that time ago, was once again so close to me that I seemed to hear still the words that had come immediately be-fore" (4:156/3:154). The basic structure of involuntary memory is the same in all the cases recounted by Marcel. An identical sensation (of uneven cobblestones, the sound of a spoon, the taste of a madeleine) recurs at two different times and causes a past self to be resuscitated. The question, however, is *why* the experience of involuntary memory is of such importance for Marcel, *why* it makes him believe in his ability as a writer and gives him the idea for his book.[3]

The established answer in Proust scholarship is that the experience of involuntary memory reveals a timeless essence. According to Samuel Beckett's influential study, "the Proustian solution" consists in "the negation of Time and Death, the negation of Death because the negation of Time."[4] Beckett's book on Proust was published in 1931, but across all the developments in Proust scholarship the account of his basic ontological commitments has remained remarkably constant. In different variations, Proust's major readers reiterate that the *Recherche* expresses a desire to transcend temporal finitude. For Georges Poulet, Marcel's aesthetic experience reveals "an essential self, liberated from time and contingency, a primal and perpetual being, the creator of itself," so that "the existence traveling in search of its essence finds it in timelessness."[5] When Marcel in the last volume "regains" time through the experience of involuntary memory, he effectively gains access to a realm that is exempt from time. In Poulet's formula: "time regained is time transcended" (320). The same figure of thought recurs in Paul Ricoeur, for whom "the revelation of art" leads to an "exaltation of the extratemporal" and allows one to reconcile time lost with the overcoming of time in aesthetic experience.[6] Gerard Genette, in his turn, argues that "the difference caused by the final revelation, the decisive experience of involuntary memory and aesthetic vocation" has a structural similarity to "certain forms of religious literature, like Saint Augustine's *Confessions:* the narrator does not simply know *more,* empirically, than the hero: he *knows* in the absolute sense, he understands the Truth."[7] René Girard is even more emphatic and claims that Proust's novel "espouses the Christian structure of redemption more perfectly than the carefully planned efforts of many conscientious Christian artists."[8] While Girard concedes that Proust was not a confessional Christian, he holds that the revelation of involuntary memory fulfills the same function as a religious revelation: "Marcel knows that his body is going to die, but this does not trouble him, for his spirit has just been resurrected in memory. And this new resurrection, unlike the first one, is permanent and fruitful: it will be the foundation of the great work of art which Marcel had despaired of writing" (7). What is at stake in the *Recherche* would therefore be the conversion to an aesthetic religion. After having been led astray by the desires and fears of mortal life, Marcel at last finds the immortal Truth of art.

The above readings can indeed find support in the text. In several places, Marcel presents his experience of involuntary memory—and the aesthetic revelation that is connected to it—as a transcendence of temporal finitude. Through the experience of involuntary memory, Marcel claims to have discovered "the eternal man" in himself (6:227/4:497), an "extra-temporal being" who resides "outside of time" (6:179/4:450) and consequently has no reason to fear death: "We can understand how the word 'death' has no meaning for him; situated outside time, what should he fear from the future?" (6:181/4:451). I will argue, however, that these remarks are contradicted by the logic of Marcel's own text. The experience of involuntary memory does not yield an identity that is exempt from time. On the contrary, it highlights a constitutive temporal difference at the heart of the self. While a past self is retrieved through involuntary memory, the one who remembers can never be identical to the one who is remembered.

Furthermore, as we saw in the scene with which I began, it is precisely by resuscitating a past self that involuntary memory makes vividly clear that the past is irredeemably lost. One of the few readers to address this problem is Gilles Deleuze. While pointing out that Marcel's mourning of his grandmother may *seem* different from the other experiences of involuntary memory—since it "makes us feel a painful disappearance and constitutes the sign of a Time lost forever instead of giving us the plenitude of the Time we regain"[9]—Deleuze argues that the same negativity is at work in all involuntary memories. Even the most ecstatic experiences of involuntary memory recall the death of the past, so the joy of involuntary memory gives way "to a sentiment of collapse, of irreparable loss, in which the old sensation is pushed back into the depths of lost time" (20).

For Deleuze, however, the temporal finitude of involuntary memory entails that it has an "inferior" status. Involuntary memory is bound to the time of finite life and must therefore be transcended by the "eternal" time of art. According to Deleuze, "the superiority of art over life consists in this: all the signs we meet in life are still material signs, and their meaning, because it is always in something else, is not altogether spiritual" (41). In contrast, the signs of art are *immaterial* because they find their meaning in "an ideal essence" (13) that does not depend on anything other than itself. "As long as we discover a sign's meaning in something else, matter still subsists, refractory to spirit. On the contrary, art gives us the true unity: unity of an immaterial sign and of an entirely spiritual meaning. The essence is precisely this unity of sign and meaning as it is revealed in the work of art" (40). Deleuze is quite clear that this spiritual unity requires the sublation of time in eternity. In opposition to "passing time, which alters beings and annihilates what once was," Deleuze posits "an absolute, original time, an actual eternity that is affirmed in art" (17). The crucial move is to transcend the passage of time—which Deleuze describes as "time wasted" on being worldly and being in love with what passes away—in favor of the eternal spirit that is affirmed in creating a work of art.

Deleuze's supposedly heterodox reading of Proust thus reinforces the most orthodox understanding of his work, namely, that the guiding vision of the *Recherche* is the transcendence of time through the eternity of art. Deleuze famously asserts that the *Recherche* is about the future rather than the past, but the future in question adheres to the traditional notion of a *telos*. Indeed, Deleuze elaborates a strictly teleological reading of Proust, where everything is oriented toward "the final revelation of art" (65) that purportedly transcends time and death.

All versions of the teleological reading appeal to the last volume of the *Recherche,* which Girard eloquently describes as "the choir toward which all architectural lines converge and from which they all originate" (10). Yet for all the importance ascribed to the last volume, the proponents of the teleological reading are remarkably silent with regard to what actually happens in the closing pages of the book. Rather than celebrating aesthetic redemption, Marcel is preoccupied by how brain damage or various accidents may prevent him from completing his great work of literature. "It needed only the car I would take to crash into another for my body to be destroyed," Marcel observes, "and for my mind, from which life would be withdrawn, to be forced to abandon forever the new ideas which at this very moment, not having had the time to put them in the securer surroundings of a book, it was anxiously keeping locked up within its quivering, protective, but fragile pulp" (6:347/4:614). Instead of exempting him from death, Marcel's sense of literary vocation thus increases his fear of death. "I felt myself enhanced by the work I carried within me," he writes, but "feeling myself the bearer of a work of literature made the idea of an accident in which I might meet my death seem much more dreadful" (6:346/4:613–14). An accident does indeed happen to Marcel after his aesthetic revelation, as he falls in a staircase and suffers from memory loss. Marcel insists, however, that "an accident affecting the brain was not even necessary" (6:347/4:614) for his memory to be threatened. Rather than positing himself as a being outside of time who recalls the past to perfection, he portrays himself as "a hoarder [un *thésauriseur*] whose strong-box had a hole in it through which the riches were progressively disappearing. For a while there existed a self which deplored the loss of these riches and tried to marshal the memory to resist it, but soon I felt that the memory, as it contracted, took this self with it" (6:347/4:615). Far from redeeming this temporal finitude of memory, Marcel's aesthetic revelation and his investment in writing make him all the more aware of the threat of mortality. Marcel has discovered that his life is the "rich mining-basin" for the work of art he wants to create, but he is seized by fear because his death will entail "the disappearance not only of the one mineworker capable of extracting these minerals, but also of the mineral deposit itself" (6:346–47/4:614).

Both the subject and the subject matter of the book are thus destructible and no power of art can offer an antidote to the radical mortality of life. On the contrary, Marcel maintains that "no doubt my books too, like my mortal being, would eventually die, one day. . . . Eternal duration is no more promised to books than it is to men" (6:353/4:620–21).[10] It follows that writing never can transcend temporal finitude but only serve as a resistance to and postponement of death. Comparing his position as a writer to that of Scheherazade in the *Arabian Nights,* Marcel points out that "I would need a good number of nights, perhaps a hundred, perhaps a thousand. And I would be living with the anxiety of not knowing whether the Master of my destiny, less indulgent than the Sultan Shahriyar, when I broke off my story each morning, would stay my death sentence, and permit me to take up the continuation again the following evening" (6:353/4:620).

The desire that drives Marcel to write is therefore not a desire for immortality but a desire for *survival.* The desire for survival is a desire to live on *as mortal,* since the death that one defends against in the movement of survival is internal to the life that is defended. On the one hand, to survive is to keep the memory of a past and thus to resist forgetting. On the other hand, to survive is to live on in a future that separates itself from the past and opens it to being forgotten. Marcel can only protect his past by exposing it to a future that may erase it, but which also gives it the chance to live on.

The desire for survival is on display throughout the *Recherche*, but it has never, to my knowledge, been analyzed as such by Proust critics. To the extent that Marcel's articulation of an essential mortality has been recognized, it has not been employed to call into question the desire for immortality that is regarded as fundamental to the concluding aesthetic vision of the novel. A telling example is Malcolm Bowie's acclaimed and indeed brilliant study *Proust Among the Stars*. On the one hand, Bowie rehearses the traditional teleological reading of the novel, where Proust is seen as providing a "convincing answer" to the riddle of temporality: "In due course, time will be redeemed and the dying creature's messianic hopes will be fulfilled."[11] According to this reading, "the plot leads slowly toward a grandly orchestrated redemptive view" (62) and the experience of involuntary memory offers "a celestial exit from loss and waste" (65). On the other hand, Bowie offers an incisive critical resistance to this "supposedly overriding ontological programme of the novel" (6) and seeks to highlight structures in the book that do not adhere to the teleological schema. As Bowie emphasizes, even "the last cadence of the book, its last well-made proposition, is a call back to the unredeemable temporal process which makes writing possible. At the close, closure is most to be resisted" (67). Paradoxically, however, the latter observation does not lead Bowie to challenge the legitimacy of the teleological reading. Bowie provides deeply insightful readings of the theme of temporality and mortality in Proust, but he does not employ his observations to provide a new analysis of the aesthetic presented in the last volume or to undercut Marcel's supposed vision of immortality and redemption. Rather, Bowie maintains two positions that are mutually exclusive: "The Platonic dream of eternal life is not countermanded by these mesmerizing images of mortality at work upon the human frame. The redemptive power of art and the vanity of art are both to be recognized and no resolution between them is to be sought" (318).

In contrast, my chronolibidinal reading of Proust will seek to demonstrate that the so-called desire for immortality is contradicted from within by the desire for survival. The chronolibidinal conception of desire holds the key to a new reading of both the aesthetics that Marcel presents in the last volume and the perennial Proustian themes of time, self, and memory. Indeed, the logic of chronolibido is not simply an extrinsic theory to be applied to Proust's text; it is intrinsic to his own writing, which exhibits remarkable insights into the chronolibidinal constitution of desire.

A good place to begin is a scene in the second volume of the *Recherche*. The young Marcel has just arrived in Balbec for the first time, and he is trying to fall asleep in an unfamiliar hotel room (the same room where he will come to mourn his grandmother years later). Plagued by his nervous disposition, he is unable to feel at home in the new room because of his attachment to the room he has left behind in Paris. Marcel explains that "the anguish and alarm I felt when lying beneath a ceiling that was unknown and too high was nothing but the protest of my surviving attachment to a ceiling that was known and lower"; an attachment that was "in revolt at being confronted with a future which had already taken place, in which there was no role for it" (2:250–51/2:32). The operative anxiety here is not only an anxiety over having abandoned his room in Paris but also an anxiety that he will abandon his attachment to that room, that he will become attached to other rooms and thereby betray the affective commitments of his present self.

The attachment to a particular room—and the resistance to letting go of this attachment—may seem like a trivial example of the problem of desire. Marcel, however, regards it as symptomatic of a pathos that is at the heart of any libidinal attachment. When Marcel loves someone, he fears not only external factors (e.g., that the beloved may betray him) but also his own internal ability to have a change of heart. To cease to love someone is for Marcel not simply an alteration within a self that persists as the same; it is to become *another self* whose life depends on the death of the former self. This temporality of the self is a persistent theme throughout the novel. The temporality that makes Marcel a unique, irreplaceable being is also what makes him liable to betray himself and become someone else than the one he has been. Consequently, in being bound by love, Marcel is haunted not only by the possibility that the beloved may leave him behind but also by the possibility that he may leave himself behind:

> The fear of a future deprived of the faces and voices of those we love, those who today give us our dearest happiness, this fear, far from being dispelled, is made worse by the thought that the pain of this

deprivation is to be compounded by something which at the moment seems even more unbearable—our no longer being affected by it as a pain, but being indifferent to it—for that would mean our self had changed, and not just that we had lost the delight in our parents' presence, the charm of a mistress, the warmth of a friend; it would mean that our affection for them had been so utterly obliterated from our heart, of which it is an integral part today, that we would be able to take pleasure in a life spent without them, horrible though that seems at present; it would amount to a death of our self, albeit followed by a resurrection, but a resurrection in the form of a different self, whose love will remain forever beyond the reach of those parts of the former self that have gone down to death. It is those parts of us, even the most insubstantial and obscure of them, such as our attachment to the dimensions or the atmosphere of a particular room, which take fright, withhold consent, and engage in rebellions that must be seen as a covert and partial yet tangible and true mode of resistance to death, that lengthy, desperate, daily resistance to the fragmentary and successive death which attends us throughout our lives, stripping off bits of us at every moment, which have no sooner died than new cells begin to grow. (2:250/2:31–32)

The problem of desire here emerges as a problem of time. The life Marcel desires is temporal in its essence: he wants to keep *this* particular life and *these* particular emotions, so the prospect of replacing them with a different life or a different set of emotions is deemed to be unbearable. A future self with a new set of attachments would supposedly not mourn the loss of the former attachments. From the perspective of the self who is defined by these attachments, however, the prospect of another life without them is perceived as a threat rather than a consolation, since it would obliterate the constitution of the present self. Thus, the succession from one self to another cannot be reduced to a peaceful alteration but is described by Marcel as a violent process, where the subsequent self is unfaithful to or even kills the preceding self. This violence is ultimately irreducible because it is intrinsic to the passage of time itself, which is "stripping off bits of us at every moment." While libidinal attachment consists in "a covert and partial yet tangible and true mode of resistance to death," the life that struggles to maintain itself is subjected to a "successive death" in and through the movement of its own survival. This movement allows for the regeneration of life across time as "new cells begin to grow" when others die away, but from the perspective of the attachment to a particular life the regeneration of another life is not a consolation, since it is predicated on the loss of the life one wants to keep.

It follows that every libidinal attachment is both chronophilic and chronophobic. On the one hand, it is chronophilic, since it is invested in maintaining something that is temporally finite and irreplaceable. On the other hand, it is chronophobic, since it fears and seeks to resist the passage of time that negates every irreplaceable moment. Marcel's apparently hyperbolic insistence on his attachment to a particular room can thus serve to elucidate the chronolibidinal nature of attachment in general:

> The trepidation that overwhelmed me at the prospect of sleeping in an unfamiliar bedroom—which is felt by many—may be nothing more than the most humble, obscure, organic, almost unconscious form of the supreme and desperate refusal, by the things that make up the best of our present life, to countenance even our theoretical acceptance of a possible future without them: a refusal which was at the core of the horror I had so often felt at the thought that my parents would one day be dead, that the requirements of life might force me to live apart from Gilberte or just make me settle for good in a country where I would never see my friends again: a refusal which was also at the core of the difficulty I found in trying to think about my own death or the kind of afterlife promised by Bergotte in his books, in which there would be no place for my memories, my defects, my very character, all of which found unconscionable the idea of their own nonexistence and hoped on my behalf that I was fated neither to unbeing nor to an eternity that would abolish them. (2:249/2:30–31)

Marcel here elucidates how the attachment to a temporal being gives rise to the fear of losing the same temporal being. This fear of death does not stem from a desire for immortality but rather from an investment in survival. Marcel explicitly wants to hold onto his mortal being ("my memories, my defects, my very character"), which makes him fear death *and*

reject the idea of immortality ("an eternity that would abolish [his de-
fects]") as an undesirable state of being. Precisely because of his investment in survival, Marcel cannot accept either his own death or the
prospect of an eternal life that would abolish his temporal being. The care
for mortal life is rather inseparable from the struggle against the immortality of death and cannot even in principle cure itself from the agony
of loss.

Accordingly, Marcel's attachment to mortal life leads to an incurable
chronophilia *and* an incurable chronophobia. Rather than coming to
terms with death, he seeks to keep alive what will die, to remember what
will be forgotten. The nature of this desire for survival is further elabo-
rated in the fourth volume of the *Recherche:*

> We desire passionately that there should be another life in which we
> would be similar to what we are here below. But we do not reflect that,
> even without waiting for that other life, but in this one, after a few
> years, we are unfaithful to what we have been, to what we wanted to
> remain immortally. Even without supposing that death might modify
> us more than the changes that occur in the course of a lifetime, if in
> that other life we were to meet the self that we have been, we would
> turn away from ourselves as from those people to whom we have been
> close but whom we have not seen for a long time—those friends of
> Saint-Loup's, for example, that I was so pleased to find again every
> evening at the Faisan Doré but whose conversation I would now find
> simply out of place and an embarrassment. In this respect, and be-
> cause I preferred not to go and rediscover what had pleased me there,
> a walk through Doncières might have seemed to me to prefigure my
> arrival in paradise. We dream a great deal of paradise, or rather of
> numerous successive paradises, but they are all, long before we die,
> paradises lost, in which we would feel lost. (4:253–54/3:253)

Marcel here glosses the desire for immortality as a desire for survival.
When we dream of being immortal we dream of *living on* as the same being. But since our being is temporal, it bears within itself the necessity of
becoming other than itself and the possibility of betraying "what we had
wanted to remain immortally." The dream of an immortal paradise is thus

undercut from within, since it dreams of keeping a mortal life that according to its own essence cannot finally be kept: it may always leave behind or change its desire in successive dreams of paradise. The chronolibidinal point, however, is not only that any paradise can be compromised by loss but also that it would not be desired as a paradise unless one could lose it. The threat of loss is *internal* to the paradise that is desired; it cannot be removed without removing the paradise itself.[12]

The same logic of chronolibido can be discerned in Marcel's most famous but also most enigmatic statement on paradise: "the true paradises are the paradises that one has lost" *(les vrais paradis sont les paradis qu'on a perdus)*. The context of this statement is Marcel's ecstatic experience of involuntary memory in the last volume.[13] A series of intense visceral sensations have brought back his memory of Venice and Balbec, just as the taste of the madeleine in the first volume brought back the memory of his childhood in Combray. When glossing these experiences, Marcel maintains that, while his present circumstances in the end won out over the resurgence of the past, "the loser always seemed to me to be the more beautiful; so beautiful that I remained in ecstasy on the uneven paving-stones, as before the cup of tea, attempting to retain, when it appeared, and bring back, the moment it escaped me, this influx and rejection of Combray, or Venice, or Balbec, which surged up only to abandon me a few moments later" (6:183/4:453). The sense of lost time, rather than eternal being, is thus crucial for the experience of involuntary memory. As Marcel explains, involuntary memory "suddenly makes us breathe a new air," but it is "new precisely because it is an air that we have breathed before" and "could not provide this profound feeling of renewal if it had not already been breathed" (6:178–79/4:449). Consequently, the joy and rejuvenation of involuntary memory is one that "the poets have tried in vain to make reign in paradise" (6:179/4:449), since it depends on the passage of time for its effect. Marcel's experiences of Combray, Venice, or Balbec were not particularly happy when first imprinted, but when they return through involuntary memory their unique qualities are luminous, precisely because they appear as irreplaceable in the light of loss.

Hence, if all true paradises are lost paradises, it is not because true paradise would consist in a timeless state of being that is lost or unattainable because we are temporal beings. On the contrary, Marcel's chronolibidinal insight is that nothing can be experienced or desired as paradise without the sense that it can be lost. Far from devaluing temporal life, the dimension of loss is precisely what makes it emerge as valuable. Following this logic, the valuation of a past experience may be enhanced when it is infused with the pathos of being lost, just as the value of a current experience may be enhanced by the sense that it will be lost.[14]

In his reflections on erotic love, Marcel tirelessly emphasizes such interdependence of desire and loss. The sense that the beloved can be lost does not decrease but rather *increases* the libidinal flow toward the beloved. Indeed, the sense that the beloved can be lost is intrinsic to the sense of the unique value and irreplaceable quality of the beloved. Yet while this logic can be discerned in Marcel's reflections on erotic love, it has traditionally been disregarded or degraded in favor of the supposed transcendent realm of involuntary memory and artistic creation. Marcel himself invites such a reading when he claims that the "contemplation of eternity" offers the only pleasure that is "real and fertile" (6:183/4:454), in contrast to the transience of social pleasures, friendship, and erotic love. The "joy" of involuntary memory supposedly consists in such a contemplation of eternity, which would make "death a matter of indifference" (6:176/4:446). Once we examine the experience of involuntary memory, however, we can see that it has nothing to do with a contemplation of eternity and most certainly does not make one indifferent to death. Involuntary memory is "extra-temporal" not because it transcends time (as Marcel sometimes claims) but because it intensifies the experience of time.

Consider the basic structure of involuntary memory. The repetition of an identical sensation in the past and the present allows for a bridge between the two, but the repetition does not abolish the temporal difference. On the contrary, it underlines it. According to Marcel's own description, the present sensation of an absent past "allowed my being to obtain, to isolate, to immobilize—for the duration of a flash of lightning—the one thing it never apprehends: a bit of time in its pure state *[un peu de temps à l'état pur]*" (6:180/4:451). This pure time, I will argue, is not eternity but the negativity of time. Precisely through the repetition of the past, Marcel apprehends that the past is no longer and will never be again. This irrevocable difference between the present and the past reveals time in its "pure" state because it is the negativity of time—its destruction of what has been—that accounts for why one cannot return to the past. The past can be recalled, remembered, and even relived, but in all these repetitions there is an experience of temporal difference that cannot be sublated.

A paradigmatic example is the scene with which I began this chapter. When Marcel remembers his grandmother on that solitary evening in Balbec, his experience has the same ecstatic quality as in the other instances of involuntary memory: he is "filled with an unknown, divine presence" that rescues him from his "aridity of soul" and resurrects the past (4:154/3:153). Yet the joy of resurrection is immediately traversed by the pain of mourning. His involuntary memory does not reveal a timeless essence but rather the "strange contradiction of survival and extinction, intertwined within me" (4:158/3:156). While his grandmother survives in his memory, Marcel is confronted with the fact that she herself has been extinguished and is lost forever:

> Lost forever; I could not understand, and I struggled to endure the pain of this contradiction: on the one hand, an existence, a tenderness, surviving in me such as I had known them . . . on the other hand, as soon as I had relived, as though present, that felicity, to feel it traversed by the certainty, springing up like a repeated physical pain, of a nothingness that had effaced my image of that tenderness, had destroyed that existence. . . . (4:156–57/3:155)

The pathos of survival is thus inherent in the experience of involuntary memory. If there is a resurrection in the experience of involuntary memory, it is the resurrection of a mortal life that lives on. The death of the beloved underlines this mortality of survival in the most agonizing way. The memory that reawakens the proximity of the beloved is powerless to make the beloved come back to life. Rather, the memory that recalls a certain life also recalls that the same life has been irredeemably lost.

In confronting this experience of loss, Marcel does not try to attenuate the pain by deluding himself into thinking that his grandmother is still alive or may come back from the dead: "I never did this, for I was determined not only to suffer, but to respect the originality of my suffering, such as I had suddenly endured it against my will, and I wanted to continue to endure it, following its own laws" (4:158/3:156). Marcel's effort here is the same as in the other instances of involuntary memory. The return of the past does not stem from an act of will—it happens to Marcel by virtue of contingent circumstance—but in the wake of the experience he mobilizes his willpower to retain the impression it has left. The significance of the latter move is highlighted in the last volume, where Marcel repeatedly maintains that the work of art should devote itself to extracting the "truth" of the impressions of involuntary memory.[15] The truth in question has traditionally been taken to be the revelation of a timeless essence, but in fact it is the truth of temporal finitude that is at the root of the impressions of involuntary memory. Thus, when Marcel examines the involuntary memory of his grandmother and seeks to extract its "element of truth," he emphasizes that such truth can be found only in the impression that "death itself, the abrupt revelation of death, had hollowed out in me like a thunderbolt" (4:158/3:156). The truth of this impression, revealed by involuntary memory, is not immortal being but rather "the painful synthesis of survival and extinction [la douloureuse synthèse de la survivance et du néant]" (4:159/3:157).

The synthesis of survival and extinction, I will argue, is the most congenial formula for the condition of time as it is rendered in the *Recherche*. Already the basic scene of the book (Marcel writing his life) stages the contrast between the remembering self who still survives and the remembered past that is already extinct. Yet the co-implication of survival and extinction is operative not only in the relation between the present and the past, but also in the constitution of presence itself. The succession of time entails that the present moment never exists in itself but is immediately negated. For one moment to be succeeded by another, it cannot *first* be present in itself and *then* be extinguished. Rather, the moment must extinguish itself as soon as it comes to be. It is in this precise sense that "pure" time is nothing but negativity. The past is no longer, the future is not yet, and the present itself can come into being only by ceasing to be.

To insist on the negativity of time is far from sufficient, however. While the passage of time requires the negation that is intrinsic to succession, it also requires that something survive to mark the passage of time. Indeed, there could be no experience of time without a synthesis that relates the past to the future and thus allows something to persist over time. For

example, if I listen to a succession of musical notes, I can only appre-
hend it as a melody by retaining what has passed away and joining it to
what follows. The same goes for the temporal extension of every individual note and indeed for the experience of anything that happens.
Even the most immediate experience depends on a succession that cannot be given as a simple unity but requires a minimal synthesis in order
to be apprehended as such.[16]

The question, then, is how the synthesis of succession is possible.
When Charles Swann listens to a piece of music in the first volume of the
Recherche, the description emphasizes that "his memory at once fur-
nished him with a transcription that was summary and temporary but at
which he could glance while the piece continued, so that already, when
the same impression suddenly returned, it was no longer impossible to
grasp" (1:217/1:206). The inscription of sound in memory here performs
a minimal synthesis of the successive notes. To be sure, Marcel suggests
that this synthesis of time can be opposed to an impression that would be
"purely musical" and "immaterial" (1:216/1:206). But his own account
directly refutes this idea by emphasizing that "the notes vanish before
these sensations are sufficiently formed in us not to be submerged by the
succeeding or even simultaneous notes" (1:217/1:206). It follows that
there can be no impression of music without the inscription of memory,
since the notes pass away as soon as they come to be and do not exist as
such without retention. While the melody successively recedes, memory
is "fabricating for us facsimiles of these fleeting phrases," thereby allowing us "to compare them to those that follow them and to differentiate
them" (1:217/1:206).

This operation of synthesis exemplifies the general structure of the
trace. Given the immediate negation of every moment in succession, it
depends on the tracing of time from the first inception. The inscription of
the trace is the condition for the synthesis of time, since it enables the past
to survive and be related to the future. Yet the survival of the trace cannot
be exempt from the negativity of time. In order to survive—even for a
moment—a trace cannot have any integrity as such but is already marked
by its own ceasing to be. The notion of the trace thus allows us to articulate the synthesis of survival and extinction that is at work throughout the
Recherche. The immediate extinction of the moment in succession makes

any synthesis dependent on the survival of a trace that retains the past for the future. The eradication of this trace is a *possibility* that is not immediately actualized (otherwise there would be no trace at all), but it already presupposes the *necessity* of extinction that is at work in succession. Given that nothing can survive without succession, extinction is at work in survival itself.

It is here instructive to contrast the notion of survival with the notion of duration formulated by Henri Bergson, to whom Proust has often been compared. Bergson too emphasizes that the succession of time cannot be understood in terms of a transition from one discreet state to another. Rather, even the most immediate temporal state is itself in transition and therefore always already involved in succession. As Bergson puts it, "there is no essential difference between passing from one state to another and persisting in the same state," since "the truth is that we change without ceasing, and that the state itself is nothing but change."[17] By appealing to this notion of ceaseless change, Bergson seeks to elucidate the fundamental difference between space and time. The spatial can remain the same, since the simultaneity of space allows one point to coexist with another. In contrast, the temporal can never remain the same, since the succession of time entails that the present immediately passes away. For Bergson, however, this passage of time does not involve any negation or negativity. The temporal moment passes away, but it does not disappear or cease to be. On the contrary, it immediately belongs to the continuous movement of duration *(la durée)*. This duration provides an absolute ground for the synthesis of succession, since it includes all of the past in an "undivided present" and continues to assimilate everything that happens in "a perpetual present" that never ceases to be but rather constitutes "an eternity of life."[18]

By denying negativity, Bergson effectively denies time. If the past has not ceased to be, it is not past but present, and by the same token there is no passage of time. To be sure, Bergson maintains that the perpetual presence of duration is not immutable, since it is always in a process of change. But given that nothing ceases to be in duration, there is nothing that can distinguish the past from the present. Symptomatically, Bergson holds that the absolute continuity of duration is like the continuity of a melody—provided that one effaces all the differences between sounds and all the distinguishing characteristics of the sound itself.[19] A melody without sounds would not be a melody at all, however, just as a time that were absolutely continuous would not be temporal at all. Bergson himself grants that the constitution of time requires the distinction between "a *before* and an *after*," since "time is succession" (66). If duration were absolutely continuous, it would therefore eliminate the very condition of time, since it would eliminate the difference that distinguishes before from after. This necessary difference is not a positive spatial difference but the negativity of time, which undermines both the idea of a discrete moment *and* the idea of an absolute continuity. Only if something is *no longer*—that is, only if there is negativity—can there be a difference between before and after, past and present. This negativity must be at work in presence itself for there to be succession. If the moment is not negated in being succeeded by another moment, their relation is not one of temporal succession but of spatial coexistence.

Despite his indictments of philosophical accounts that confuse time with space, Bergson's notion of duration thus eliminates the succession of time and absolutizes the spatial attribute of coexistence. Bergson himself confirms this by emphasizing that all of the past *coexists* with the present in duration. Of course, he emphasizes that this coexistence is not actually spatial, since it does not depend on any external, material support to retain the past. Rather, the coexistence of past and present is a virtual coexistence that is internal to duration itself. Given that the past never ceases to be, it preserves itself and everything that happens without relying on anything other than itself. For the same reason, however, the duration of the past is not temporal at all but an eternal substance. It exists absolutely in itself and is not susceptible to destruction.

Consequently, we should not be surprised to find that Bergsonian interpretations of Proust promote a notion of eternity. A prominent example is Miguel de Beistegui's *Jouissance de Proust,* which provides the most philosophically sophisticated reading of Proust in terms of a Bergsonian ontology. De Beistegui is well aware that the *Recherche* is haunted by the drama of time as *chronos*. Several times he alludes to Goya's painting of Saturn (the Roman version of Chronos) devouring his own children. As de Beistegui notes, this drama of destruction is internal to the being of chronos itself, since the succession of time destroys the moment that it engenders. For de Beistegui, however, the "destructive and saturnian time of succession" is counteracted by the "creative, artistic, and redemptive time of eternity."[20] While temporal *existence* is subjected to succession, de Beistegui holds that the *essence* of time is a pure past that "registers and preserves every detail of our existence, every fragment of our experience" (93), thus ensuring that nothing is ever lost. Like Bergson, de Beistegui maintains that this virtual memory is "spiritual" and "immaterial" since it does not depend on any spatial, material support to retain time. As in Bergson, however, the supposedly pure time of duration turns out to be the pure space of coexistence. De Beistegui explicitly holds that all events "coexist" on the virtual plane of memory, which is endowed with "a totality and a coherence that is only accessible to a divine gaze, but of which we sometimes have the intuition" (134). According to de Beistegui, it is the intuition of such an absolute past—existing in itself and never passing away—that is given by the experience of involuntary memory. The "joy" of involuntary memory would then be the joy "of *being* this pure past, this moment that does not pass" (109). Furthermore, de Beistegui maintains that the "life" of this pure past "is not survival and does not age," just as the "true time" of duration "never effaces itself and immediately eternalizes itself " (177–78).

The synthesis of time would thus be grounded in the supposed eternity of a pure past. The account of temporality in the *Recherche,* however, directly contradicts this notion of a spiritual movement of absolute duration. When the past returns through involuntary memory, it is not because it persists in itself but because it has been inscribed as a trace that remains across time. Far from being immaterial or eternal, this inscription of time is explicitly material and destructible. Indeed, already in the famous madeleine episode that concludes the first section of the novel, Marcel vividly describes the precarious support of memory:

> When nothing subsists of an old past, after the death of people, after the destruction of things, alone, frailer but more enduring, more immaterial, more persistent, more faithful, smell and taste still remain for a long time, like souls, remembering, waiting, hoping, upon the ruins of all the rest, bearing without giving way, on their almost impalpable droplet, the immense edifice of memory. (1:47/1:46)

In contrast to the Bergsonian notion of duration, the past is here explicitly recognized as being *no longer:* it is destroyed and dead. It follows that the past (being nonexistent in itself) must be retained by something other than itself: in this case a smell or a taste that allows the past sensation to be repeated. The memory is thus involuntary in the precise sense that it exceeds the power of the will and marks our dependence on circumstances that ultimately are beyond our control. A certain time has been inscribed as a trace that can be reactivated through visceral sensations, but one may never again come across the relevant taste or smell, and the past self may never be resuscitated. As Marcel points out in the madeleine episode, whether or not we encounter the thing that will trigger an involuntary memory is a matter of chance and "a second sort of chance, that of our own death, often does not allow us to wait long for the favors of the first" (1:44/1:43).

Furthermore, as is clear from the passage above, the traces that remain and provide the support for involuntary memory are not eternal but only endowed with the capacity to "still remain for a long time" *(restent encore longtemps)*. Between what remains and what has ceased to be there is not a difference of essence but a difference of degree. If what remains is *more* enduring, *more* immaterial, *more* persistent, *more* faithful, it can also be described as *less* momentary, *less* material, *less* transient, and *less* unfaithful. In either case, the persistence remains bound to the temporal finitude that it modifies. While the trace of memory allows the past to survive, it can only do so through a temporal repetition that exposes it to loss and erasure.

By revealing how the past can be reactivated through visceral sensations, the experience of involuntary memory leads Marcel to the conception of "embodied time" *(temps incorporé)* that concludes the novel. Marcel may here seem to confirm a Bergsonian notion of duration by emphasizing that we carry the past with us and can connect to it by descending deeper into ourselves. Yet Marcel's notion of embodied time in fact provides an elaborate parody of Bergson's notion of duration. As we have seen, Bergson holds that the pure past preserves everything that happens in an eternal duration. Given that nothing ceases to be, the past is "continually swelling with the duration that it accumulates; it goes on increasing—rolling upon itself, as a snowball on the snow."[21] Although this idea amounts to a complete spatialization of time, Bergson insists that all of the past is preserved without any need for a space that preserves it. When Marcel picks up the notion of embodied time, however, he employs the spatial metaphor to devastating effect. The Bergsonian idea of duration—that the past carries us with it in a constant accumulation of the time that has passed—is translated into the disconcerting image of how "all men are perched on top of living stilts which never stop growing, sometimes becoming taller than church steeples, until eventually they make walking difficult and dangerous, and down from which, all of a sudden, they fall" (6:357/4:625). Accordingly, we find the Duc de Guermantes "shaking like a leaf, on the scarcely manageable summit of his eighty-three years" (6:357/4:625). Similarly, Marcel finds himself perched on the "vertiginous summit" (6:357/4:624) of the past, and he worries that "the stilts on which I myself was standing had already reached that height [of the downfall to death] and it did not seem to me that I would for very long have the strength to keep this past attached to me which already stretched so far down" (6:358/4:625). Rather than being a vital, continuous movement, the accumulation of the past is thus described as a weight that man "has to drag with him wherever he goes," that grows "more and more enormous, and which in the end defeats him" (6:355/4:623).

A similar ironic fate befalls Bergson's notion of introspection. According to Bergson, an introspective "attention to life, sufficiently powerful and sufficiently removed from all practical interest" would reveal that all of our past is "continually present" in a vital duration.[22] In contrast, when Marcel descends into himself to discover the nature of duration, he is seized by "a sense of tiredness and fear at the thought that all this length of time had not only uninterruptedly been lived, thought, secreted by me, that it was my life, that it was myself, but also that I had to keep it attached to me at every moment" (6:357/4:624). It is this embodied time that Marcel—in the very last sentence of the *Recherche*—declares as the primary subject of his book. "If enough time was left to me to complete my work," he writes, "my first concern would be to describe the people in it, even at the risk of making them seem colossal and unnatural creatures, as occupying a place far larger than the very limited one reserved for them in space," namely, a "place—in Time" (6:358/4:625).

On the one hand, then, Marcel spatializes time by describing it as a place or a height that is inscribed in the body. This spatialization is not a failure of poetic imagination or conceptual rigor but follows from the constitutive negativity of time. Given that time is nothing but negation, it has to be spatialized to be anything at all. The very concept of duration presupposes that something remains across an interval of time and only that which is spatial can remain. On the other hand, Marcel temporalizes space in the same gesture, since the place we occupy in time is shown to be inhabited by the negativity of decay, destruction, and loss. The body that keeps traces of time—thus allowing us to extend our place in time—is itself destructible. Accordingly, Marcel emphasizes that "I really had to start from the fact that I had a body, which is to say that I was perpetually under threat from a twofold danger, external and internal" (6:345/4:612). Even if all external threats are evaded, the body still bears the cause of its own destruction within itself because it is mortal. When Marcel discovers the importance of embodied time, he is consequently haunted by an awareness of all the factors that may eradicate the memories that are retained in the body: "I felt the present object of my thought very clearly within myself, and understood how entirely dependent on chance it was, not only that this object had not entered my thoughts before, but also that, along with my body, it might be annihilated at any moment" (6:345–46/4:613).

Yet the idea of being exempt from the negativity of time persists not only in Bergsonian readings of Proust but also in those readings that seek to challenge the Bergsonian framework. The most influential example is Georges Poulet's *Proustian Space.* The strength of Poulet's reading is that he clearly acknowledges the necessity of spatializing time. As he formulates his guiding thesis: "If Bergson denounces and rejects the metamorphosis of time into space, Proust not only accommodates himself to it, but installs himself in it, carries it to extremes, and makes of it finally one of the principles of his art."[23] Poulet thematizes the relation between time and space in terms of the relation between superposition and juxtaposition. To superimpose is "to act like the reality of time does" (92), since superposition "requires the disappearance of the one so that the appearance of the other may take place" (91). In contrast, juxtaposition does not replace one moment at the expense of another but places the moments next to one another. Juxtaposition is thus a spatial relation of coexistence whereas superposition is a temporal relation of succession. Following this schema, Poulet argues that the distinctive operation in Proust's novel is *the juxtaposition of superposition,* which is to say the spatialization of time. When the past returns through involuntary memory, two successive, superimposed moments (the past sensation and its repetition in the present) are juxtaposed.

The question, however, is how the juxtaposition of memory should be understood. Poulet himself insightfully argues that involuntary memory does not disclose a "positive existential dimension" (47), namely, a plenitude of life where nothing is lost. Rather, when memories make the past return it is "a past irremediably finished that they relate, a past that never ceases to be separated from us by the very distance, so that the latter, far from being suppressed, is on the contrary rendered more cruelly distinct by the movement of mnemonic thought, which, in traveling all the way, has more clearly revealed the length of time" (46). For the same reason, the one who recollects his own past "remembers also, in a certain way, the interval that separates him from it" (46). The juxtaposition of memory, then, does not overcome the negativity of time. Rather, it is precisely through the spatial juxtaposition of moments that the negativity of time becomes palpable, in terms of an interval that cannot be sublated. Instead of developing this interpretation, however, Poulet recuperates a version of the traditional *telos* of Proust's novel. The "negative space" (43) of interval and distance is for Poulet overcome by the full positivity of "a space *finally regained*" (58). This absolute space is a "memory total in itself, which conserves and reproduces the mass of episodes, as if they had never been a part of time, had never been menaced by forgetfulness" (104–05).

Hence, despite his critique of Bergsonian readings of Proust, Poulet too promotes a notion of absolute duration. That Bergson calls absolute duration "time" and Poulet calls it "space" makes no essential difference, since both notions invoke a duration that is exempt from negativity and loss. Thus, while Poulet recognizes the necessity of spatializing time, he ultimately exempts space from time. Indeed, Poulet holds that Proust "has exactly transposed, in the realm of space, this victory over the destructive forces of time, which precisely in its essence constitutes the novel" (14).

The space of memory discovered by the *Recherche,* however, does not lead to a victory over the destructive forces of time. On the contrary, the novel ends with the discovery of the "embodied time" that entails the destructibility of every space of memory. By spelling out the co-implication of time and space, Marcel's notion of embodied time undermines the positions held by both Bergson and Poulet. *Pace* Bergson, embodied time displays the necessity of spatializing time. The duration of the past is not spiritual and immaterial but depends on the inscription of time in a material body. *Pace* Poulet, this embodied time also displays the necessity of temporalizing space. The spatial body that survives—whether the body of the self or the work of art—is in its turn temporal and exposes the traces it keeps to the possibility of effacement. As Marcel makes clear with a poignant phrase at the end of the book, the body that is the site of time, memory, and desire is also the site of radical destruction: "after death, Time leaves the body, and the memories—so indifferent, so pale now—are effaced from her who no longer exists and soon will be from him whom at present they still torture, but in whom they will eventually die, when the desire of a living body is no longer there to support them" (6:357/4:624).

The stakes of embodied time can be further clarified in relation to Joshua Landy's important study of Proust, *Philosophy as Fiction.* Landy offers an incisive account of how the self in Proust is divided not only "synchronically, into a set of faculties or drives" but also "diachronically, into a series of distinct organizations and orientations of those faculties or drives, varying according to the phase of life (or even the hour of the day)."[24] On the one hand, there is a succession of selves that come into being and pass away as Marcel changes over time. This alteration is intrinsic to temporal being and accounts for why "today's 'moi' cannot predict tomorrow's, nor even always remember that of yesterday" (105). On the other hand, the successive selves do not simply disappear but are sedimented as a multiplicity of selves in the same body. As a result, we are liable to change not only with regard to the emergence of future selves but also with regard to the resurgence of past selves. Even when we apparently remain the same "we cannot achieve unanimity within ourselves at any given moment" (101). Due to the sedimentation of past selves, "previously unseen sub-selves may at any moment float to the surface of consciousness" (122), reigniting a passion or despair that we thought was buried and, in the process, transforming our conception of who we are.

Despite his careful account of the temporality of subjectivity, however, Landy subscribes to a version of "the timeless essence of my *vrai moi*" (84) that is supposedly revealed by involuntary memory. According to Landy, the experience of involuntary memory enables Marcel to write his book because it discloses a true self that is the foundation of all the successive selves and thus provides a ground for the narrative. "What involuntary memory gives to the future book is less its content than its *form*, if not its very condition of existence: a narrating instance sufficiently unified as to be able to say 'I' and to speak for a multiplicity of selves in past and present tenses" (111). While Marcel's temporal being is divided between successive selves, the experience of involuntary memory gives him access to an essence of the self that persists as the same across the passage of time: "If today's madeleine tastes the same as it did thirty years ago, it is because there must be a part of us at least that has not changed in between times, *a permanent aspect underlying all of the mutable selves*" (112).[25] Landy himself concedes that such a "permanent aspect" is not sufficient to constitute what he calls a "total Self" and grants that temporality necessarily intrudes on Marcel's "communion with the atemporal" (116). Unlike the true self that is "entirely static" (163n.12), the total Self evolves in time and cannot achieve an abiding unity except by reaching "the personal equivalent of the End of History—something Marcel, for one, considers an impossibility" (122). Nevertheless, Landy holds that "for Proust, it is preferable to imagine such a *telos* and live accordingly than to face the fact of its nonexistence" (125). The guiding aesthetic principle would therefore be to organize "the various lines of one's development toward their point of convergence at infinity, an ideal *telos* from which one projects . . . consistency and indeed purpose into a life of chaos and contingency" (125).

In contrast, I argue that the experience of involuntary memory does not reveal the timeless essence of a true self and that Marcel does not promote the fictional unity of a total Self. The reason why one self can connect with another is not because there is an underlying subject that unites the two, but because a trace of the past survives across the interval of time. The survival of this trace depends on its inscription in the body of a temporal being. It is this retention of time in the body—rather than a timeless essence of subjectivity—that enables the synthesis of successive selves. Furthermore, the synthesis is always one of both survival *and* extinction. Far from dissimulating this temporal finitude, Marcel's aesthetic efforts are devoted to making it palpable. The very pathos of the experience of involuntary memory—and the aesthetic to which it gives rise—presupposes that mortal life is the object of libidinal investment. If one were not invested in the fate of a mortal life, one would never be moved by what happens to it or concerned for its survival in memory.

My argument, then, is that the experience of involuntary memory leads Marcel to pursue a chronolibidinal aesthetics. For a chronolibidinal aesthetics, the point is not to redeem the condition of temporality but, on the contrary, to mobilize it as the source of pathos. Indeed, there would be no pathos without the drama of temporal finitude that exposes every libidinal investment to the possibility of loss. The key to generating aesthetic pathos is therefore to intensify the sense of the passage of time:

> Theoretically, we are aware that the earth is spinning, but in reality we do not notice it: the ground we walk on seems to be stationary and gives no cause for alarm. The same happens with Time. To make its passing perceptible, novelists have to turn the hands of the clock at dizzying speed, to make the reader live through ten, twenty, thirty years in two minutes. At the top of a page, we have left a lover full of hope; at the foot of the following one, we find him again, already an octogenarian, hobbling his painful daily way round the courtyard of an old-people's home, barely acknowledging greetings, remembering nothing of his past. (2:55–56/1:473–74).

This juxtaposition of two moments in time—revealing the inherent contradiction between survival and extinction in the duration of a life—is precisely what characterizes involuntary memory. Like the narrative technique described by Marcel, the experience of involuntary memory makes the passage of time appear at "dizzying speed" *(en accélérant follement)* by contracting two moments that can never be united. If the experience of involuntary memory serves as an aesthetic inspiration, then, it is not because it reveals a timeless essence. On the contrary, it is because involuntary memory recalls Marcel to the pathos of mortal life.

Throughout the novel, he searches for a subject that would be elevated enough for his literary ambitions, only to discover that the drama of mortal life, the vicissitudes that follow from the sheer passage of time, are the source of the aesthetic pathos he seeks. As he puts it in the last volume: "I understood that all these raw materials for a literary work were actually my past life . . . without my ever having realized that there should be some contact between my life and the books that I had wanted to write and for which, when I used to sit down at my table, I could not find a subject" (6:208/4:478). Rather than a transcendent topic of writing, which has always left Marcel's imagination blank, it is "this life, the memories of its times of sadness, its times of joy" (6:208/4:478) that he comes to see as the basis for his book. "The greatness of true art," he argues, "lies in rediscovering, grasping hold of, and making us recognize . . . this reality which we run a real risk of dying without having known, and which is quite simply our life" (6:204/4:474). This life does not receive its aesthetic meaning or existential truth from the projection of a *telos* beyond time. On the contrary, the "truth" that Marcel sets out to elucidate is the truth that we are essentially temporal: "the fact that we occupy an ever larger place in Time is something that everybody feels, and this universality could only delight me, since this was the truth, the truth suspected by everybody, that it was my task to try to elucidate" (6:355/4:623).

The ambition to stage the pathos of mortal life can thus be traced in Marcel's basic aesthetic impetus. When affirming his vocation as a writer, Marcel emphasizes that his work will be devoted to "the thing that ought to be most precious to us," namely, "our true life, our reality as we have felt it *[telle que nous l'avons sentie]*" (6:189/4:459). The experience of involuntary memory is central for this conception of aesthetics, since it discloses "the qualitative difference in the ways we perceive the world, a difference which, if there were no art, would remain the eternal secret of each individual" (6:204/4:474). The task of writing is therefore to convey the unique texture of individual experience, which is always a texture of time. If our selves were not temporal, there would be no qualitative difference between the ways in which we perceive the world, since our selves would not be irreplaceable. Accordingly, Marcel advocates a form of realism that is attuned to the subtle nuances of experience and displays how "an hour is not just an hour, it is a vessel full of perfumes, sounds, plans and atmospheres. What we call reality is a certain relationship between these sensations and the memories which surround us simultaneously . . . a unique relationship which the writer has to rediscover" (6:197–98/ 4:467–68).

Like the realism advocated by the painter Elstir, Marcel's realism is not concerned with objective data but with the way in which reality is given in a singular experience. The ambition is to break away from "the falsity of so-called realist art, which would not be so untruthful if life had not given us the habit of expressing our experience in ways that do not reflect it" (6:189/4:460). In contrast, Marcel seeks to create a style of writing that conveys the unique texture of an irreplaceable life. If he succeeds in this ambition, however, his writing is necessarily haunted by the drama of temporal finitude that he identifies in one of Elstir's paintings:

> [Elstir's] eye had been able to arrest the passage of the hours for all time in this luminous moment when the lady had felt hot and stopped dancing, when the tree was encircled by a ring of shade, when the sails seemed to be gliding over a glaze of gold. But precisely because that moment had such a forceful impact, the fixity of the canvas conveyed the impression of something highly elusive: you felt that the lady would soon return home, the boats vanish from the scene, the shadow shift, night begin to fall; that pleasures fade away, that life passes, and that the instant, illuminated by multiple and simultaneous plays of light, cannot be recaptured. (3:417/2:714)

The ability to capture a given moment in art is inseparable from an aesthetic practice that highlights the evanescence of the moment. One cannot retain the moment without also retaining that it was temporal in its very event and never will return. As we have seen, the same synthesis of survival and extinction is internal to involuntary memory. On the one hand, involuntary memory allows the past to return with a "forceful impact," since it retrieves the self who experienced a given moment. On the other hand, the forceful impact of involuntary memory also serves as a reminder that the past no longer exists and that life irrevocably passes

away, since the memory cannot sublate the difference in time that separates one self from another.

The painful synthesis of survival and extinction is brought to the fore
when Marcel contemplates his aesthetic project at the end of the *Recherche*. After the revelation of involuntary memory on the courtyard and in
the library of the Princesse de Guermantes, Marcel joins the party to
which she has invited him. Marcel has been away from life in high society
for several years, and at first he believes that the Guermantes's party is a
masked ball, where the guests are dressed up as old men and women.
"Everybody seemed to have put on make-up, in most cases with pow-
dered hair which changed them completely" (6:229/4:499). He realizes,
however, that the old age of the people he once knew is not cosmetic but
due to the passage of time. The contrast between his memory of the guests
in their youth and their present state of decay makes him acutely aware of
"all the time that had passed in their lives, an idea which overwhelmed me
with the revelation that it had passed equally for me . . . their old age devastated me by its announcing the approach of my own" (6:235/4:505). As
Marcel observes, the aging bodies make Time visible by displaying how
the past has been overtaken by the present and how the present will be
overtaken by the future: "it was not only what had become of the young
people of the past, but what would become of the young people of today,
that was giving me such a strong sensation of time" (6:251/4:521). Moreover, Marcel offers a striking inversion of the classic metaphysical premise
that the passage of time is merely an appearance whereas real being is a
permanent entity. When describing the revelation of the aging body, he
emphasizes that it reveals life "not as it appears to us, that is as permanent,
but in its reality" (6:233/4:503), namely, the "chronological reality"
(6:234/4:504) that becomes painfully palpable in the contrast between the
past that is no longer and the trace of the past that still remains.

Proust scholars have traditionally maintained an opposition between
the revelation of Time at the Guermantes's party and the preceding revelation of involuntary memory in the Guermantes's library. Beckett articulates the most influential view when he argues that Time and Death only
come to power when Marcel "leaves the library and joins the guests,
perched in precarious decrepitude," whereas the experience of involuntary memory, according to Beckett, obliterates Time and Death in favor of

timeless being.[26] Similarly, Girard asserts that in the experience of involuntary memory "time is replaced by a sensation of eternal youthfulness, in violent contrast to the horrible spectacle of degeneration and decay offered by the guests of the Guermantes" (6). Again, one may certainly find support for such a reading in some of Marcel's own remarks. For example, he contrasts the "destructive action of Time" to the "genuinely full impressions" of involuntary memory, which supposedly "exist outside time."[27] My point, however, is that these remarks are incompatible with Marcel's actual description of the experience of involuntary memory. The destructive action of Time is just as legible in the revelation of involuntary memory as it is in the revelation of the aging body.[28] The painful synthesis of survival and extinction that we traced in the experience of involuntary memory is precisely what emerges in the confrontation with the aging body. To recognize the one who was young in the one who has become old is "to think two contradictory things under a single heading, to admit that what was here, the individual one remembers, no longer exists, and that what is here is a being one did not formerly know" (6:248/4:518). As Marcel goes on to admit, "it was difficult to reconcile the two appearances, to think of the two people under a single heading; for just as it is hard to imagine that a dead person used to be alive, or that somebody who was alive is now dead, it is almost as difficult, and of the same order of difficulty (for the annihilation of youth, the destruction of a person full of energy and light-heartedness, is already a form of oblivion), to conceive that she who was young is now old" (6:249/4:519).

The power of death is thus intrinsic to every body that lives on, and it gives rise to the chronolibidinal pathos that characterizes both the experience of involuntary memory and the testimony to old age at the Guermantes's party. When retrieving his memories of the young while confronted with the altered body of the old, Marcel insists that "nothing is sadder than this contrast between the way individuals change and the fixity of memory, when we understand that what we have kept so fresh in our memory no longer has any of that freshness in real life, and that we cannot find a way to come close, on the outside, to that which appears so beautiful within us" (6:296/4:565). Far from being restricted to the display of "decrepitude" at the Guermantes's party, this painful synthesis of survival and extinction is internal to Marcel's experience of involuntary memory in the Guermantes's library. When he picks up a copy of *François le Champi* by George Sand, the childhood self who had the book read to him by his mother is resuscitated "with the same impression of the weather outside in the garden, the same dreams as he formed then about other countries and about life, the same anxiety about the future" (6:194/4:464). The resurrection of his childhood self, however, is concomitant with the insight that the child is dead, so once again we find "the painful impression" *(la douloureuse impression)* at the heart of involuntary memory and Marcel is moved to mournful tears (6:191–92/4:461–62).

Consequently, there is no opposition between the revelation in the Guermantes's library and the revelation at the Guermantes's party. At stake in both cases is a revelation of what Marcel calls "the form of Time" (6:354/4:622). This form becomes visible in the contrast between the memory that still survives and the past that already is extinguished. Without such a synthesis of survival and extinction, there would be no form of time in the first place. Without extinction, nothing would pass away, and without survival, nothing would relate the past to the future. In writing his book, Marcel neither can nor aspires to transcend this painful synthesis of survival and extinction. On the contrary, it is operative on every level of experience and generates the dramatic pathos of the *Recherche*.

In a final twist, the painful synthesis of survival and extinction also provides Marcel with the very impetus to write his book. It is precisely because Marcel's existence will be extinguished that he is concerned with its survival and compelled to write his life. The form of time gives him not only the idea for his book but also "the fear of not being able to accomplish it" (6:354/4:622), and this fear precipitates him to write: "Finally, this idea of Time was valuable to me for one other reason, it was a spur, it told me that it was time to start" (6:342/4:609). Accordingly, it is the destructive action of time—and the concomitant sense that his life is limited by its own duration—that motivates Marcel to recreate the memories of his life:

> The idea of Time that I had just formed was telling me that it was time
> to apply myself to the work. It was high time; but, and this was the
> explanation for the anxiety which had beset me as soon as I entered
> the drawing-room, when the made-up faces had given me the idea of

lost time, was there still time, and was I even still in a sufficiently fit condition? The mind has its landscapes and only a short time is allowed for their contemplation. My life had been like a painter who climbs up a road overhanging a lake that is hidden from view by a screen of rocks and trees. Through a gap he glimpses it, he has it all there in front of him, he takes up his brushes. But the night is already falling when there is no more painting, and after which no day will break. Only, one prerequisite of my work as I had just recently conceived it in the library was the thorough investigation of impressions which needed first to be recreated through memory. But that was threadbare. (6:344-45/4:612)

The co-implication of chronophilia and chronophobia is thus at the genesis of Marcel's book. Because he is attached to his temporal being (chronophilia) and afraid of the same being passing away (chronophobia), he seeks to record it for the future. The recording of time does not redeem the temporal condition but is itself subjected to it. The threads of memory may be broken and the piece of writing may be destroyed.

The question we need to ask, then, is why Marcel's concluding aesthetic reflections persistently have been read in terms of a desire for immortality, when the logic of his own writing exhibits a desire for survival. The first thing to remember here is that we are reading a *narrative* and not a philosophical treatise. The propositions put forward are thus signed by Marcel as a narrator in a particular situation (which is not to be conflated with that of Proust the author). Specifically, Marcel is composing the text under the pressures of illness and impending death, which generates an extraordinary instability and range of intonations in the closing pages of the *Recherche,* when he is trying to make sense of his life and his purpose in writing. If one follows the sequence of articulation here (rather than isolating a certain statement), one will see how the apparent commitment to a state of eternity is repeatedly undone by the recognition of temporal finitude. Even on the explicit level of Marcel's aesthetics, the articulation of an essential temporality is far more prevalent than the remarks about the revelation of a timeless being. If the latter remarks nevertheless have been highlighted at the expense of the former, it is because there is no available model for reading how the purported desire for immortality is contradicted from within by the desire for survival. By providing such a model, the notion of chronolibido allows for an analysis of the *Recherche* that challenges not only the redemptive readings of Proust but also those readings that dismiss the grand declarations of the final volume as the expression of an untenable metaphysics.[29] From the beginning, Proust scholarship has been divided between those who appropriate the concluding aesthetic-philosophical program as the key to the novel and those who dismiss it as a misleading superstructure in favor of other aspects of the *Recherche*.[30] What is precluded in both cases is a counter-reading of the aesthetic-philosophical program itself, which is what I seek to provide in light of the condition of chronolibido.

It is here particularly instructive to compare my approach to Leo Bersani's influential reading of Proust in *The Culture of Redemption*. Bersani targets the "redemptive" readings of modernist literature, which hold that "a certain type of repetition of experience in art repairs inherently damaged or valueless experience."[31] Proust—and the dominant reading of Proust—is for Bersani the paradigmatic example of such a redemptive aesthetics. Bersani's "frankly polemical study" of claims concerning the supposed "redemptive virtues of literature" (1) may thus seem to have the same target as I do. Yet once we examine Bersani's account, we can see that his critique of "the culture of redemption" is itself based on an idea of redemption that is undermined by the insights of the *Recherche*.

For Bersani, the culture of redemption is complicit with the inclination of the self to "annihilate" others in favor of transcendence, and one can certainly find passages in Proust that would seem to support such a reading. Consider, for example, the following famous declaration from the last volume of the *Recherche:*

> Every person who makes us suffer can be linked by us to a divinity of which he or she is only a fragmentary reflection at the lowest level, a divinity (Idea) the contemplation of which immediately gives us joy instead of the pain we felt before. The whole art of living is to use those who make us suffer simply as steps enabling us to obtain access to their divine form and thus joyfully to people our lives with divinities. (6:207/4:477)

This is the passage that is most often adduced in support of the redemptive reading of Proust. Art would have the capacity to transform suffering into joy by allowing us to transcend the attachment to a particular individual—which makes us susceptible to the pain of loss or betrayal—in favor of a general truth that is immune to the vicissitudes of mortal life. We can thus understand why Bersani maintains that the aesthetics of redemption is ultimately premised on an "annihilating salvation" (11), since only the annihilation of the particularity of others could end "all resistance to Marcel's voracious desire to appropriate them" and allow him "to reconstruct the objects of his desires as invulnerable truths" (14).

Yet the passage above is in fact a fragment that does not have a clear place in the closing pages of the *Recherche*[32] and the logic it proposes is contradicted only a few pages later. Rather than celebrating the transformation of particular others into examples of general truths as an aesthetic redemption, Marcel goes on to lament that "even those who were most dear to the writer have in the end done no more than pose for him like models for a painter," an idea that he does not embrace but to which he has to "resign" himself (6:214/4:484). Consequently, while Marcel maintains that "the supreme truth of life resides in art" (6:211/4:481) and seeks "to extract from our grief the generality that lies within it, to write about it" (6:210/4:480), he acknowledges that such writing does not offer any redemption for those who have passed away. On the contrary, Marcel expresses an "infinite pity" for all those "whom my thought, in its attempt to understand them, had reduced to their suffering or merely to their follies" and he confesses to a feeling of "horror" at himself, as if he were "some nationalist party" which "alone had profited from a war in which many noble victims had suffered and died" (6:211/4:481). Far from holding forth his book as a glorious body of redeemed life, he describes it as "a huge cemetery where the names have been effaced from most of the tombs and can no longer be read" (6:212/4:482).

Furthermore, the violence of death and forgetting applies not only to the treatment of others in his book but also to the treatment of himself. "Saddening too was the thought that my love, to which I had clung so tenaciously, would in my book be so detached from any individual that different readers would apply it, even in detail, to what they had felt for other women" (6:211/4:481). He goes on to observe, however, that "this infidelity, this division of love between a number of women" had already begun in his own lifetime and even before he started to write. "It was true that I had suffered successively for Gilberte, for Mme de Guermantes, for Albertine. But successively I had also forgotten them, and only the love, dedicated to different women, had lasted. The profanation of one of my memories by unknown readers was a crime that I myself had committed before them" (6:211/4:481).

The double bind of survival—as the source of both desire and fear—is thus operative both in relation to the survival of his book and the survival of his life. In the first case, survival enables him to live on after his death but by the same token exposes him to the "posthumous infidelity" (6:211/4:481) of readers appropriating his experiences beyond anything he ever intended. In the second case, survival enables him to live on after the death of a given love but by the same token makes him liable to betray himself and the one he was.

Inversely, the survival of the other is also the source of both desire and fear. When Marcel glosses his discovery of embodied time in the closing pages of the novel, he emphasizes how embodied time gives rise not only to an individual history but also to a violent jealousy. Precisely because human bodies "contain within themselves the hours of the past" they have "the power to hurt so terribly those who love them, because they contain the memories of so many joys and desires already effaced for them, but still cruel for the lover who contemplates and prolongs in the dimension of Time the beloved body of which he is jealous, so jealous that he may even wish for its destruction" (6:357/4:624). The latter observation is certainly inflected by the misogynic jealousy that Marcel displays throughout the novel. One can and should be critical of misogyny, however, while still recognizing the irreducible double bind of attachment and loss, desire and fear, at the heart of libidinal being. This is exactly the distinction that Bersani does not heed. Having noted the violent tendencies of relational desire, he does not articulate the double bind of relationality as a condition that needs to be negotiated, but rather advocates a retreat from the very relation to others in favor of a "self-shattering and solipsistic *jouissance*" (4). This *jouissance,* which consists in "both a turning away from others and a dying to the self" (45), is for Bersani the site of nonviolence. Indeed, Bersani advocates self-shattering *jouissance* as a "primary, hygienic practice of nonviolence," since it "dissolves the person and thereby, at least temporarily, erases the sacrosanct value of selfhood, a value that may account for human beings' extraordinary willingness to kill" (3–4).

Ironically enough, Bersani thereby repeats a version of the most traditional trope for a redemptive aesthetics. Following his notion of a *jouissance* that would redeem us from violence, Bersani's reading of Proust seeks to promote "an erotic art independent of the anxieties inherent in desire" and a "disinterested mode of desire for objects" (28). It should come as no surprise if Bersani has difficulty finding support for this aesthetics in Proust. While Marcel repeatedly lays claim to having attained an aesthetic state that would allow him to contemplate the world without the anxieties of desire, these moments are undercut from within by the sense of temporal finitude that animates and sustains them. As soon as Marcel declares that he no longer fears death in light of the book he will write, he begins to fear that he will die before he has written it. And even when he is animated by the hope that the book will be written and live on, its very ability to survive becomes a painful reminder of the dead who are left behind.

If these threats of loss persistently emerge, it is because of the chronolibido that sustains the project of redemption itself. The sense of temporal finitude—the sense of the possibility of loss—is part of the desire to save anything in the first place. The threat of loss is thus not merely an external threat but is internal to whatever one wants to save. That desire and loss are interdependent does not mean that there is a given way to deal with loss or that one can be immune from responding to it in reactive or violent ways. The chronolibidinal investment in survival is rather coextensive with an exposure to *traumatic* events, and the response to these events cannot be given in advance.

CHAPTER 2

Trauma

Woolf

O N A WINTER afternoon in the alpine region of Norway, a man begins to read Virginia Woolf's novel *To the Lighthouse*. He is seized by how she manages to convey the smallest movements of thought, sensation, and everyday life. Woolf's writing makes him think about the very activity of thinking, sense the very texture of sensation, and his life opens itself to him with a new depth. As he proceeds to the second part of *To the Lighthouse*, however, everything changes. A major character such as Mrs. Ramsay, whose life he previously could follow second by second over the space of numerous pages, is now disposed of in a parenthesis. Indeed, no less than three of the main characters die in parentheses, as time indifferently passes away. For the man who was seized by the fate of these characters, the insight is unbearable. The depth of life that he had begun to appreciate suddenly appears terrifying. He closes the book, never to open it again.

This scene from Jan Kjaerstad's novel *Oppdageren* captures the sense of temporality in Woolf's writing that I want to explore in this chapter. On the one hand, Woolf has a celebrated ability to depict moments of time in their unique texture, as in the first part of *To the Lighthouse*. On the other hand, Woolf also depicts the relentless negativity of time that destroys the moments to which it gives rise, as in the second part of *To the*

Lighthouse. It would be a mistake to oppose these two types of temporality to one another. Rather, the violent passage of time is at work even in the most immediate and fully experienced moment.

Consequently, I will focus on what has come to be known as Woolf's aesthetics of the moment. Ann Banfield has provided the most comprehensive account of this aesthetics, linking it to a literary impressionism whereby a "unit of experienced time" is rendered in vivid detail.[1] While Banfield offers a rich and wide-ranging discussion of Woolf's notion of the moment, she ultimately understands the being of the moment as a timeless presence. On Banfield's account, the fleeting world of temporal existence is opposed to the atemporal being of the moment. Accordingly, she reads Woolf's aesthetic ambition to "crystallize" moments of being as a way to transform the ephemeral into the eternal.[2] Banfield here understands the eternal as presence in itself, quoting the early Wittgenstein's claim that "he lives eternally who lives in the present."[3]

In contrast, I will argue that Woolf's aesthetics of the moment reveals how even the most immediate presence passes away as soon as it comes to be. Precisely because Woolf seeks to convey singular moments, she has to convey that these moments are temporal rather than eternal. If the moment were not temporal, it could not be distinguished *as* a moment, since it would not be irreplaceable. Furthermore, it is the temporality of the moment that precipitates the desire to crystallize it. It is because the moment is passing away that one seeks to keep it as a memory for the future. Contrary to Banfield's thesis, to crystallize the moment is not to render it eternal but to record it so that it may *live on* in time.

An instructive example is the opening of *To the Lighthouse.* The young James Ramsay is here endowed with the ability "to crystallize and transfix the moment" (3) precisely because he is hypersensitive to how his present experience already is becoming past and becoming related to the future. James cannot repose in the present "but must let future prospects, with their joys and sorrows, cloud what is actually at hand" (3). Thus, when his mother declares that they will go to the lighthouse if the weather is fine tomorrow, the picture James is looking at is "fringed with joy" (3) because it is associated with his positive anticipation of the event. But when his father interjects that the weather will not be fine tomorrow, James's joy turns into despair. In accordance with a pattern that Woolf explores to great effect, the future as a source of excitement may always become a source of dreaded disappointment. This double relation to the future is not something that can be overcome in a crystallized moment of plenitude. On the contrary, it is intrinsic to the crystallization of the moment itself. As the narrator points out a propos James, "any turn in the wheel of sensation has the power to crystallize and transfix the moment upon which its gloom or radiance rests" (3). The power of crystallization, then, depends on a libidinal investment in the temporal fate of the moment. Without the chronophilic hope for and chronophobic fear of what may come, there would be no radiance or gloom that could transfix the moment in memory and thus "crystallize" it. The aesthetic and affective power of this crystallization does not stem from an intimation of eternity but from the investment in a life that is susceptible to transformation and loss. If the moment is glowing with expectation or burdened by disappointment, it is because one is invested in the fate of a temporal life. Crystallization is not a matter of timeless presence but of how the moment is refracted in memory and anticipation.

Accordingly, we can trace the logic of chronolibido in the aesthetics of the novel's modernist painter, Lily Briscoe, whose explicit ambition is "to make of the moment something permanent" (161). Her method for achieving this crystallization is to capture the present in painting:

> One must keep on looking without for a second relaxing the intensity
> of emotion, the determination not to be put off, not to be bamboozled.
> One must hold the scene—so—in a vise and let nothing come in and
> spoil it. One wanted, she thought, dipping her brush deliberately, to be
> on a level with ordinary experience, to feel simply that's a chair, that's
> a table, and yet at the same time, It's a miracle, it's an ecstasy. (202)

This ecstatic experience of the moment does not suspend time; it is rather an effect of temporal being. When Lily experiences a miraculous moment and tries to seize its quality, it is because she senses how it is in the process of being lost and never will return. Following her own simile, the experience of an ecstatic moment is like that of a traveler who is looking out of a train window and suddenly knows "that he must look now, for he will never see that town, or that mule-cart, or that woman at work in the fields, again" (194). For the same reason, even when Lily experiences "the perfection of the moment," she is already "burying" it (172), as it is never present in itself and needs to be commemorated.

Lily's aesthetic ambition to crystallize the moment is thus haunted by the double bind that is inherent in any act of living on. Through her painting, the "passing and flowing" of time is supposed to be "struck into stability" (161) and preserved in the moment. Yet the very form of preservation is itself temporal. The spatial painting that retains moments of time can only remain for a future that may obliterate it, as Lily herself acknowledges when contemplating the painting: "it would be hung in the attics, she thought; it would be destroyed" (208).

The same problem of survival haunts Mrs. Ramsay's attempts to make the moment permanent. Lily points to the parallel between her own aesthetic practice and the dictum she has inherited from Mrs. Ramsay: " 'Life stand still here' " (161). Mrs. Ramsay does not pursue her resistance to the passage of time through the medium of art, but rather through what she describes as the "merging and flowing and creating" (83) of social relationships. The apparent consummation of Mrs. Ramsay's efforts to halt time is the famous dinner party scene in the first part of *To the Lighthouse*. When observing her family and friends together, Mrs. Ramsay has the sense of how "there is a coherence in things, a stability; something, she meant, is immune from change, and shines out . . . in the face of the flowing, the fleeting, the spectral, like a ruby. . . . Of such moments, she thought, the thing is made that endures" (105). This passage may seem to confirm Banfield's reading of the crystallized moment as an eternal presence. Yet such a reading is undercut by the logic of the passage itself. At the very moment of Mrs. Ramsay's ecstatic experience—when she reposes "in an element of joy" which fills "every nerve of her body fully and sweetly"—she thinks to herself: "this cannot last" (104–05). Moreover, the reflection on the transience of the moment is inserted between two temporal markers in her train of thought: "*Just now* (but this cannot last, she thought, dissociating herself from the moment while they were all talking about boots) *just now* she had reached security" (104–05, my emphasis). The repetition of the "now" is already a function of temporal difference, which marks that the moment is passing away and cannot be immune from alteration. Accordingly, the very "thing" that Mrs. Ramsay describes as "enduring" cannot be immune from alteration either, since it is composed of moments that belong to the experience of finite beings. What Mrs. Ramsay is passionate about is not endurance as eternal being but endurance as *living on* in time.

The idea of such endurance is intrinsic to the value placed on family and friends by Mrs. Ramsay. Through their lives and their memories, she herself can live on. Having facilitated the engagement between Paul and Minta, Mrs. Ramsay thinks to herself after the dinner party: "however long they lived, [they would] come back to this night; this moon; this wind; this house; and to her too. . . . All that would be revived again in the lives of Paul and Minta. . . . Paul and Minta would carry it on when she was dead" (113–14). Mrs. Ramsay's declared desire to make life stand still—to keep it as it is—is thus contradicted from within. The life she wants to hold on to is temporal in itself and can only be kept for a future that may allow it to live on, but also will alter and destroy it. For the same reason, the "stability" or "coherence in things" that is created by intimate bonds is essentially liable to break down. Those who are supposed to keep the memories or ensure the legacy are themselves mortal, and while they are still alive they can forget or reject what has been handed down to them.[4]

Consequently, when we move from the first part of the novel to the second (entitled "Time Passes"), Mrs. Ramsay and two of the children die, leaving Mr. Ramsay and Lily Briscoe to mourn them in the third part of the novel. This tripartite division of *To the Lighthouse* reflects the structure of survival, where the anticipated future always can turn out to shatter expectations and leave the survivor in mourning. I want to emphasize again, however, that the threat of temporal finitude does not supervene upon something that precedes it but is at work in every experience. Already in the first part of the novel, Mrs. Ramsay's intense happiness in being alive—captured in a scene where "ecstasy burst in her eyes and waves of pure delight raced over the floor of her mind and she felt, It is enough! It is enough!" (65)—is deeply equivocal. The emphatic "It is enough!" may express a sense of satisfaction and fulfillment, but also a sense of having had enough, of not being able to take more of the life that nevertheless keeps on giving. Accordingly, the receptivity to life is also a susceptibility to becoming overwhelmed, and the ecstasy of being alive is intertwined with the sense of life as a cruel "antagonist" (79). While Mrs. Ramsay has a famous capacity for rejoicing in life, Woolf makes clear that she also "felt this thing that she called life terrible, hostile, and quick to pounce on you if you gave it a chance. . . . And yet she had said to all these children, You shall go through it all" (59–60). The value of life is thus never given once and for all but is strictly undecidable: life is the source of both the desirable *and* the undesirable, so the promise of the future is at the same time a threat.

The undecidability of life is central to what I will analyze as the *traumatic* conception of temporality in Woolf's writing. A traumatic event is minimally defined by being *too much*. In the event, one is flooded with stimulus that one cannot master. Something happens so brutally and so fast that it exceeds one's capacity to experience it and to feel its impact. The time factor here is crucial. On the one hand, the traumatic event happens *too soon*, since it happens too unexpectedly to be fully comprehended in the event. On the other hand, the traumatic event happens *too late*, since the event is not available to consciousness until it imposes itself again, as in nightmares or intrusive memories. The experience of trauma is therefore both deferred and delayed: it exposes the psyche to the force of a temporality that it cannot master.

What I want to emphasize here is that the same structure of deferral and delay characterizes temporal experience in general. A temporal event can never be present as such, since it comes into being only by becoming past and becoming related to the future. The experience of the event is always given *too late* (in relation to what is no longer) and *too soon* (in relation to what is not yet). Following Derrida's provocative formulation, we can therefore say that *every event is traumatic*, in the sense that what happens exceeds any given anticipation and only can be apprehended in retrospect, when it has already passed.[5]

In Woolf studies, the theme of trauma has gained prominence as a number of scholars have focused on her accounts of war and sexual violence. These themes are important, and I will return to them further on. My analysis, however, proceeds from the structural link between the possibility of trauma and the constitution of time. To proceed from the structural possibility of trauma, rather than from the specificity of certain historical traumas, is not to deny the urgency or intricacies of the latter.

Rather, it is to begin with the question of why it is *always possible* to become traumatized. As Lily Briscoe reflects in *To the Lighthouse:*

> What was it then, what did it mean? Could things thrust their hands up and grip one; could the blade cut; the fist grasp? Was there no safety? No learning by heart the ways of the world? No guide, no shelter. . . . Could it be, even for elderly people, that this was life?—startling, unexpected, unknown? (180)

The answer conveyed by Woolf's writing is an emphatic yes. She persistently returns to how any psychological structure—any configuration of expectation and hope—is vulnerable to breaking down. Of course, the general susceptibility to trauma does not mean that everyone is *equally* susceptible to trauma. The different degrees of susceptibility, however, all presuppose the structural possibility of trauma that is concomitant with temporal experience in general. A temporal being is by definition vulnerable to trauma, since it can never repose in itself and is exposed to an undecidable future.[6] The notion of undecidability that I employ is thus a feature of temporal experience itself. The condition of temporality is, strictly speaking, "undecidable," since it consists in a relentless displacement that unsettles any definitive assurance or given meaning. One can never know what *will have happened,* since the succession of time may always alter the character of the anticipated event. It is precisely this experience of time that is intensified in the experience of trauma, when the horizon of expectation breaks down because of an unexpected event.

My argument, then, is that Woolf's aesthetics of the moment highlights the traumatic deferral and delay at the heart of temporal experience. Precisely by narrating immediate experience, she conveys how it is always mediated across a temporal interval that exposes it to the possibility of trauma. This exposure to trauma should not be understood as merely a negative determination. Rather, the exposure to trauma is inseparable from the very opening of the future and thus inseparable from the possibility of living on in the first place.

I will focus on *Mrs. Dalloway,* which is the groundbreaking novel both for Woolf's narration of time and her treatment of trauma. These two aspects of her work should not be considered separately. If *Mrs. Dalloway* is "a masterpiece from the point of view of the perception of time," as Paul Ricoeur has claimed,[7] it is precisely because it relates the traumatism that haunts the movement of temporalization.

On the thematic level, trauma is prevalent in *Mrs. Dalloway*. The novel takes place on a day in June after the end of the First World War, the effects of which linger among all the characters. The traumatic aftermath of the war comes to the fore in the character Septimus Warren Smith, whose life is disintegrating due to his experiences as a soldier. The other main character—Clarissa Dalloway—is not subjected to the same psychological suffering, but she too is clearly marked by traumatic experiences. As a young girl she witnessed her sister being killed by a falling tree, and when the novel begins she has just recovered from an illness that threatened her life.

Beyond the depiction of specific traumas, however, Woolf displays how experience in general is characterized by a delay and deferral that can be described as traumatic. The characters' streams of consciousness convey how they are always in the process of comprehending past experience (delay) and how their present experience can be apprehended only in retrospect (deferral). For example, in the opening scene of the novel, Clarissa Dalloway steps out onto the streets of London and is seized by the radiance of the early summer morning. Her present experience is immediately informed by the past, since the morning awakens the memory of another morning in her youth. The memory of that day in Clarissa's youth comes back throughout the entire novel, as she assesses the significance of her past experience and reckons with her delayed understanding of what happened. Inversely, Clarissa's present experience is necessarily deferred, since it is never given as such. The present moment can only be apprehended through the repetition of memory, which is marked by the haunting phrase through which Clarissa expresses what she loves: "life; London; this moment of June" (4). This phrase is the culmination of a sentence that captures Clarissa's excitement at the details of London in early morning. Far from expressing the timeless plenitude of the moment, the phrase underlines that the experience of plenitude is always already temporalized. In repeating to herself what she loves ("life; London; this moment of June"), Clarissa imprints it as a memory for the future. This act would be unthinkable unless the apprehension of temporality—of ceasing to be—were intrinsic to the experience of presence itself.

The link between the movement of temporalization and the experience of the moment is further clarified when Clarissa returns home later the same morning and pauses before her reflection in the mirror. The doubling of Clarissa in this scene is not only an effect of her physical reflection but also answers to how her identity is divided by temporality. Rather than being given as an indivisible unity, she has to "collect" herself in order to appear as such and "transfix" the present as a memory in order to resist the coming of time:

> She was not old yet. She had just broken into her fifty-second year. Months and months of it were still untouched. June, July, August! Each still remained almost whole, and, as if to catch the falling drop, Clarissa (crossing to the dressing-table) plunged into the very heart of the moment, transfixed it, there—the moment of this June morning on which was the pressure of all the other mornings, seeing the glass, the dressing-table, and all the bottles afresh, collecting the whole of her at one point (as she looked into the glass), seeing the delicate pink face of the woman who was that very night to give a party; of Clarissa Dalloway; of herself. (36–37)

As in the opening scene of the novel, Clarissa here "plunges" into the moment, not because it offers a consummate plenitude but because of its intrinsic temporality. Her sensation of how the moment is precious—its quality of being a unique "drop" of life—is concomitant with her sensation of how the moment is already dissolving, as in the figure of the falling drop and the impetus to catch it. Thus, Clarissa's chronophilic desire to "transfix" the moment—to imprint it in memory—stems from her chronophobic awareness of the moment passing away. Even in the sentences that establish persistence across time, discrete adverbs remind us of the possibility of loss: "She was not old *yet* . . . months of it were *still* untouched. . . . Each *still* remained."

Persistence itself thus emerges as a temporal form that is susceptible to trauma. The most general name for this temporal form is what I analyze as the condition of survival, which is an explicit concern already in the opening pages of *Mrs. Dalloway*. As Clarissa enjoys the summer morning in London, her thoughts open onto the problem of living on:

> What she loved was this, here, now, in front of her; the fat lady in the cab. Did it matter then, she asked herself walking towards Bond Street, did it matter that she must inevitably cease completely; all this must go on without her; did she resent it; or did it not become consoling to believe that death ended absolutely? but that somehow in the streets of London, on the ebb and flow of things, here, there, she survived, Peter survived, lived in each other, she being part, she was positive, of the trees at home; of the house there, ugly, rambling all to bits and pieces as it was; part of people she had never met; being laid out like a mist between the people she knew best, who lifted her on their branches as she had seen the trees lift the mist, but it spread ever so far, her life, herself. (9)

The affirmation of beloved presence is concomitant with the awareness of its possible negation. No sooner has Clarissa affirmed her love for "this, here, now" than she is contemplating the disappearance of the very being that harbors this love. The ensuing reflection may seem paradoxical, since it maintains both that death is an absolute end *and* that there is the chance of survival. The paradox vanishes, however, when we recognize that the survival beyond a given individual death does not transcend the condition of mortality but is itself subjected to it. As Christine Froula has shown, the arboreal metaphor in the passage above extends throughout *Mrs. Dalloway*, where moments are described as "buds on the tree of life, flowers of darkness" (29) and people branch out into each other's lives through a vast network of connections. Yet the tree of life that sustains connections beyond individual death is itself subject to perishing. Following Froula, the arboreal metaphors should be understood in relation to Shakespeare' *Cymbeline*, which is an intertext throughout *Mrs. Dalloway* and where Posthumus declares: "Hang there like fruit, my soul, / Till the tree die!"[8] Analogously, the survival of a given life in memories or other material traces does not release it from the threat of death but marks its dependence on a support system that itself is destructible.

Nevertheless, readers of *Mrs. Dalloway* persistently conflate the notion of survival with a notion of immortality. Despite her astute observations about the problem of survival in *Mrs. Dalloway,* Froula holds that the power of art and memory "defeats time and loss" in "a diamantine 'present' preserved from time, death, loss, absence."[9] J. Hillis Miller is more emphatic in his reading of *Mrs. Dalloway* and maintains "the possibility that repetition in narrative is the representation of a transcendent spiritual realm of reconciliation and preservation, a realm of the perpetual resurrection of the dead."[10] For Hillis Miller, the "undecidable" question is whether such a transcendent realm exists only in the words of Woolf's novel "or whether the words represent an extralinguistic realm which is 'really there' for the characters, for the narrator, and for Woolf herself" (201–02). From my perspective, however, neither of these alternatives is the right one, since there is no transcendent realm even in the words of Woolf's novel. The structures of memory and repetition in *Mrs. Dalloway* do not point toward immortality (a "perpetual resurrection of the dead") but toward the precarious possibility of survival through finite traces.

The finitude of survival is clearly marked when, later in the novel, Peter Walsh returns to Clarissa's theory of life and death. Confirming her notion that they live on in each other, Peter remembers how Clarissa in their youth proposed a "transcendental theory" to alleviate her "horror of death":

> Clarissa had a theory in those days. . . . It was to explain the feeling they had of dissatisfaction; not knowing people; not being known. For how could they know each other? You met every day; then not for six months, or years. It was unsatisfactory, they agreed, how little one knew people. But she said, sitting on top of the bus going up Shaftesbury Avenue, she felt herself everywhere; not "here, here, here"; and she tapped the back of the seat; but everywhere. She waved her hand, going up Shaftesbury Avenue. She was all that. So that to know her, or any one, one must seek out the people who completed them; even the places. Odd affinities she had with people she had never spoken to, some woman in the street, some man behind a counter—even trees, or barns. It ended in a transcendental theory which, with her horror of death, allowed her to believe, or say that she believed (for all her skepticism), that since our apparitions, the part of us which appears, are so momentary compared with the other, the unseen part of us, which spreads wide, the unseen might survive,

be recovered somehow attached to this person or that, or even haunting certain places after death . . . perhaps—perhaps.

Looking back over that long friendship of almost thirty years her theory worked to this extent. Brief, broken, often painful as their actual meetings had been what with his absences and interruptions . . . the effect of them on his life was immeasurable. There was a mystery about it. You were given a sharp, acute, uncomfortable grain—the actual meeting; horribly painful as often as not; yet in absence, in the most unlikely places, it would flower out, open, shed its scent, let you touch, taste, look about you, get the whole feel about it and understanding, after years of lying lost. Thus she had come to him; on board ship; in the Himalayas; suggested by the oddest things. (152–53)

The basic problem here concerns the interval of time that separates one self from another. To remedy the separation, Clarissa proposes that the self survives ("attached to this person or that, or even haunting certain places") so that connections may be established across time. The survival that allows a given life to extend beyond itself, however, is necessarily marked by the death it seeks to resist. In order to live on—and thus counteract the separation of time—one must be separated from oneself at the very moment of the event. Already when Clarissa is sitting on the bus, she is being separated from herself in order to be inscribed as a memory. If she were not separated from herself—namely, if she were not ceasing to be— she could never leave a trace for the future and be remembered by Peter, herself, or anyone else. The connection across time is thus predicated on a separation in time that opens it to the possibility of disconnection. The "unseen part" of Clarissa that survives beyond her visible apparition is not an immortal soul; it is the mortal traces she has imprinted upon the world and others. By living on in something else or someone else, she can be said to resist the separation in time, but by the same token she is at the mercy of an other who may forget, distort, or erase the memory of herself. Far from redeeming death, her transcendental theory of survival bears time and loss within itself.

Furthermore, there is no guarantee that it is better to have something survive rather than killed off. In the passage quoted above, we see how Clarissa lives on in Peter, but her surviving impact has the structure of a trauma. His understanding of their meetings only emerges across a delay in time ("after years of lying lost"), and their significance is never given as such. The event in question may "flower out, open, shed its scent" in a positive manner, but it may equally well be a ghost that drains him of life. Indeed, we learn that "Clarissa had sapped something in him permanently" (159), and it is clear throughout the novel that Peter hangs on to his surviving memories of Clarissa in a self-destructive way.

My point here is not to cast Peter as a victim, and one should certainly note his implication in the exercise of imperial and patriarchal power. In order to assess Woolf's rendition of war trauma and sexual violence, however, we need to take into account the general undecidability of the value of survival, which is operative in Peter's life as well as in everyone else's. Recent studies of the problem of trauma in Woolf's work have tended to valorize either a "melancholic" refusal to let go of the lost object or a "mourning" process of consolation. Following the chronolibidinal logic of survival, I will show why both of these approaches are contradicted from within and why neither can be recommended over the other a priori.

A good place to start is the juxtaposition of Septimus and Clarissa. Their relation is an organizing principle of the novel, which Woolf famously underlined by describing Septimus as Clarissa's "double."[11] Through the way they are reflected in one another, we can observe the complex interplay of melancholia and mourning in the response to trauma. In contradistinction to the upper-class Clarissa, Septimus comes from the working class, having gradually ascended the social ladder in England and served with great distinction in the First World War. "He had gone through the whole show, friendship, European War, death, had won promotion, was still under thirty and bound to survive" (86). In the war he cultivates detachment and emotional restraint, congratulating himself "upon feeling very little" when his friend Evans dies and watching "with indifference" (86) as the shells explode around him. In accordance with the experience of many soldiers, it is only afterward—upon returning home to the supposed normality of peace—that his experience of trauma and sense of guilt begin to emerge. When we encounter Septimus on the fateful day in June, he is wandering the streets of London with his wife Rezia, who herself is haunted by a sense of loss and alienation, having left her home in Italy for a country she does not understand and a husband who is increasingly deprived of his sanity. Septimus hears voices, lapses into visions, and is frequently visited by the ghost of Evans, whose death he witnessed with stoic acceptance but for which he now cannot forgive himself.

As Karen DeMeester has shown, Woolf here provides a compelling dramatization of a psychological condition that the discipline of psychiatry would not understand for another fifty years, namely, post-traumatic stress disorder (PTSD).[12] Given the magnitude of Septimus's experiences during the war, he can only process them in retrospect, and the repetition of the traumatic past is a way of working through what happened as well as the guilt of having survived. This process of working through is short circuited, however, since the source of Septimus's suffering is not recognized and addressed. He is stranded in a society that wants to move on and forget about the war. Even the doctors who treat him reinforce that he has no reason to suffer or feel guilt but rather should be proud of his service to his country.

Given such a politically repressive mourning, the act of holding on to the past and refusing consolation can be seen as a form of resistance. Along these lines, the most insightful "melancholic" reading of Woolf is the one pursued by Tammy Clewell. Arguing against readings that fault Woolf with an inability to mourn, Clewell maintains that "Woolf's refusal to engage a process of mourning aimed at 'working through' despair and grief" is not pathological; instead it forms part of a consistent anticonsolatory and anti-redemptive aesthetics.[13] Clewell argues that Woolf's aesthetic response to the traumas of the First World War "sought not to heal wartime wounds, but to keep them open" (198) and created "commemorative forms intended to provoke and hurt, rather than console and heal" (199). Clewell is right to emphasize the antiredemptive force of Woolf's aesthetics, and one can certainly adduce many cases where the refusal of consolation may serve politically progressive ends. It does not follow, however, that it is a priori better to refuse consolation than to accept it, better to keep wounds open than to close them. Yet it is precisely such an a priori argument to which Clewell succumbs when she moves from accounting for Woolf's anticonsolatory aesthetics to promoting an anticonsolatory ethics. As she concludes her study, "*only* by refusing consolation and sustaining grief can we accept responsibility for the difficult task of performing private and public memory" (219, my emphasis). The ethical status of this argument is unclear. The fact that there can be no redemptive consolation—no final healing of wounds—does not entail that it is better to offer less consolation and healing rather than more consolation and healing. The cultivation of wounds and the refusal to mourn does not necessarily result in a more ethical response to trauma; it can just as well breed destructive rage and hatred. Moreover, the refusal to mourn may be destructive not only for others but also for the self. Septimus, for one, is never able to "work through" his experiences from the war but is rather locked in a repetition of traumatic events, which eventually leads him to commit suicide.

Now, it is precisely because of the destructive effects of the melancholic attachment to the past that the therapeutic effects of mourning traditionally have been recommended. To mourn is to learn to accept the loss of the past and to form new attachments in its place. The most prominent advocate for the "mourning" reading of Woolf is Christine Froula. Froula offers a powerful reading of *Mrs. Dalloway* as a modern form of elegy that explores "the genre's deep resources for dramatizing and mediating violence both psychic and social: the violence of war and of everyday death; the violence of everyday life; and the violence intrinsic to mourning, the grief-driven rage that threatens to derail the mourner's progress toward acceptance and consolation."[14] Acceptance and consolation are thus posited as the goal for the elegy's work of mourning. While Froula does speak of a "violence" that is intrinsic to mourning, she restricts it to the perversion of mourning in grief-driven rage. Revenge tragedy is according to Froula the elegy's "bad other" (88), which fails to mourn and rather engages in violent rage to make up for grievances. By maintaining this opposition between peaceful acceptance and violent revenge, however, Froula does not thematize the violence that is intrinsic to elegiac mourning itself. If "the elegy's very principle" is "the necessity of relinquishing the dead and of forming new attachments in order to carry on with life"—as Froula herself eloquently formulates it (91)—it follows that the principle of the elegy necessarily is violent. To relinquish an attachment is by definition a violent act, and no consolation for the living can redeem the forgetting of the dead. Thus, while one may certainly argue that it is often crucial to let go of the attachment to the dead in order to live on, the act of letting go cannot be exempt from violence.

Furthermore, Froula's own reading of *Mrs. Dalloway* undermines the idea that the principle of elegy always is preferable to the principle of revenge tragedy. By paying close attention to "the sexual violence buried in this novel's news of the day no less than to the war on its front page" (126), Froula comes upon the case of Sally Seton. In Clarissa's youth, Sally represents the values of female emancipation: sexual freedom, education, and progressive political struggle. Clarissa falls in love with her, describing the moment she kissed her as "the most exquisite moment of her whole life . . . she felt that she had been given a present, wrapped up, and told just to keep it, not to look at it—a diamond, something infinitely precious" (35). When Clarissa receives the news of Septimus's suicide, it is to this "treasure" that she first associates, feeling how she has allowed it to be "defaced, obscured in her own life, let drop every day in corruption, lies, chatter" (184). In contrast to her own letting go of the past, she perceives Septimus's suicide as an act of "defiance" and "an attempt to communicate" (184). Clarissa understands that this defiance is aimed at men like Sir William Bradshaw (Septimus's doctor), whom she describes as "obscurely evil" and "capable of some indescribable outrage—forcing your soul, that was it. . . . Life is made intolerable; they make life intolerable, men like that" (184–85). Yet Clarissa pursues neither a critique of the repression of the war nor a critique of the patriarchal repression of her desire for female emancipation. Rather, she contributes to maintaining the political status quo precisely to the extent that she is successful in mourning her past and Septimus's fate.

Far from dissimulating the violence of this mourning, Woolf makes it explicit in an extraordinary sequence. In a first move, Clarissa identifies with Septimus: "She felt somehow very like him—the young man who had killed himself" (186). Upon hearing of his suicide, she even viscerally empathizes with how it must have felt: "her body went through it . . . her dress flamed, her body burnt. He had thrown himself from a window. Up had flashed the ground; through him, blundering, bruising, went the rusty spikes" (184). In a second move, however, Clarissa displays her ability to find consolations in everyday life—to let go of the past in favor of living on—with a lighthearted cruelty: "The young man had killed himself; but she did not pity him. . . . She felt glad that he had done it; thrown it away. . . . He made her feel the beauty; made her feel the fun" (186). Froula herself observes that the emotional logic of this passage reveals the "brutal principle of substitution" at work in mourning, but this observation does not lead her to question the inherent desirability of an "elegiac progress" from "perilous grief and rage" to "existential consolation."[15]

Nevertheless, Froula's own reading allows us to see that elegiac acceptance is intrinsically violent and always may be mortgaged to political compromise. Froula convincingly argues that Sally is sexually assaulted by the conservative Hugh Whitbread and that Clarissa contributes to silencing this crime. Clarissa urges Sally "not to denounce him at family prayers" (*Mrs. Dalloway* 181) and to repress what has happened. Apparently, the repression is successful as the rebellious Sally is transformed into the conventional Lady Rosseter, who is dutifully married and has "five enormous boys" (*Mrs. Dalloway* 171). As Froula points out, Sally has thereby avoided the revenge tragedy of denouncing the patriarchal power represented by Hugh in favor of the "elegiac conversion narrative" that Clarissa advocates.[16] As is clear, however, elegiac acceptance is here in the service of political conformity, whereas revenge tragedy would have been in the service of the progressive transformation of gender relations that Froula herself advocates. Violent rage can be a much more powerful political weapon than elegiac acceptance. Moreover, to discount violence in advance as the "bad other" of proper action is to limit the possible range of women's political struggle in a traditional manner.

Let me emphasize that I am not arguing a relativist thesis here. The point is not that everything is equally violent but that the response to violence necessarily is violent and nothing can ensure that it is better to be more forgiving rather than less forgiving. Woolf's achievement is not to have offered a cure for the violent condition of survival but to have rendered its complexities.[17] The power of her depiction of trauma does not consist in the proposition of a formula for how to respond to trauma. On the contrary, it consists in the depiction of the undecidable value of survival, which entails that the response to trauma cannot be given once and for all but has to be decided from time to time.

Furthermore, *Mrs. Dalloway* dramatizes how the undecidability of survival pertains to the desire for life itself. Clarissa expresses an emphatic love of life, "loving it as she did with an absurd and faithful passion" (5), and she is endowed with the gift of appreciating the details of everyday existence. The chronophilic love of life cannot, however, be dissociated from the chronophobic fear of death. Clarissa feels how it is "very, very dangerous to live even one day" (8) and she fears "time itself . . . the dwindling of life; how year by year her share was sliced; how little the margin that remained was capable any longer of stretching" (30). The "divine vitality" (7) affirmed by Clarissa is thus haunted from within by its own finitude and by the possibility of suffering. Alongside the ecstasy of being alive there is "the terror, the overwhelming incapacity, one's parents giving it into one's hands, this life, to be lived to the end, to be walked with serenely; there was in the depths of her heart an awful fear" (185). Even on a radiant June morning, "soft with the glow of petals," she comes to experience herself as standing "alone against the appalling night . . . feeling herself suddenly shriveled, aged, breastless, the grinding, blowing, flowering of the day, out of doors, out of the window, out of her body and brain" (30–31).

The threat of trauma, then, is latent even in the most precious experience. The beloved good life bears within itself the possibility of becoming intolerably bad. To resolve this predicament, one may seek to eliminate life altogether. Such a "solution" to the problem of survival figures in *Mrs. Dalloway* via two lines from *Cymbeline* ("Fear no more the heat o' the sun / Nor the furious winter's rages") that both Clarissa and Septimus repeat to themselves during the day. The lines belong to a funeral song and have often been read as promoting the "peace" of death beyond the exigencies of life. Hillis Miller, for example, holds that the lines indicate that one "will reach peace and escape from suffering only in death" (198). According to Hillis Miller, this is the central insight of *Mrs. Dalloway*. "Septimus chose the right way," he maintains, since "death is the place of true communion" (196) and "self-annihilation is the only possible way to embrace that center which evades one as long as one is alive" (197). A similar reading is pursued by John Graham, who argues that the lines from *Cymbeline* convey a sense of "peace and reassurance" corresponding to the vision of "cosmic unity" that supposedly leads Septimus to kill himself in order to "exist independently of time."[18] These metaphysical readings misconstrue what is at stake in the employment of the lines from *Cymbeline*. Both Clarissa and Septimus repeat the lines *not* as an affirmation of death but as a conjuration to help them to go on living by tempering their fear of survival. To be sure, it is always possible that one may not be able to bear the exigencies of living on—and that one will respond by short-circuiting life—but this response itself presupposes a libidinal investment in survival. If one were not invested in survival, one would not experience any fear in the first place and never try to master one's affective response to being alive.

Far from transcending the investment in survival, the drama and significance of Septimus's suicide is altogether dependent on it. The metaphysical reading of Septimus's death as an ascent to transcendent "peace" is quite at odds with the operative logic in *Mrs. Dalloway* for at least three reasons. First, if death were a spiritually higher state of being—and if Septimus consequently did the right thing in taking his own life—there would be no reason to agonize over the political system that is implicated in his suicide. The critique of mechanisms that lead to the destruction of the self or others would lose all force, since death would not be something negative but rather the path to spiritual salvation. Second, if Septimus *wanted* to die due to a spiritual insight, there would be no tragedy in the event of his suicide, since there would be no conflict between what is desired and what happens. Third, the scene of Septimus's suicide in fact makes clear that he does *not* want to die. His last thoughts explicitly read: "He did not want to die. Life was good. The sun hot" (149). He nevertheless ends up killing himself because he cannot accept being taken away and kept under surveillance by a doctor he does not trust. Rezia tries to stop the doctor from entering their home and taking Septimus away, but the doctor pushes past her and goes after Septimus, who in response throws himself out of the window and dies. This death is a tragic descent and not a spiritual ascent.

Last but not least, the pathos of Woolf's writing here depends on the resistance to—rather than the embrace of—death and madness. The sequence that leads up to Septimus's suicide begins by slowing down the pace of his thoughts, letting the rage and rambling subside. Up to this point of the novel, Septimus has been dominated by his visions, but he now makes a concerted effort to return to reality. "He began, very cautiously, to open his eyes, to see whether a gramophone was really there. But real things—real things were too exciting. He must be cautious. He would not go mad. . . . None of these things moved. All were still; all were real" (142). The insistent repetition of the word "real" here operates like a magical spell against the threat of madness, and Septimus gradually finds himself in the apartment where he lives with Rezia. She is making a straw hat for Mrs. Peters, and Septimus comes to help her with the task. He opens up to her with playful comments, and for the first time in the novel they reconnect to one another beyond his trauma, with the narrative relaying their respective thoughts and feelings. "How it rejoiced her that! Not for weeks had they laughed like this together, poking fun privately like married people," Rezia thinks to herself, "Never had she felt so happy! Never in her life!" (143). Septimus in turn echoes her feelings: "It was wonderful. Never had he done anything which made him feel so proud. It was so real, it was so substantial, Mrs. Peters' hat" (144). The joyfully repeated "Never" serves to underline the singularity of the moment, the preciousness of the feelings circulating between them on this particular day that never will return. The precarious temporality of the moment is then underlined when their presence together is juxtaposed with Rezia's solitary future. Alongside their shared joy over the hat—" 'Just look at it' " he says to her in a moment of happiness—we read the thoughts that will have been hers when he is gone: "it would always make her happy to see that hat. He had become himself then, he had laughed then. They had been alone together. Always she would like that hat" (144). The joyful "Never" here gives way to a mournful "always" and an equally mournful "then," resonating with the grief over what will have happened. Woolf thus builds a remarkable scene of everyday happiness in the wake of imminent loss. She mobilizes all of her ability to make the moment vivid—to give the sense of a unique and irreplaceable time—in order to contrast it all the more sharply against the death that arrives.

The scene of Septimus's suicide thereby takes us to the heart of Woolf's aesthetics of the moment and the chronolibidinal experience that it dramatizes. The sense of temporal irreplaceability is here what gives the sense of a singular value to the moment and precipitates the investment in a singular life. But the same temporality and the same investment also make one susceptible to a suffering that may make it impossible to go on living. The ambition to convey this double bind of temporal life informs both Woolf's aesthetic innovations and her accounts of traumatic experience. Reflecting on her own aesthetic sensibility, she famously maintains that it originates in "violent moments of being" and that "the shock-receiving capacity is what makes me a writer. I hazard the explanation that a shock is at once in my case followed by the desire to explain it. I feel that I have had a blow."[19] In Woolf's description, a moment of being is thus equivalent to a traumatic event. The force of what happens precipitates the compulsion to return to the event in order to comprehend its meaning and survive its impact. The temporality of the event is such, however, that it will always exceed any final comprehension and threaten any given survival. Moments of being are not moments of timeless plenitude but testify to the inherent traumatism of temporal life. They may intensify one's attachment to life—endow events with a new radiance—but they may equally well shatter one's attachment to life and make survival unbearable.

Nevertheless, the dominant reading of Woolf's aesthetics of the moment aligns it with an aspiration to transcend time. For example, in her introduction to the collection of Woolf's writings entitled *Moments of Being*, Jeanne Schulkind maintains that Woolf's aesthetics is centered around "a privileged moment when a spiritually transcendent truth of either personal or cosmic dimensions is perceived in a flash of intuition."[20] According to Schulkind, a moment of being is the experience of "a timeless unity which lies beneath the appearance of change, separation, and disorder" (18). Schulkind thus anticipates the reading of Woolf proposed by Banfield, specifically the idea of a "crystallized" moment of timeless presence with which I began. These readings are in turn versions of the notion of *epiphanic* time that has been deeply influential for the understanding of modernist aesthetics. Accordingly, in a wide-ranging study of modernism that explicitly focuses on epiphanic time, Karl Heinz Bohrer claims that for Woolf the transitoriness of the moment "can only be redeemed by lifting it out of time."[21]

My argument is, on the contrary, that the affective and aesthetic impact of the moment depends on its temporality. The moment can only be given *as* a moment by passing away, and it is the passing away of the moment that makes it a matter of passion, whether positive or negative. If the moment were not passing away, nothing would happen and no one would be affected.

In Woolf's own account of her life, she records how "many of these exceptional moments brought with them a peculiar horror and a physical collapse."[22] The moment of being is experienced "as if I were passive under some sledge-hammer blow; exposed to a whole avalanche of meaning that had heaped itself up and discharged itself upon me, unprotected, with nothing to ward it off" (78). Woolf's response is the attempt to "bind" the stimulus of these events in works of art that allow their force to be processed and understood. As she puts it, the traumatic event "is or will become a revelation of some order; it is a token of some real thing behind appearances; and I make it real by putting it into words. It is only by putting it into words that I make it whole; this wholeness means that it has lost its power to hurt me; it gives me, perhaps because by doing so I take away the pain, a great delight to put the severed parts together" (72).

The binding of the event into a coherent whole does not, however, make the whole immune from being shattered in its turn. The "real thing behind appearances" is not a timeless being but the force of time itself, which is the force that Woolf seeks to capture in her practice of writing. Reflecting on how to describe her self as a child, she emphasizes that the dimension she must seek to convey is the dimension of temporality that made her subject to a process of alteration from the first inception:

> One must get the feeling of everything approaching and then disappearing, getting large, getting small, passing at different rates of speed past the little creature; one must get the feeling that made her press on, the little creature driven as she was by growth of her legs and arms, driven without her being able to stop it. . . . That is what is indescribable, that is what makes all images too static, for no sooner has one said this was so, than it was past and altered. (79)

The "indescribable" that Woolf seeks to describe is thus not a transcendent being; it is rather the intrinsic alteration of temporal being. The point is not to overcome time but to render its effects palpable. By the same token, the binding of events into a coherent "whole" can never be final but must remain open to the future in order to mark the movement of temporalization.

We can thus return to the scene with which I began this chapter. The intensified affective experience of being alive—which Kjaerstad describes as quintessential to the experience of reading Woolf—is an effect that she herself explicitly sought to create. When Woolf calls for the reformation of the modern novel, it is persistently in the name of *life*. Her experiments with narrative technique, structure, and style are not a turn away from realism but a challenge to those conventions of realism that fail to do justice to the texture of temporal experience. As she argues in her essay "Modern Fiction," the problem with conventional narrative techniques is that in their depiction of reality "life escapes; and perhaps without life nothing else is worthwhile" (149). Woolf's proposed remedy is to pursue the very strategy that guides *Mrs. Dalloway* and *To the Lighthouse,* namely, to "examine for a moment an ordinary mind on an ordinary day" in order "to come closer to life":

> Examine for a moment an ordinary mind on an ordinary day. The mind receives myriad impressions—trivial, fantastic, evanescent, or engraved with the sharpness of steel. From all sides they come, an incessant shower of innumerable atoms; and as they fall, as they shape themselves into the life of Monday or Tuesday, the accent falls differently from old; the moment of importance came not here but there. . . . Let us record the atoms as they fall upon the mind in the order in which they fall, let us trace the pattern, however disconnected and incoherent in appearance, which each sight or incident scores upon the consciousness. . . . This method has the merit of bringing us closer to what we were prepared to call life itself.[23]

My concern in this chapter has not been to establish the verisimilitude of Woolf's narrative techniques. Rather, I have sought to demonstrate that her aesthetics of the moment—and the affective experience of being alive that this aesthetics seeks to call forth—depends for its effect on a chronolibidinal investment in the fate of temporal existence. If we are moved by how Woolf records atoms of experience, it is because we care about the survival of the ephemeral—of incidents and details that may be lost. The pathos of Woolf's *moments of living* stems from the fact that they are always already *moments of dying.* For this reason, however, the experience of reading Woolf may not only enhance one's feeling of being alive, it may also leave one devastated. No matter how vital the affirmation of life in Woolf's prose may be, it inscribes within itself the possibility that it may be unable to bear survival. There is no way to come to terms with the double bind of finitude, no way of approaching life that would allow one to accept death resolutely or immunize oneself from the traumatic impact of being mortal. Like the character in Kjaerstad's novel, even the most devoted reader of Woolf may thus have to close the book, never to open it again.

CHAPTER 3

Writing

Nabokov

W HEN THE PHONE rings, it will have been seventeen years since he heard her voice. It is July 14, 1922, and he has been driving all night to meet her at the hotel where they parted in 1905. He has aged, time has been lost, and faced with the prospect of seeing her again, he finds himself in a state of "exhilaration, exhaustion, expectancy, and panic."[1] He does not know who they have become to one another and which possibilities remain. Yet her voice on the phone cuts through his anxiety and resuscitates the past in spite of all the years that have passed:

> Now it so happened that she had never—never, at least, in adult life— spoken to him by phone; hence the phone had preserved the very essence, the bright vibration, of her vocal cords, the little 'leap' in her larynx, the laugh clinging to the contour of the phrase, as if afraid in girlish glee to slip off the quick words it rode. It was the timbre of their past, as if the past had put through that call, a miraculous connection ('Ardis, one eight eight six'—*comment? Non, non, pas huitante-huit— huitante six*). . . .
>
> That telephone voice, by resurrecting the past and linking it up with the present, with the darkening blue-slate mountains beyond the

lake, with the spangles of the sun wake dancing through the poplar, formed the centerpiece in his deepest perception of tangible time, the glittering 'now' that is the only reality of time's texture. (436)

This scene from Nabokov's *Ada or Ardor: A Family Chronicle* recounts the reunion of the lovers Van and Ada Veen, whose memoir we are reading. The telephone call connects Van to the memory of their first reunion in the summer of 1886, when he called Ada and they met at the same place where they had first parted in 1884. This repetition of the past is now reflected as if in a mirror, when Ada calls him and the hotel that witnessed their final parting becomes the scene of their final reunion. It is an ecstatic moment—"the glittering 'now' that is the only reality of time's texture"—but one that is shot through with the sense of separation and loss that haunts the story of their love. Almost half the book is devoted to their first two summers together (1884 and 1888). In between, only a few fleeting meetings take place, and after the second summer another four years pass before they meet again. They spend a winter together in 1892 and barely a week in 1905. Not until 1922 (the time of the telephone call) are they reunited to live together for the rest of their lives.

If their relationship weaves a texture of time, then, it is one that stretches across long periods of absence and is torn by interruptions. In order to counteract this loss of time, Van and Ada persistently trace patterns of repetition. In narrating their story they emphasize reflections of the past that not only yield an experiential texture but also display apparently perfect symmetries. Yet in each repetition of the past, in each mirrored reflection—however perfect it may be—there is a displacement of time that testifies to temporal finitude. If the only reality of time's texture is the "now" (as Van maintains a propos the telephone call), it depends on an instance that ceases to be as soon as it comes to be. The drama of *chronos*—of a being that is the source of its own destruction—therefore haunts the insistence on the "now," which characterizes both levels of Van and Ada's autobiography. On the level of the narrative, they seek to hold on to the fleeting moments of their lives. On the level of narration, the same chronolibidinal desire recurs when they not only inscribe the past but also reckon with the temporality of the act of writing and seek to preserve its traces.

If this drama of *chronos* is intensified in *Ada,* it is because the lovers hyperbolically insist on the unique value of their lives. Constituting what Ada calls a "super-imperial couple" (60), they do not hesitate to underscore the incomparable quality of their love. This arrogance has been a source of disapproval even among inveterate Nabokophiles and it is true that "vain Van Veen" (one of his many alliterations) at times becomes a quite intolerable narrator. Nevertheless, it would be a mistake to dismiss Van and Ada's vainglorious attitude as a mere character flaw or eccentric indulgence. Rather, it serves to highlight the chronolibidinal notion of writing that informs Nabokov's aesthetic practice. Precisely because of Van and Ada's excessive chronophilic investment in themselves, the chronophobia that haunts any chronophilia is made all the more visible and is acted out in a number of intricate ways.

The paradigm for such chronolibidinal writing is Nabokov's own autobiography, *Speak, Memory.* Nabokov ascribes a tremendous power to his proper consciousness, emphasizing in particular his ability to recreate the past in a clear and distinct fashion. This posture may seem to confirm Nabokov's notorious hubris, but at the same time it underscores the precariousness of any affirmation of one's life, however self-assured it may be. Nabokov mobilizes his power of recollection against the threat of forgetting, but everything he wants to remember was transient from the beginning.[2] The very first sentence of *Speak, Memory* invokes the existence of consciousness as "a brief crack of light between two eternities of darkness," and Nabokov goes on to note that one is heading toward death "at some forty-five hundred heartbeats an hour" (17).[3]

The celebrated consciousness in *Speak, Memory* is thus not an idealized entity but one hypersensitive to the temporality of its own existence. In a discreet but important episode, Nabokov recounts how his mother—"as if feeling that in a few years the tangible part of her world would perish"—was led to cultivate "an extraordinary consciousness of the various time marks distributed throughout our country place" (33). The careful attention to memory is a response to the awareness of temporal finitude and leads to the "almost pathological keenness of the retrospective faculty" that Nabokov describes as "a hereditary trait" (60) of his family. When the young Vladimir went walking with his mother, she would pinpoint some cherished detail and in "conspiratorial tones" say *Vot zapomni:* an imperative Nabokov translates as *now remember* (33).

The explicit memorization of the present recurs with a remarkable frequency in Nabokov's writings and is symptomatic of his "chronophobia," a term that he himself introduces in *Speak, Memory* (17). The main symptom of chronophobia is an apprehension of the imminent risk of loss and a concomitant desire to imprint the memory of what happens. It follows that chronophobia—in spite of what Nabokov sometimes claims—does not stem from a metaphysical desire to escape "the prison of time" (*Speak, Memory,* 18). On the contrary, it is because one desires a temporal being (chronophilia) that one fears losing it (chronophobia). Without the chronophilic desire to hold on to the moment, there would be no chronophobic apprehension of the moment passing away. It is this chronolibidinal desire to keep temporal events that motivates Nabokov's autobiographic protagonists. They seek to record time because they are hypersensitive to the threat of oblivion.

Nabokov's first great work, *The Gift,* is an instructive example. Berlin's Russian émigré culture here provides the backdrop for a chronicle of the young author Fyodor's life between 1926 and 1929. This chronicle turns out to have been in search of lost time, when Fyodor in the last chapter decides to write the book we are about to finish. It is intended as a declaration of love for his beloved Zina, who finally has come to illuminate his life after a number of complications have prevented them from meeting. Fyodor conceives the idea for the book on a glorious summer day while sunbathing in the Grünewald. It is the happiest time of his life: full of a sense of anticipation, of love, of creative inspiration. Yet in and through the very experience of happiness, he is "seized by a panicky desire not to allow it to close and get lost" (337). It is precisely this desire to keep what can be lost that is the impetus for his decision to write.

Thus, the inception of *The Gift* testifies to Fyodor's chronophilia and chronophobia. The gift refers to Fyodor's life (and especially his relationship with Zina) but also to his literary talent. This other "gift" will result in the book we are reading and includes some of Fyodor's preliminary efforts, among them a biography of his deceased father and commemorative love poems to Zina after their nightly meetings. The act of writing is thus explicitly an endeavor to remember, which is underlined when Fyodor tells Zina about his idea to write an autobiography. *The Gift* shall commemorate the history of their love, Fyodor promises at the end of the book. In making this promise, he must figure the presence of the promise as a memory for the future. "One day we shall recall all this," Fyodor pledges on the last page of *The Gift* (366). This promise of memory leads him to inscribe the details of the fleeting evening with lyrical precision, as he and Zina leave a restaurant and wander out into the summer night.

The final scene is thus Fyodor's version of *now remember,* pervaded by a remarkable happiness but also by a sense of "the weight and the threat of bliss" (366) that is due to the precarious "gift" of life. It is precisely by affirming the finite gift of his life that Fyodor is seized by the "panicky desire" to preserve it through narration. This narration must inscribe the past *and* the present with regard to the future, but it can do so only by entrusting survival to a medium that is itself destructible. Accordingly, in the last paragraph of *The Gift,* Fyodor marks the finitude of every writer and reader ("Good-bye, my book! Like mortal eyes, imagined ones must close some day") while at the same time expressing his desire to retain and prolong the experience of his finite life: "And yet the ear cannot right now part with the music and allow the tale to fade . . ." (366).

A parallel example is Nabokov's short story "The Admiralty Spire." Here the narrator recalls his first love, one distant summer when the gramophones played Russian *tsyganskie romansy:* a kind of pseudo-gypsy, sentimental music. The mood of the music, with its invocations of bygone landscapes and bittersweet memories, would seem suitable for the one who is writing in retrospect. Yet the young couple already apprehends their present happiness in the same spirit. The sense of temporal finitude—of how their tangible circumstances at any time can be taken away—leads them to "counterfeit the remoteness of time" (348). Anticipating loss in the very experience of bliss, they approach the present as if in retrospect, keeping its happening as a beloved memory. "We transformed everything we saw into monuments to our still nonexistent past by trying to look at a garden path, at the moon, at the weeping willows, with the same eyes with which *now*—when fully conscious of irreparable losses—we might have looked at that old, waterlogged raft on the pond, at that moon above the black cow shed" (348).

Given the prevalence of the motif *now remember,* we can understand why a large number of Nabokov's novels have the form of memoirs, where the protagonists narrate their own lives. These protagonists are all in the position of living on, since they have survived a time to which they return in memory. In writing their lives, they seek to reconstruct a past that otherwise would be lost but are themselves exposed to a future that may erase what has been inscribed. Furthermore, the act of writing does not supervene on a given consciousness but is at work in the experience of presence itself. This necessity of writing—of inscribing the present as a memory for the future—follows from the negativity of time. Every moment immediately negates itself—it ceases to be as soon as it comes to be—and must therefore be inscribed as a memory in order to be apprehended at all. Without the inscription of memory nothing would survive, since nothing would remain from the passage of time. The passion for writing that is displayed by Nabokov and his protagonists is thus a passion for survival. Writing is here not limited to the physical act of writing but is a figure for the chronolibidinal investment in living on that resists the negativity of time while being bound to it.

Nabokov scholarship, however, is dominated by the thesis that his writing is driven by a desire to transcend the condition of time. The most influential proponent for this view is Brian Boyd, who in a number of books has argued that Nabokov aspires toward "the full freedom of timelessness, consciousness without the degradation of loss."[4] According to Boyd, the possibility of such a life beyond death is a pivotal concern in Nabokov's oeuvre. Boyd is well aware that Nabokov and his protagonists are resolute chronophiles who treasure their memories and temporal lives. As he eloquently puts it, "the key to Nabokov is that he loved and enjoyed so much in life that it was extraordinarily painful for him to envisage losing all he held precious, a country, a language, a love, this instant, that sound."[5] At the same time, however, Boyd maintains that Nabokov regards temporal consciousness as a "prison" that he hopes to transcend through death.[6] Boyd's reconstruction of Nabokov's metaphysics hinges on the assumption that these two positions are compatible. For his account to work, the desire to retain temporal experience must be compatible with the desire for a timeless state of being. As I will argue, however, it is precisely the idea of such compatibility that

Nabokov undermines. Contrary to what Boyd holds, "the full freedom of timelessness" could never allow one "to enjoy endlessly the riches of time."[7] In a timeless state of being there are, by definition, no riches of time. The chronophilic desire to hold on to temporal experience is therefore incompatible with a metaphysical desire to transcend the condition of time.

Let me emphasize that I am not charging Boyd with having misconstrued Nabokov's philosophy. Boyd's account clearly draws on statements made by Nabokov himself, and we have already seen that *Speak, Memory* begins with a description of time as a "prison" that it supposedly would be desirable to escape. My aim, however, is not to make Nabokov's philosophy consistent but to elucidate how the logic of chronolibido is operative in his writing. This logic opens a new way of reading Nabokov's work, which does not rely on his philosophy but rather reveals the internal contradictions in the metaphysics reconstructed by Boyd. The philosophical position that Boyd rehearses does not become any more coherent just because the incoherence in question can be traced back to Nabokov's own thinking. My argument is rather that the logic of chronolibido undermines the Nabokovian metaphysics that Boyd assumes must serve as the foundation for a reading of his work.[8]

The logic of chronolibido emerges clearly in the preoccupation with death and the afterlife that runs throughout Nabokov's work. His protagonists are typically haunted by ghosts of the dead—Fyodor in *The Gift* by his dead father, Nabokov himself in *Speak, Memory* by his dead father, John Shade in *Pale Fire* by his daughter Hazel who committed suicide, Van and Ada by their sister Lucette who also committed suicide, and so on. In all these cases of mourning, the refusal to accept death is equally the refusal to accept an immortal state of being, since the latter would not allow the mortal beloved to live on.

A paradigmatic example is *Pale Fire*, where Shade's long autobiographical poem broaches the question of survival and immortality. The same poem reverberates in *Ada*, where Van and Ada translate Shade into Russian with particular attention to his notion of the afterlife. In response to his fear of death and Hazel's suicide, Shade holds out the hope "that we survive / And that my darling somewhere is alive" (58). As is clear from Shade's reasoning, however, the state of immortality cannot give him what he asks for, namely, the survival of a mortal life. Shade frankly declares that he will "turn down eternity unless / The melancholy and the tenderness / Of mortal life; the passion and the pain. . . . Are found in Heaven by the newlydead / Stored in its stronghold through the years" (44). Insofar as Shade desires to keep these traits of mortal life, he cannot desire an immortal state of being. The pain and passion of mortal life would be inconceivable for an immortal being, since the latter could never fear or suffer from loss.

Boyd tries to solve the problem by understanding the timeless state of immortal being as an unlimited access to the temporal states of mortal being, namely, "an immortal consciousness" that would have access to "an always available past."[9] This argument presupposes that there could be a realm where the experiences of a temporal life remain intact and ready to be reactivated for a timeless consciousness. Shade's poem, however, provides an elaborate parody of exactly this idea. As he puts it:

> Time means succession, and succession, change:
> Hence timelessness is bound to disarrange
> Schedules of sentiment. We give advice
> To widower. He has been married twice:
> He meets his wives; both loved, both loving, both
> Jealous of one another. . . . (46)

The scenario makes vividly clear that one cannot eliminate the temporality of relations without eliminating the sense and meaning of the relations themselves. The same problem of temporality applies to the idea of resurrecting one's own mortal life. "What moment in the gradual decay / Does resurrection choose?" Shade asks rhetorically. "What year? What day?" (35). Shade's poem thereby targets the basic assumption of the metaphysics reconstructed by Boyd, namely, that a timeless consciousness could have access to the sense and meaning of a temporal life. For the latter argument to work, it must be possible to abstract the sense of a life from temporal relationality and finite embodiment. Even if such an operation were possible, however, it would eliminate the sense of the mortal lives that Nabokov and his protagonists want to keep. In a conversation about Shade's poem toward the end of *Ada,* Van makes precisely this point:

Van pointed out that here was the rub—one is free to imagine any type of hereafter, of course: the generalized paradise promised by Oriental prophets and poets, or an individual combination; but the work of fancy is handicapped—to a quite hopeless extent—by a logical ban: you cannot bring your friends along—or your enemies for that matter—to the party. The transposition of all our remembered relationships into an Elysian life inevitably turns it into a second-rate continuation of our marvelous mortality. (458)

Both Shade's poem and Van's commentary thus undermine the idea that our memories or relationships could be transposed to an eternal life. When Boyd comments on Van's reading of Shade, however, he dissimulates the stakes. According to Boyd, Van's argument shows "the absurdity of merely eternalizing human life" and thereby teaches us to leave behind our "anthropomorphic confines" when we imagine the afterlife.[10] This reading is untenable for a number of reasons. Van does *not* seek to rehabilitate the idea of an afterlife beyond the reach of anthropomorphic imagination. On the contrary, he argues that the desire for an afterlife *is* anthropomorphic and therefore bears a contradiction—a "logical ban"— within itself. The desire for an afterlife is, on Van's account, motivated by a desire for one's mortal life to continue. By the same token, he is lead to "turn down eternity" since it would not allow for the "continuation of our marvelous mortality."

When Boyd himself recognizes that "an eternalization of anything resembling his mortal life is logically impossible" and concedes that "anything we *can* imagine collapses under the absurdity of trying to transpose the conditions of temporality into eternity,"[11] he in fact concedes the ground for his own reading of Nabokov. If it is absurd to transpose the conditions of temporality into eternity, then it is equally absurd to hold out the possibility of a timeless consciousness that would have access to the personal past of a temporal consciousness. Boyd's self-contradictory reasoning is evident even within single paragraphs of his text. "Scrupulously avoiding the logical absurdity of eternalizing the necessarily finite condition of human consciousness," Boyd asserts, "Nabokov satisfies his desire for freedom by imagining the various limitations of the mind transcended in death. Death could offer us a completely new relation to time: freedom of our being pegged to the present, freedom of access to the whole of the past."[12] The idea of a realm where past events would be accessible forever is a clear example of eternalizing the finite, since past events had to be finite in order to become past in the first place. The only way to avoid this "logical absurdity" is to say that being in a state of eternity has nothing to do with preserving events of temporal life, since an eternal state of being would make one indifferent to the past as well as the future. That is why it is consistent to emphasize (as many religious sages do) that *detachment* is the path to the salvation of eternity. Only by becoming indifferent to the fate of temporal life can one embrace the absolute quietude of eternity. Following a chronolibidinal insight, however, Nabokov's protagonists insist that there is a constitutive *attachment* to temporal life, which undercuts the supposed desirability of eternity. Precisely because they are invested in the survival of temporal life, they turn down the prospect of eternity.

The chronolibidinal logic at work here does not deny that we dream of paradises and afterlives. Rather, it seeks to demonstrate that these dreams themselves are inhabited and sustained by temporal finitude. The fictional universe of *Ada* is organized around this idea. *Ada* is set on a planet called Demonia, or "Antiterra" in what appears to be the colloquial usage. With the invention of Antiterra, Nabokov rewrites the history of our world in an apparently wishful way, so that Russia and America, for example, belong to the same country. Taken together with Van and Ada's insistence on their exceptional happiness, it may thus seem as though Nabokov has created a "paradisal Antiterra," as John Updike puts it in a blurb that appears on most covers of the book. Yet the inhabitants of Antiterra dream of Terra as another world or as a life beyond death. The point here is not whether those who envision Terra on Antiterra are right or wrong (some people in the novel consider them as mad, others consider them as visionaries) but that the Terra they envision, by all appearances, is identical to life on Earth. Inversely, the Antiterra of the novel is just as marked by temporal finitude as our own Terra. The world of Antiterra thereby serves to underline—in both directions—that wherever you go or dream of going you will take time with you.

If this drama of chronolibidinal attachment becomes particularly visible in *Ada,* it is because the protagonists so strongly emphasize the investment in their singular lives and depict the happiness of their love as paradise itself. The first lines of the novel set the tone by reconfiguring the first lines of Tolstoy's *Anna Karenina.* In *Ada* it is unhappy families that are all alike, while happy families are happy each in their own special way. This inversion of Tolstoy's premise permeates the book. As in so many nineteenth-century novels, the romance of Van and Ada is set against a dark family secret. Officially they are cousins, but in fact they are brother and sister, the products of a confidential love affair they unravel during their first summer together. At that time, Ada is twelve years old and Van fourteen, but neither their age nor the incest taboo can soften their passion. On the contrary, the young siblings soon become lovers in every sense of the word.

That their forbidden love does not lead to a predestined tragedy but lives on for more than eighty years is of course a cunning demonstration of the happy family. Despite a number of *contretemps* that keep them separated for long stretches of time, the story elides traditional tragic narratives of love by letting Van and Ada emerge from their partings to reunite and live happily ever after. The very actuality of happiness, however, is haunted by the threat of loss. As Michael Wood has argued in an insightful reading of *Ada,* Nabokov does not treat happiness as something that is unattainable or impossible but rather as something whose precious quality depends on being susceptible to loss. The actuality of happiness in *Ada* makes clear that the threat of loss is *internal* to the experience of happiness itself, "not because happiness is doomed, or because fate is unkind, but because happiness is intelligible only under threat; intelligible only as its own threat."[13]

Accordingly, even in the most brazenly blissful moments of the book there is an apprehension of possible mourning. Within the space of single sentences, the affirmation of love is haunted by its opposite and contrary categories clash: passion/pain, beau/beast, tenderness/torture, happiness/helplessness. The logic of chronolibido thus emerges in beautiful, entangled phrases—as when Van describes how the sight of Ada's twelve-year-old hands gave rise to "agonies of unresolvable adoration" (85). Van's adoration here signifies an irrevocable emotion; it is "unresolvable" in the sense that it cannot be dissolved. At the same time, even the seemingly perpetual bond of love can always be broken and is thus characterized by an "unresolvable" contradiction that permeates Van's adoration with symptomatic agonies.

Almost four hundred pages later, the same word reappears concerning Van's aging: "physical despair pervaded his unresolvable being" (448). Van's being is here "unresolvable" because his resistance to its approaching death yields a conflict that cannot be resolved. This "unresolvable" problem of aging is staged on both levels of *Ada,* as the novel divides into two narratives. The main narrative spans from 1884 to 1922, recounting the intricate love story of Van and Ada, with an epilogue from 1967 when they are on the verge of death. We here find them worrying about who will die first and leave the other in solitary mourning. Indeed, "each hoped to go first, so as to concede, by implication, a longer life to the other, and each wished to go last, in order to spare the other the anguish of widowhood" (457). The happy ending is thus shown to be essentially compromised by finitude. Van and Ada have managed to survive almost all the classical *contretemps* of a great romance, but the *contretemps* of death cannot be avoided, only delayed.

The writing of the book begins in 1957 and probably comes to an end sometime in 1967, when Ada is ninety-five and Van ninety-seven. We learn that it took six years to write and dictate the first draft of the book (1957–1963), after which Van revised the typescript and rewrote it entirely in long hand (1963–1965). He then redictated the entire manuscript to his secretary, Violet Knox, who finished typing up the new version in 1967. For Van's ninety-seventh birthday, Violet prepares a special edition of the supposedly finished memoir, "ideally clean, produced on special Atticus paper in a special cursive type (the glorified version of Van's hand), with the master copy bound in purple calf " (459–460). Yet this pristine copy is "immediately blotted out by a regular inferno of alterations in red ink and blue pencil" (460) that Van and Ada continue to inscribe in the text up until their death. The book has thus been interrupted, rather than finished, and the text we read is a posthumously published manuscript. Although the manuscript does not relate exactly when Van and Ada died or who died before the other, an editorial note asserts that neither one of them is alive at the time of publication.

Nabokov's ingenious move is to stage the ten-year period of writing (1957–1967) parallel with the narrative running from 1884 to 1922. By way of interpolated parentheses, we get to witness Van and Ada in the process of writing their past. Van is the main signatory of the text, but Ada takes over from time to time, and both of them interrupt the narrative of the past to refer to circumstances at the time of writing, comment on certain details, admit lapses in memory, or demand that certain passages be eliminated or rephrased. Ada, especially, inserts a large number of additions that supplement, correct, and quarrel with Van's version of their life. In effect, the act of writing emerges as a chronolibidinal drama in itself. The moods of the narrators range from exorbitant self-confidence to elegiac intonations and nervous arrogance. The emotional shifts are due not only to their love story being perforated by partings, or to the depicted young lovers being so distant in time, but also to Van and Ada as writers being marked by impending death. Telling takes time, and we are not allowed to forget the irrefutable process of aging. On the contrary, it breaches the act of narration. For example, an enchanting episode in the first half of the novel is disrupted by an inserted addition that might be Van's last words. Via an editorial note informing us that "the end of the sentence cannot be deciphered but fortunately the next paragraph is scrawled on a separate writing-pad page" (173), we are displaced from Van and Ada as young lovers in 1888 to Van reading the proofs in 1967, pointing out that he is sick, that he writes badly and can die at any moment, in a note that ends with an instruction to the editor of the book: "Insert" (174).

The imminent threat of death that is explicit in Van's note is implicit throughout the text, not only because the protagonists are shadowed by their writing selves but also because the negativity of time is at work in the very presence of life. "We die every day; oblivion thrives / Not on dry thighbones but on blood-ripe lives," John Shade writes in *Pale Fire* (44). In *Ada,* this chronophobic apprehension of finitude explicitly accompanies the chronophilic investment in temporal life. Having recently fallen in love, Ada and Van undertake an excursion in the resplendent landscape that surrounds the family estate, Ardis Hall. In a playful exchange of memories, they compare travel itineraries from childhood, trying to figure out where and when they might have seen each other for the first time. Already in the midst of this blissful experience of love, however, they are haunted by the sense of temporal finitude that is intrinsic to consummate happiness itself:

> "But this," exclaimed Ada, "is certain, this is reality, this is pure fact—
> this forest, this moss, your hand, the ladybird on my leg, this cannot
> be taken away, can it? (it will, it was). *This* has all come together *here*,
> no matter how the paths twisted, and fooled each other, and got fouled
> up, they inevitably met here!" (123–24)

Van and Ada's marginal comments are usually identifiable through an appended description, such as "Ada's note" or "late interpolation." Significantly, the interpolated parenthesis here is exempt from this practice. It would be easy to read the stealthy reminder—*it will* be taken away, *it was* taken away—as a belated insight signed by the aged couple. Yet such a reading disregards how *it will*, *it was* resonates not only in the act of retrospective narration but also in the actuality of Ada's experience. Rather than pinpointing a pure presence, her articulation of *this* is an act of memorization through which she tries to imprint details before they disappear. Such an act would be unthinkable without the sense that *this* is ceasing to be and needs to be recorded. While Ada's emphatic *this* and *here* are spatial locutions, her question is motivated by the negativity of time that inhabits the spatial determination of something as being *this* and *here*. Repeated seven times, her insistence on *this* marks temporal displacement in the very act of trying to mitigate it.

Ada's insistence on the present thus recalls the scene in *Speak, Memory* where Nabokov's mother teaches him to *now remember*. Ada turns both toward what is no longer and what is not yet by retaining the present as a memory for the future. This double temporal structure is doubled once again when the event is inscribed in the autobiography. On the one hand, Van and Ada turn backward in time by recounting past events. On the other hand, they turn forward in time by addressing readers to come, including their future selves. Both their experience and their writing are therefore haunted by the refrain *it will* be taken away, *it was* taken away. The perilous implications of this refrain are underscored by Van and Ada's decision to publish the book posthumously.

They hold on to their memories, but the desire to keep their lives is concomitant with the awareness that every detail will be taken away from them in death. Indeed, it is the sense of temporal finitude that makes Van and Ada promise each other to hold on to what happens. As Van describes it, their love gives rise to "a complex system of those subtle bridges that the senses traverse . . . between membrane and brain, and which always was and is a form of memory, *even at the moment of its perception*" (174, my emphasis).

The necessity of memorization, then, answers to a form of writing that is operative in perception itself. The inscription of memory—and thereby the writing of time—is at work in Ada's articulation of *this here* as a perceptual presence. On the one hand, she performs a *spatialization of time* since the moment is recorded as a trace of the past. On the other hand, she performs a *temporalization of space* since the trace of the past is left for the future and thereby remains exposed to the possibility of erasure. This implicit relation between time and space is explicit in the passage leading up to Ada's remark. Van recounts how on that summer day he "found himself tackling, in still vague and idle fashion, the science that was to obsess his mature years—problems of space and time, space versus time, time-twisted space, space as time, time as space—and space breaking away from time in the final tragic triumph of human cogitation: I am because I die" (123). On Van's account, the negativity of ceasing to be ("I am because I die") is thus what distinguishes time from space. As we will see, however, the negativity of time does not establish it as independent of space. On the contrary, the negativity of time makes it altogether *dependent* on space.

The interdependence of time and space is crucial for the entire novel, but given Van's allusion to "the science that was to obsess his mature years," his statement above should primarily be read against his philosophical treatise *The Texture of Time*. This treatise occupies the fourth part of *Ada* and is intertwined with a narrative of Van's journey (by car) from the Dolomites to Switzerland. We here return to the time with which I began this chapter: it is the middle of July, 1922, and Van is on his way to the hotel where he will meet Ada for the first time in seventeen years. During this journey, Van composes *The Texture of Time*. It is a measure of its pivotal status that Nabokov had first planned to use the title of the treatise for the novel itself. Nonetheless, in approaching *The Texture of Time* we need to be armed with critical vigilance. On one level, the treatise denies that time and space are interdependent. Van repeatedly maintains his search for a Pure Time that would be independent of space. On closer inspection, however, these assertions do not answer to the logic of Van's writing. What emerges is rather a necessary co-implication of time and space, which is accentuated by Van's stylistic ingenuity and subverts his philosophical claims.

We thus come to a crossroads in our reading. All of Van's metaphors—including the title of his treatise—describe time in spatial terms and thus contradict his notion of Pure Time. A sympathetic reader may try to explain away this circumstance by arguing that what Van calls pure time is something immediately given, an unmediated experience of duration that is incompatible with the spatialization intrinsic to language. From such a perspective, pure time is an interior quality that cannot be translated to external, quantitative categories. To measure time would be to distort its proper essence, to discriminate separate phases in what is originally an indivisible unity. A number of Van's formulations may seem to invite such a reading, but in fact the very idea of immediacy is undermined in his writing. The following passage is an instructive example:

> What nudged, what comforted me, a few minutes ago at the stop of a thought? Yes. Maybe the only thing that hints at a sense of Time is rhythm; not the recurrent beats of the rhythm but the gap between two such beats, the gray gap between black beats: the Tender Interval. The regular throb itself merely brings back the miserable idea of measurement, but in between, something like true Time lurks. How can I extract it from its soft hollow? The rhythm should be neither too slow nor too fast. One beat per minute is already far beyond my sense of succession and five oscillations per second make a hopeless blur. The ample rhythm causes Time to dissolve, the rapid one crowds it out. Give me, say, three seconds, then I can do both: perceive the rhythm and probe the interval. A hollow, did I say? A dim pit? But that is only Space, the comedy villain, returning

by the back door with the pendulum he peddles, while I grope for
the meaning of Time. What I endeavor to grasp is precisely the
Time that Space helps me to measure, and no wonder I fail to grasp
Time, since knowledge-gaining itself "takes time." (421)

Van's inquiry is here guided by the idea that the essence of time is an indivisible presence. When examined, however, the idea turns against itself.
Van aims at a pure interval that would harbor "true time," but he soon
realizes that the interval only comes into being through a distended temporality. The interval cannot be a pure presence. On the contrary, it divides every moment from within. Van's argument is thus haunted by
minutes, seconds, and oscillations within seconds, despite his attempt to
debase measurement as a "miserable idea." Van's philosophical ambition
is to elucidate experience at its most immediate, but what he discovers is
that there can be no presence in itself.

The impossibility of presence in itself becomes particularly evident
when Van applies a method he calls "Deliberate Presence." Deliberate
presence consists in directing the energy of thought toward what is happening *right now*. Van describes it as follows:

To give myself time to time Time I must move my mind in the direction
opposite to that in which I am moving, as one does when one is driving
past a long row of poplars and wishes to isolate and stop one of them,
thus making the green blur reveal and offer, yes, offer, its every leaf. (31)

The very focus on the present thus demonstrates that there cannot be an
immediate presence. Even if Van brought the car to a halt, he would still
be driven toward the future. Consequently, every moment—like every detail in the fleeting landscape—can only appear as past. Temporality divides not only what appears but also the self-awareness of the one to
whom it appears. Temporal division is here marked by an inherent delay
in the reflexive act of giving oneself "time to time Time." The interval
separates the present from itself in its event, and without such discrimina-
tion nothing could ever be distinguished. A page further on, Van continues in the same vein:

> Since the Present is but an imaginary point without an awareness of
> the immediate past, it is necessary to define that awareness. Not for
> the first time will Space intrude if I say that what we are aware of as
> "Present" is the constant building up of the Past, its smoothly and
> relentlessly rising level. How meager! How magic! (432)

Van here concedes that the experience of temporality depends on spatiality. Given that every temporal moment immediately negates itself, it must
be retained by something other than itself. Such retention is unthinkable
without the spatial inscription of a trace that can remain from one moment to another, thereby opening the possibility of both short-term
awareness of the past and long-term memory.

Van's desire to retain evanescent moments is therefore not compatible
with a desire for the supposed pure time of presence in itself. Rather, Van
seeks to spatialize time and temporalize space. Despite his overt denun-
ciation of space, the narrative of his treatise archives temporal events in
spatial signs. Inversely, without temporalization these spatial signs could
not persist and relay the past to the future. Such "chronographies" (88)
are necessary to keep the memory of the past. The logic of the exposi-
tion—in spacing time and timing space—thus undermines the purported
thesis of the text.

A similar complication can be tracked in Van's discussion of the future
in *The Texture of Time*. Van describes the treatise as a "Work-in-Progress"
(439) and openly addresses "the dawning desk of the still-absent reader"
(420). Nevertheless, he makes several attempts to deny that the future is a
valid temporal category, which perhaps can be ascribed to a psychological
cause. While writing *The Texture of Time,* Van is palpably nervous about
the prospect of meeting Ada after seventeen years, and he himself says
that the purpose of his philosophical speculations is to keep him from
brooding over their anticipated reunion.

In any event, Van's line of reasoning encounters severe problems. His
proclaimed stance is that anticipations of the future—whether in the form
of hope or fear—are inessential phenomena for a proper understanding of
time. When Van specifies his argument, however, he pursues a completely
different thesis: that the future is not predetermined. His simple point is
that coming events do not yet exist. This argument does not refute the

future as a temporal category, but is rather intrinsic to the definition of the future. Accordingly, we get to witness yet another U-turn in the treatise. What was supposed to be negated is instead emphatically affirmed:

> The unknown, the not yet experienced and the unexpected, all the glorious "x" intersections, are the inherent parts of human life. The determinate scheme by stripping the sunrise of its surprise would erase all sunrays—(441)

The relation to the future is here articulated as a necessary condition of experience. In spite of Van's programmatic declarations, this insight is at work in his argument from the beginning. Van has no qualms about appropriating a concept of the past while attempting to denounce what he calls the false third panel in the triptych of time. It is impossible to accept a concept of the past and deny a concept of the future, however, since the two concepts are interdependent. That something is past means that it has been overtaken by a future. Inversely, anticipations of the future are anticipations of a past to come. Whatever happens *will have been* in a future anterior that marks the becoming of every event.

Although the temporality of the future anterior operates throughout the novel, one scene in particular captures it with striking precision. The scene in question is triggered by a photograph that portrays Van and Ada as young relatives in the summer of 1884. In a stylized setting, they pose for the family photographer, and the occasion turns out to be memorable indeed:

> Van stood inclining his head above her and looked, unseeing, at the opened book. In full, deliberate consciousness, at the moment of the hooded click, he bunched the recent past with the imminent future and thought to himself that this would remain an objective perception of the real present and that he must remember the flavor, the flash, the flesh of the present (as he, indeed, remembered it half a dozen years later—and now, in the second half of the next century). (316)

Through the self-reflective movement of trying to capture himself in the photographic moment, Van illuminates how even the most immediate experience is pervaded by the negativity of time. His very act of perceiving is divided between the negative determination of being no longer ("the recent past") and the negative determination of being not yet ("the imminent future"). It is precisely because of this constitutive negativity that the experience of time depends on the material support of a spatial trace. Without the support of such a trace there could be no experience of time, since there would be nothing that could retain the recent past for the imminent future. This necessity of recording time is further underscored by the material support of the photograph, which pinpoints a certain moment by duplicating it as a trace on the film. Analogously, Van is both witness and witnessed when he *thinks to himself* that he must memorize the moment. The event is inscribed as a trace in his consciousness, while the interpolated parenthesis demonstrates how the inscription of time enables repetitions of the memory. Within the space of a single sentence we move from the summer of 1884 to the winter of 1892—when Van encounters the photograph in an apartment in Manhattan—all the way up to the 1960s, when the sequence of memories is archived in the autobiography.

The connection to technological memory in Van's series of recollections is deeply significant for the novel. Van and Ada have a tremendous ability to recall the past, but they are dependent on supplementary devices to retain the flight of time—everything from clocks and calendars to photographs and telegrams. Furthermore, the fictional universe of *Ada* gives a hint as to the importance of technology. To a large extent, the world of Antiterra corresponds to our own, but Nabokov rearranges the historical course of events. For example, in the beginning of the nineteenth century, cars, telephones, and cinemas are part of everyday life. This revision of the history of technology is not just playful but is closely intertwined with the time theme of the novel. In the foreword to *Speak, Memory,* Nabokov writes that all our memories ought to be microfilmed, and a chronophile does indeed have good reasons to be fascinated by mnemotechnical devices. The possibility of saving sense data, of transmitting visual and sonorous phenomena, increases dramatically with inventions such as the tape recorder and the film camera. "Time is but memory in the making" (440), Van claims with a striking phrase in his treatise. A decisive question, then, is what material supports are available for archiving. Time must be spatially inscribed, and an advanced technology provides a greater capacity for storing and transferring what happens.

Nevertheless, humanist ideologies have traditionally demoted technology, arguing that its artificial modes of production distort the immediacy of living presence. When phenomena are reproduced mechanically there is an inevitable spacing between origin and transmission. To surrender one's face to a camera or to deposit one's voice in a tape recorder is to be duplicated by an exterior medium that is subject to reiteration and dislocation. What becomes clear in *Ada,* however, is that such temporal spacing is not an unnatural process but is always already at work in the "interior" of the subject. Rather than being essentially different from a system of technological mediation, the perceptual apparatus itself depends on the mediation of the trace.

We can discern the necessity of mediation in Van's thoughts before the camera in 1884. Parallel to the explicit act of photography is an implicit act of *chronography* that marks the mnemotechnics of the psyche. In both cases, it is a matter of inscribing traces that give experience both the chance to live on and to be effaced. Just as photographs can easily fade or be destroyed, Van will suffer from forgetfulness and death. Yet there is a difference of degree to be noted. The photograph is described as "an objective perception of the real present," capable of preserving details independently of Van's memory and repeating them without his animating intention. While the photograph's designated mnemonic power depends on Van's ability to resuscitate "the flavor, the flash, the flesh of the present," such animation cannot sublate the inanimate repetition of the technological medium. By transferring sense data to an exterior receptacle, Van strengthens his ability to resist the threat of forgetting, but through the same gesture he commits himself to a medium that does not belong to him. When one is photographed or recorded on tape, there is always the possibility of the face or the voice being reproduced in a different context, beyond the control of its presumed origin. The same condition applies to written words, which are not only readable and repeatable in the absence of the author but also susceptible to manipulation. As we will see, this problem of technological mediation is at the heart of chronolibidinal writing in *Ada.*

A first clue is a number of connections between the project of the memoir and technical devices. On several occasions, Van and Ada imagine that
episodes from their past are displayed as a motion picture, and they are
repeatedly attracted to the idea of a particular event being accessible
through magnetic tape or cinematographic recording. A dialogue between the couple in 1884 is thus presented by Van and Ada in 1967 with
the appended regret that they did not tape the conversation, since it
would have allowed them to reactivate sonorous traces of their past.
Words printed on paper do not exhibit such an apparently direct link to
sense data, but they can nevertheless perform an analogous function. The
style of writing in *Ada* is perhaps the most elegant example of literary
mnemotechnics, since it reactivates the sense of the past by elucidating
subtle nuances of experience. Van and Ada, however, also pursue a more
advanced technology of writing. Already to inscribe an event is a form of
programming, since it relies on the ability of future readers to translate the
marks on the page into "living" impressions. The strategies of writing
in *Ada* extend the scope of such programming, since they not only narrate
the past but also *record the act of narrating the past,* thereby documenting
the ten-year period of writing as a drama in itself that gradually evolves
in the margins of the book.

For example, the episode when Van and Ada make love for the first
time is repeatedly interrupted by arguments between the two at the time
of writing, when they recall the event more than seventy years later. At
times, Van attempts to protect himself from the emotionally charged subject by having recourse to summarious or lecherous phrases, but Ada pro-
tests and gives us a more delicate description of what happened, as they
take turns writing the episode. That the alternating process of writing is
staged in the text is no coincidence; it is consistent with the chronophilic
and chronophobic sense of autobiography that pervades the memoir.
Throughout the novel, we can observe the desire *to narrate the one who is
narrating,* to integrate the process of writing the autobiography into the
autobiography itself.

The ambition to narrate the one who is narrating is brought to a head
in a number of supplementary markers that are mainly appended to Ada's
notes. An inserted comment may be followed by characterizations such as
"Marginal note in red ink" (104) or "Marginal jotting in Ada's 1965 hand;

crossed out lightly in her latest wavering one" (19). Such specifications are recurrent and typographically distinguished from the editor's notes, which are given in square brackets according to the model: [Ed.]. It is thus Ada herself who provides the additional descriptions of her marginal notes, in accordance with a chronophilic and chronophobic logic. When the manuscript is printed as a book, the marginal notes will cease to be marginal and will be transferred to the center of the page (as indeed they are in the edition we read). For the same reason, the color of Ada's ink will have been erased when her handwriting is replaced by printed letters. It is therefore necessary to describe these characteristics in order to prevent them from vanishing without a trace. When Ada writes a note in 1965, she thus adds that it is a note written by herself in 1965. This doubling is operative even when impending death has deprived Ada of physical strength: her wavering hand lightly crossing out text describes itself as a wavering hand lightly crossing out text. These inscriptions may seem to be an extreme form of chronophilia and chronophobia, but the very project of the memoir resonates in Ada's desire to record as much as possible. The text is programmed to retain its character when transmitted from one material support to another and enables us to track different dates of inscription on one and the same page.

The originality with which Nabokov stages such chronolibidinal writing is perhaps best measured against the analysis of temporality pursued by Gerard Genette in his study of narrative discourse. While the narration of time by definition takes time, Genette observes that "almost all novels in the world except *Tristram Shandy*" proceed as if the fictive narrating of the narrative has "no duration; or, more exactly, everything takes place as if the question of its duration had no relevance."[14] This idea that "narrating involves an instantaneous action, without a temporal dimension" (222) is, according to Genette, one of the most unchallenged fictions of literary narrative. What makes *Tristram Shandy* an exception is its explicit thematization of the temporality of narration. With characteristic wit, Tristram points out that he lives faster than he writes and never will be able to catch up with himself in the telling of his life story. After having managed to narrate only the first day of his life in one year of writing, he has in fact fallen behind three hundred and sixty-four days in the narration of his life.

If the articulation of Tristram's insight is rare, the way in which *Ada* stages the time of narration—including acts of revising and editing the manuscript—is all the more unique, if not unprecedented. Perhaps the most dramatic example is the pages devoted to Lucette's suicide. Here the narrative not only bears traces of Van's grief at the time of narration but also of his secretary typing the sentences he dictates to her: recording her mishearings, misspellings, and lines that testify to how Van fumbles with his notes while dictating the description of Lucette's death.[15] Even in blissful moments of the book, however, we can trace the time of writing and the emotional strain it places on those who are involved in recalling their past. The following passage, taken from the narrative of the first time Van and Ada made love, is an instructive example of how the temporally extended process of writing is staged in the text. The point of departure is a summer night in 1884:

> For the first time in their love story, the blessing, the genius of lyrical speech descended upon the rough lad, he murmured and moaned, kissing her face with voluble tenderness, crying out in three languages—the three greatest in all the world—pet words upon which a dictionary of secret diminutives was to be based and go through many revisions till the definitive edition of 1967. When he grew too loud, she shushed, shushingly breathing into his mouth, and now her four limbs were frankly around him, as if she had been love-making for years in all our dreams—but impatient young passion (brimming like Van's overflowing bath while he is reworking this, a crotchety gray old wordman on the edge of a hotel bed) did not survive the first few blind thrusts; it burst at the lip of the orchid, and a bluebird offered a warning warble, and the lights were now stealing back under a rugged dawn, the firefly signals were circumscribing the reservoir, the dots of the carriage lamps became stars, wheels rasped on the gravel, all the dogs returned well pleased with the night treat, the cook's niece Blanche jumped out of a pumpkin-hued police van in her stockinged feet (long, long after midnight, alas)—and our two naked children, grabbing lap robe and nightdress, and giving the couch a parting pat, pattered back with their candlesticks to their innocent bedrooms.

"And do you remember," said gray-moustached Van as he took a Cannabina cigarette from the bedside table and rattled a yellow-blue matchbox, "how reckless we were, and how Larivière stopped snoring but a moment later went on shaking the house, and how cold the iron steps were, and how disconcerted I was—by your—how shall I put it?—lack of restraint."

"Idiot," said Ada from the wall side, without turning her head.

Summer 1960? Crowded hotel somewhere between Ex and Ardez?

Ought to begin dating every page of the manuscript: Should be kinder to my unknown dreamers. (98–99)

At least four different time-levels can be discerned here. Initially, we are treated to an episode from 1884, which necessarily was written at a later date—in its first version probably sometime in the late 1950s. When the first parenthesis interrupts the narrative we become aware of yet another time-level, since Van here is *reworking* the section we read. The narration of the summer night is then resumed, but the depiction of the "crotchety gray old wordman" is continued in the following paragraph, which displaces us to a hotel room where Van and Ada are working on the manuscript. If we wonder exactly when this scene takes place we soon realize that the same question occupies Van ("Summer 1960? Crowded hotel somewhere between Ex and Ardez?") when he on *yet another* occasion reads the text and notes that he ought to begin dating every page of the manuscript. It seems reasonable to attribute the last comment to 1967, since a reference to this year has been inserted into the description of the episode from 1884—if the reference to 1967 does not testify to yet another date of inscription, yet another time-level.

In any event, Van and Ada enable us to track how they return to the same passage several times, as they record themselves in the act of making further additions or commenting on their comments. Their obsessive investment in recording themselves, however, also serves to accentuate their disappearance. Van and Ada apply themselves to an ingeniously programmed textual archive, but even the most advanced technology runs the risk of being distorted. The possibility of malfunction is built into the system from the beginning, due to the finitude of both the machine and its designers. It is thus significant that the book we are reading is an unfinished manuscript. This is easy to forget since the prose of the novel is so elegant and arrogant, but there are several furtive mementos to be noted. In a number of places, incomplete sentences remain in the text and are subsequently repeated and completed. These momentary disruptions of the progressing narrative create the same effect as when the needle of a gramophone is caught in a track: we become aware of how the act of reading or listening is dependent on a fragile mechanism.

The editor's remarks, which appear about twenty times throughout the novel, underline the technological corruptibility. As mentioned earlier, what might be Van's last word is a technical instruction ("Insert"). The inserted addition that interrupts an amorous scenario in 1888 is in turn interrupted in the middle of a sentence and followed by the editor's square brackets, where we learn that the rest of the sentence is illegible. Apparently, the margins of Van's proofs have not allowed sufficient space for his notes, but he has continued writing on a separate sheet and these notes have been inserted in the printed book following Van's concluding instruction. In this case, then, the editor appears to be faithful to the manuscript. At the same time, his interventions mark a series of interruptions that become more and more critical. As the book proceeds, one can observe that the editor is insolent in some of his comments. In the middle of a dialogue, he begins to speculate on whether Van has obtained the lines from other sources. Even in Van's and Ada's intimate love letters he takes note of solecisms with a pedantic *sic!* The man behind these remarks is a certain Ronald Oranger, who, as it turns out, has at least one special interest in the book. When in the final chapter Van is about to describe his beautiful secretary, Violet Knox (who was to become Mrs. Ronald Oranger), the sentences in question are replaced by an omission mark. The autobiography of our super-imperial couple has thus been bowdlerized by a jealous husband. Nabokov's stealthy irony reminds us that the written can never protect itself against being grafted onto a different context. Van and Ada inscribe layer upon layer of memories in their texture of time, but their hypermemoir also holds the threat of a lifeless repetition upon its posthumous publication, when readers and editors can do as they please with the dead letters.

Nevertheless, Nabokov scholars have sought to locate a transcendent meaning that would redeem the displacements of time that *Ada* records. A telling example is Robert Alter, who, in an otherwise valuable essay, misreads the part played by Ronald Oranger. Relying on no textual support except the possibility that Ronald Oranger is an anagram ("angel nor ardor"), Alter claims that Oranger is an angelic figure whose final responsibility for the text of *Ada* confirms the idea that art can create a "perfected state" of paradise. Indeed, in Alter's view "the ultimate sense" that *Ada* seeks to convey is that "all threats of evil, including the evil of the corrosive passage of time" can be "finally transcended by the twinned power of art and love."[16] My reading of *Ada* has argued for an opposite view. The very idea of a perfect paradise is shown to be untenable in *Ada,* since threats of destruction are intrinsic to even the most amazing happiness and the most meticulous work of art. It is thus an appropriate irony that the figure Alter assumes to be the angelic guardian of the book's metaphysical ambition in fact is a petty editor who disfigures the text and reminds us that corruption is always possible.[17] Far from redeeming corruptibility, the writing of Van and Ada highlights that the chance of inscription is inseparable from the risk of erasure. Whether their mnemotechnics are "interior" or "exterior" it is a matter of *chronographing:* of saving time in spatial marks. In the same process of preservation, however, Van and Ada are forced to underline their dependence on marks that not only are destructible but also exceed their control.

In reckoning with the problem of writing time, *Ada* can be seen to engage the legacy of the modernist novel in general and Proust's *Recherche* in particular. The latter is a recurrent intertext throughout the book, and it is instructive to compare the final pages of *Ada* with the final pages of the *Recherche*. *Ada* is divided into five parts that gradually become shorter and shorter, as if mirroring the dwindling of time left at the narrators' disposal. The epilogue that constitutes the final part is leaf-thin and situated in 1967. Van and Ada are here trying to complete their autobiography, but they do not know how to end or when to stop revising the manuscript. As Van points out, "one can even surmise that if our time-racked, flat-lying couple ever intended to die they would die, as it were, *into* the finished book" (460), but for that very reason they seek to keep the book alive through an interminable process of revision. The physical pain of dying here begins to set in and at times seems to syncopate the very syntax of the writing. This physical pain is in turn compounded by the psychological fear of death, strikingly described by Van as the chronophobic "wrench of relinquishing forever one's memories" which animates the chronophilic investment in "accumulating again and again the riches of consciousness that will be snatched away" (457).

The same chronolibidinal anxiety over keeping memory and physical health emerges in the final pages of the *Recherche*. To recall, the *Recherche* does not end with Marcel's aesthetic revelation but with a set of chronophobic speculations concerning how and if he will be able to write his book. As Marcel emphasizes, "I would need a good number of nights, perhaps a hundred, perhaps a thousand" and at any moment death could come to interrupt the telling of his story (6:353/4:620). Indeed, even before starting to work on his book, Marcel falls in a staircase and suffers from a memory loss that intensifies his anxiety over not being able to write. "I asked myself not only 'Is there still enough time?' but also 'Am I still in a sufficiently fit condition?'" (6:353/4:621). Yet, while Marcel articulates the potential difficulties of writing the book, these difficulties are not enacted as a drama within the frame of the fiction. We know that Proust was unable to finish the *Recherche* before his death and that he struggled to enter revisions in the galley proofs up until the end. Within the frame of the fiction, however, we do not get to witness an analogous struggle on the part of Marcel as the writer of the pages we are reading. There are occasional references to the present life of the narrator, but we do not learn under what circumstances he writes the book, and there are no visible traces of the different dates of inscription, revision, and proofreading.

By making all these aspects of writing visible within the frame of the fiction, Nabokov's *Ada* ups the ante on Proust's *Recherche*.[18] If one takes seriously the idea of writing one's life, one cannot simply tell a story as though one's life had come to an end. Rather, one must record both the process of writing itself and the life that continues beyond the life that is written. By the same token, it becomes clear that one's life never reaches an end in the sense of being completed. There is no completion or redemption of life, only an irredeemable interruption, and it is the traces of such interruption that *Ada* records. Interruption should not, however, be understood as the interruption of a life that would be intact or complete if it were allowed to continue. Rather, the life that continues is in itself already marked by interruption: it reckons with irreversible losses and continues to record the negativity of time in its very continuation.

To examine the seams in the texture of time is thus to see the material destructibility of every thread of memory and the inherent fragility of every cherished connection. There is here perhaps no better example than the scene with which I began this chapter. When Van picks up the phone in 1922, the sound of Ada's voice after seventeen years not only gives rise to an involuntary memory that resuscitates the past; the scene also inscribes a discrete allusion to a specific scene in Proust. In the third volume of the *Recherche*, Marcel hears his grandmother's voice on the phone for the first time, and the event gives rise to an extended reflection on the experience of telecommunication.[19] On the one hand, the telephone has a "magic" ability to transport us "hundreds of miles" in "only a few seconds" and "bring before us, invisible but present, the person to whom we wish to speak" (3:127/2:431). On the other hand, the proximity of someone who is actually absent recalls "at what a distance we can be from those we love at a moment when it seems we only have to stretch out our hands to retain them" (3:128/2:432). Thus, the telephone line that enables one to bridge spatiotemporal distances in life also anticipates the "eternal separation" (3:128/2:432) of death. "Many times," writes Marcel, "I have felt that the voice was crying out to me from depths from which it would never emerge again, and I have experienced the anxiety that was one day to take hold of me when a voice would return like this . . . to murmur in my ear words I would dearly like to have kissed as they passed from lips forever turned to dust" (3:128/2:432).

The mediators in this drama of life and death, proximity and distance, are "the young ladies of the telephone" *(les Demoiselles du téléphone)* whom Marcel describes both as "the All-Powerful Ones who conjure absent beings to our presence without our being permitted to see them" and as "the ironic Furies who, just as we are murmuring private words to a loved one in the hope that we are not overheard, cruelly call out: *J'écoute*" (3:127/2:432). When Van describes the phone call

from Ada, he seems to imagine a conversation with one of these opera-
tors, who is now not only endowed with the power to connect a call to
another spatial location but also to another time in the past, with the
year he wants to reach turned into a telephone number: "It was the
timbre of their past, as if the past had put through that call, a miraculous connection ('Ardis, one eight eight six'—*comment? Non, non, pas
huitante-huit—huitante six*)." While the structure of recollection is parallel, it seems to lead to opposite effects in the *Recherche* and *Ada* re-
spectively. For both Marcel and Van, the separation between the body of
the other and her voice on the phone leads them to perceive her differ-
ently, since they cannot follow what she says "on the open score of her
face," as we read in Proust (3:128/2:433). For Marcel, this separation
from the body leads him to hear the "actual voice" (3:128/2:433) of his
grandmother for the first time, but what the voice reveals is "how pain
had cracked it in the course of a lifetime" (3:129/2:433) and how she is
about to die: "I wanted to kiss her; but all that I had beside me was her
voice, a ghost as bodiless as the one that would perhaps come back and
visit me when my grandmother would be dead" (3:129–30/2:434). For
Van, too, the separation between Ada's body and her voice on the phone
leads him to perceive "the very essence, the bright vibration, of her
vocal cords," but what the voice reveals is how this essence—"the little
'leap' in her larynx, the laugh clinging to the contour of the phrase"—
has been preserved despite all the years that have passed.

In place of the intimation of death in the *Recherche, Ada* thus insists on
the vigorous resurgence of life. Yet the resurgence of life cannot ultimately
be separated from the intimation of death, since both have their source in
the spacing of time that makes it possible to separate the voice from the
body in the first place. This spacing may allow the voice to survive at odds
with the dramatic aging of the body, but it may also leave one with the
ghost of a voice after the body has ceased to be alive. Up until the end, Van
and Ada will insist on keeping their lives and their memories, but they can
do so only through the spacing of time that exposes them to the threat of
loss and the possibility of having their words repeated or manipulated
after they have died.

It is thus by dramatizing the spacing of time that *Ada* manages to
tackle what Van in the closing pages calls the "one great difficulty" of

writing the book: "The strange mirage-shimmer standing in for death should not appear too soon in the chronicle and yet it should permeate the first amorous scenes" (456–57). Indeed, the sense of death comes to permeate every scene of love and affirmation in *Ada* precisely because of the insistence on life. Even at the height of youth and in the midst of a summer day there is a sense of ceasing to be that induces the passion for the moment. This spacing of time—and the interdependence of love and loss that follows from it—is the cause of the chronophobia that haunts chronophilia from beginning to end.

CHAPTER 4

Reading

Freud, Lacan, Derrida

I N HIS ESSAY "On Transience," Freud recounts a summer walk through the countryside with a famous poet. The scenery is resplendent, but the poet is haunted by the sense that all the beauty will be destroyed by the passage of time. Everything that may be desired as beautiful bears its own destruction within itself because it is temporal and begins to pass away as soon as it comes to be. The poet's conclusion is that such temporal finitude deprives beauty of its value. As Freud explains: "All that he would otherwise have loved and admired seemed to him shorn of its worth by the transience which was its doom."[1]

The dialogue that follows exhibits two paradigmatic ways of denying the co-implication of chronophobia and chronophilia that I have sought to analyze in this book. The poet exhibits clear symptoms of chronophobia, since he is hypersensitive to how the beauty around him is "fated to extinction" (14:305/10:358). The poet does not acknowledge, however, that his chronophobia stems from a chronophilia. Rather than recognizing that transience is internal to the beauty he desires, he claims that it deprives beauty of its value. The experience of temporal finitude would thus be the experience of an ontological *lack*, since it can never measure up to the ideal of eternal being.

For all its groundbreaking achievements, the psychoanalytic conception of desire has generally not questioned the supposed experience of an ontological lack. Both Freud and Lacan assume that temporal being is a lack of being that we desire to transcend, while emphasizing that the idea of a timeless state of being is an illusion that we should learn to leave behind. Thus, in seeking to cure the poet of his melancholia, Freud does not acknowledge the chronophobia that is intrinsic to chronophilia. Responding to the poet, Freud claims that there is no reason why "the thought of the transience of beauty should interfere with our joy in it" (14:305/10:359). Rather, if we learn to let go of the fantasy of timeless being, we should be able to free ourselves from the phobic relation to the passage of time and enjoy the transience of life. Following the logic of chronolibido, however, this argument cannot be sustained. If one removes the fear of what may happen to a temporal being (chronophobia) one removes the attachment to the same temporal being (chronophilia), since one no longer cares if what happens to it is vital or lethal, beneficial or devastating. Indeed, attachment to a temporal being means that every affirmation is inhabited by negation from the start and even the most active embrace of life cannot be immune from the reactive mourning of death.

Chronophilia, then, cannot cure chronophobia. Philia and phobia are rather two aspects of the same chronolibidinal condition. The psychoanalytic logic of lack fails to articulate this condition, since it assumes that chronophobia derives from the desire for a timeless, eternal being. This assumption has two major consequences. First, it assumes that the fundamental drama of desire resides in the conflict between the temporal being that we are and the timeless being that we desire to be, rather than in the double bind of chronophilia and chronophobia. Second, because it does not articulate this double bind, the logic of lack invites the assumption that chronophobia could be cured by chronophilia.

In "On Transience," however, Freud opens the possibility for a different diagnosis of chronophobia. On Freud's reading, the poet's denigration of temporal being does *not* stem from the lack of a timeless being. Rather, it is a defense mechanism against the threat of loss. By denigrating the value of temporal being, the poet seeks to avoid the experience of mourning that follows from the attachment to a being that is lost. As

Freud puts it, those who "seem ready to make a permanent renunciation because what was precious has proved not to be lasting, are simply in a state of mourning for what is lost" (14:307/10:360–61). Importantly, what has been lost is not a timeless being but a temporal being: something that was precious but could not last and leaves the survivor in mourning. Furthermore, the mourning in question does not have to be the mourning of something that already has been lost; it can also be the mourning of what *will be* lost, as is the case when the poet finds his enjoyment of beauty "interfered with by thoughts of its transience" (14:306/10:359).

Hence, although the poet claims that he is lacking a timeless being, he is in fact mourning a temporal being. Freud himself does not elaborate this argument, but we can trace it through the account he gives. It is because the poet fears to lose a temporal being that he seeks to detach himself from it by renouncing its value. The apparent *detachment* thus presupposes *attachment* to a temporal being. If the poet were not attached to a being that could be lost, he would never anticipate the painful experience of mourning that motivates the act of detachment. What comes first, then, is not the desire for a timeless being that cannot be lost, but the attachment to a temporal being that can be lost. In my terminology, this attachment is the source of *both* chronophilia *and* chronophobia. The one cannot be disentangled from the other, since the chance of what one desires is inseparable from the threat of losing it. While this double bind is at work in every moment of life, it becomes poignant upon the death of the beloved. To mourn the beloved is precisely to experience how he or she or it could always become the source of radical loss.

The condition of mourning can thus be seen as paradigmatic for the general condition of chronolibido. Mourning requires both a chronophilic attachment to a temporal being and a chronophobic resistance to the loss of the same temporal being. Without the attachment, one would have nothing to lose, and without the resistance, one would have nothing to mourn, since one would not care about the loss of the temporal being.

For the same reason, the condition of chronolibido is inextricable from the condition of *survival* that I have analyzed throughout this book. To survive is necessarily to be haunted by mourning, both in relation to what has been lost in the past and what will be lost in the future. The *actual* experience of mourning is preceded by the *possible* mourning that is at work from the first moment of experience, since everything that may be experienced is temporal and will be lost. It follows that every libidinal investment—what Freud describes as the "cathexis" *(Besetzung)* of an object—has an essential relation to time. The temporal finitude of the cathected object calls forth the economic capacity to redistribute resources or withdraw investments as a strategic response to being dependent on what may change or be lost.[2] Inversely, the calculation of libidinal investments is necessarily exposed to the incalculable temporality of the cathected object. The temporal finitude of the cathected object is thus what gives rise to a libidinal economy. It is *because* things are mutable and can be lost, because they have not always been and will not always be, that one cares about them. If things were fully present in themselves, if they were not haunted by alteration and loss, there would be no reason to care about them, since nothing could happen to them.

To elaborate this point, it is instructive to turn to Freud's essay "Timely Reflections on War and Death," written the same year as "On Transience," and in particular to the section entitled "Our Attitude Towards Death." Freud's argument here is apparently directly at odds with the notion of chronolibido, since he claims that the unconscious ("the deepest strata of our psyche") is unaware of either temporality or mortality. As Freud puts it, "our unconscious does not believe in its own death" (190/10:350) and for that reason "in the unconscious each of us is convinced of his immortality" (183/10:341). These claims resonate with assertions made in *Beyond the Pleasure Principle,* where Freud famously maintains that "unconscious psychic processes are in themselves 'timeless.'"[3] "This means," he goes on to explain, "that they are not ordered temporally; that time does not change them in any way; and that the idea of time cannot be applied to them" (18:28/13:28).

As I will seek to demonstrate, these assertions are incompatible with the logic of Freud's own arguments. First, while the unconscious certainly does not have to obey the chronology of *linear* time, this does not mean that it can be exempt from the *succession* of time. On the contrary, the retroactive temporality of the unconscious itself presupposes the notion of time that I derive from the implications of succession. The deferral and delay that Freud calls *nachträglichkeit* is on my account characteristic of temporal experience in general. A temporal event can never be present as such, since it comes into being only by becoming past and becoming related to the future. The experience of the event is always given *too late* (in relation to what is no longer) and *too soon* (in relation to what is not yet). *Every experience* is thus characterized by a retroactive temporality, since what happens exceeds any given anticipation and can be apprehended only in retrospect, when it has already passed. If the unconscious was not marked by this succession of time, nothing would happen in it and nothing would happen because of it.

Second, when Freud asserts that the unconscious operates without regard for time and death, or believes that it is immortal, he does not rely on the evidence of psychoanalytic experience but on speculative concepts through which the evidence is interpreted. To challenge the coherence of these concepts, as I seek to do, is thus also to challenge the interpretation of the evidence. The most important move here is to distinguish between immortality and survival. Freud argues that because we cannot imagine our own death, we unconsciously believe that we are immortal. Freud is certainly right that we cannot imagine the state of being dead—this is the evidence of psychoanalytic experience to which he appeals—since in order to do so we have to imagine ourselves as surviving to witness our own death and thus necessarily fail to imagine ourselves as dead. It does not follow from this argument, however, that we are unconsciously convinced that we are immortal. Rather, what follows from Freud's argument is that even in our relation to death we fantasize about survival. To fantasize about *living on* after death is not to fantasize about being immortal, since to live on is to remain subjected to temporal finitude.

The distinction between immortality and survival is not incompatible with Freud's reasoning, but rather an expressive tool that enables a different reading of the same text. By distinguishing between immortality and survival we can thus unearth a wealth of chronolibidinal insights in Freud's essay. Despite Freud's claim that the unconscious does not have a sense of mortality, his own account shows that the fundamental conflicts of the unconscious emerge from an experience of survival and mourning that would be impossible without a sense of mortality. Contrary to Freud's tacit assumption, the sense of mortality does not depend on the ability to imagine or experience oneself *as dead*. On the contrary, the sense of mortality—the sense of oneself *as mortal*—is characterized by the exposure to a disappearance that exceeds one's grasp and can only be experienced in relation to an other, or in relation to oneself as an other. It is indeed impossible to experience one's own death, since in order to do so one could not be dead. The only death one can experience is rather the death of an other whom one survives. Inversely, the relation to one's own death marks the exposure to a future that will survive oneself and cannot be appropriated by oneself.

Now, it is precisely in the experience of survival that Freud locates the fundamental conflict of the unconscious with regard to death. While we cannot imagine our own death, we are nevertheless confronted with mortality through "the death or the threatened death of our loved ones."[4] This experience of mourning—or the mere anticipation of mourning—reveals an inherent contradiction in the unconscious between "two opposing attitudes to death, the one that acknowledges it as the annihilation of life, and the other that denies it as unreal," which "collide and come into conflict" upon the death of the beloved (192/10:353). Far from being unaware of mortality, then, the fear of death is operative in the unconscious. As I have argued throughout this book, to fear death is not to fear the state of being dead but to fear the loss of what one wants to keep. Rather than being limited to organic death, the fear of death is operative in relation to everything one cares about and can lose against one's will.

The significance of the fear of death and the experience of survival is further underlined by Freud's account of "primeval man," whose experience in this regard would be isomorphic to that of the unconscious. "When primitive man saw someone close to him die," Freud writes, "he was brought up against the fact that he himself could also die and his whole being raged against admitting this" (187/10:346). In a remarkable move, Freud goes on to suggest that it was this conflicted experience of survival that gave rise to the notion of an immortal soul as well as the sense of a moral conscience and ethical duty. "What came into being by the side of the loved one's corpse," Freud argues, "was not only the theory of souls, belief in immortality and a powerful root for the human sense of guilt, but also the first ethical commandments. The first and most significant prohibition of the awakening conscience was: *Thou shalt not kill*"

(189/10:348–49). What interests me here is not Freud's speculative invocation of the experience of "primeval man," but rather the structural significance of the double bind of survival that can be extracted from his mythical narrative. What this narrative indicates is first of all that the notion of immortality derives from the experience of survival. According to Freud, "the physical changes of death" first gave rise to "the division of the individual into a body and a soul," since "the constant memory of the dead person became the foundation of the hypothesis of other forms of life" and specifically "the idea of life continuing after apparent death" (188/10:347–8). The capacity to remember someone even after his or her body has ceased to be alive would thus be the origin of the idea of an immortal soul. By the same token, the very idea of a capacity to transcend death—of an immortal soul—derives from and depends on the memory of a mortal life that survives in others who themselves are mortal.

Furthermore, Freud makes clear that the survival of the dead is not simply something that is desired; it is not only the wishful projection of someone who does not want to let go of the beloved but also inflected by hostility toward the other and thus by guilt over having wished for or being satisfied by the death of the beloved. As Freud observes, "there adheres to the most tender and profound of our loving relationships a little piece of hostility which can stimulate the unconscious desire for death" (192/10:353), and this "law of emotional ambivalence, which still governs our emotional relationships with the people we love, would certainly have applied even more generally in primeval times" (187/10:346). Accordingly, "it was by the corpse of the beloved person that [primeval man] invented spirits, and it was his sense of guilt over the satisfaction that was mixed with his grief that meant that the first spirits he created were fearful, evil demons" (188/10:347).

The same ambivalence informs the ethical injunction "Thou shalt not kill." While it expresses care for the other through the recognition of his or her mortality, the same recognition is at the root of all sorts of aggression. As Freud puts it, "the very emphasis on the commandment: Thou shalt not kill, makes us certain that we are descended from an endless series of generations of murderers who had the lust to kill" (190/10:350). The double bind of survival, then, gives rise to and continues to haunt not only the notion of the immortality of the soul but also the sense of moral conscience and ethical duty. The investment in survival is the condition for any care for life and resistance to death, but it is also the condition for any resentment of life and desire for death.

If the experience of mourning is exemplary of this double bind, it is because it elucidates the inherent violence of living on. On the one hand, mourning is an act of fidelity, since it stems from the attachment to a mortal other and from the desire to hold on to this mortal other. On the other hand, mourning is an act of infidelity, since it stems from the decision to live on without the other and thus leave him or her or it behind. This betrayal is certainly unavoidable—the only alternative to surviving the other is to kill oneself and thereby kill the memory of the other as well—but the violence of survival is nonetheless real. As Freud puts it in a letter to Jones, in mourning one is left with "the choice of dying oneself or of acknowledging the death of the loved one, which again comes very close to your expression that one kills the person."[5] Similarly, Freud offers a striking analogy between the process of mourning, in which the beloved object is declared dead, and the process of overcoming the libidinal fixation to an object "by disparaging it, denigrating it, and even as it were killing it."[6] The point is not that these two processes are necessarily the same, but that even the most peaceful mourning relies on a violent severing from the other. In order to live on, I cannot be absolutely faithful to the other. I have to mobilize my ability to do without the other and in the process "kill" my previous attachment to a greater or lesser degree.

Rather than valorizing either "mourning" or "melancholia" as an adequate response to loss, one should therefore analyze their co-implication. In "Mourning and Melancholia"—yet another essay written the same year as "On Transience"—Freud himself begins by elucidating the common traits of the two conditions. In both mourning and melancholia, we have "the same painful frame of mind, the same loss of interest in the outside world—insofar as it does not recall the deceased—the same loss of capacity to adopt any new object of love (which would mean replacing the one who is mourned) and the same turning away from any activity that is not connected with thoughts of the deceased" (14:244/10:429). Thus, in resistance to an actual absence, both the mourner and the melancholic seek to ensure the survival of what has been lost by keeping it within themselves. The crucial difference, for Freud, is that the melancholic fails to recognize the reality of loss and instead incorporates the lost other in him- or herself through "an *identification* of the ego with the abandoned object" (14:249/10:435). As a consequence, the melancholic suffers not only from the loss of the other but also from a loss of the sense of self, expressed through an "extraordinary diminution" (14:246/10:431) of his or her self-regard. "In mourning it is the world which has become poor and empty; in melancholia it is the ego itself" (14:246/ 10:431). Furthermore, due to the law of emotional ambivalence, the ego who is identified with the lost other becomes not only the subject of love but also the subject of hate. In the absence of an other to whom grievances can be addressed, the melancholic turns the aggression against his or her own ego: "abusing it, debasing it, making it suffer and deriving sadistic satisfaction from its suffering" (14:250–51/10:438).

Now, it is precisely in order to break the self-destructive circle of melancholia that Freud advocates a mourning that is able to recognize the reality of loss and sever the attachment to the lost other. In mourning, the attachment is first internalized through a process where "each single one of the memories and expectations in which the libido is bound to the object is brought up and hypercathected" (14:245/10:430). But unlike in melancholy—where the attachment to what has been lost "takes refuge in narcissistic identification" and refuses to let go (14:251/10:438)—the attachment in mourning "is met by the verdict of reality that the object no longer exists; and the ego, confronted as it were with the question of whether it shall share this fate, is persuaded by the sum of the narcissistic satisfactions it derives from being alive to sever its attachment to the object that has been extinguished" (14:255/10:442). The aim of the work of mourning is thus, according to Freud, to retract the libido that was invested in the lost object and make it available for investment in new objects. Freud recognizes that this work of mourning is slow and painful—"carried out bit by bit, at great expense of time and cathectic energy" (14:245/10:430)—but he holds that if it succeeds, "the ego will have succeeded in freeing its libido from the lost object," and through this completion of mourning, the ego supposedly "becomes free and uninhibited again" (14:245/10:430). The same notion of successful mourning recurs in "On Transience," where Freud claims that "if the objects are destroyed or if they are lost to us, our capacity for love (our libido) is once more liberated; and it can then either take other objects instead or can tempo-rarily return to the ego" (14:306/10:360). Indeed, Freud maintains that mourning "comes to a spontaneous end. When it has renounced every-thing that has been lost, then it has consumed itself, and our libido is once more free (insofar as we are still young and active) to replace the lost ob-jects by fresh ones equally or still more precious" (14:307/10:361).

Freud's notion of successful mourning has been subjected to consider-able critique in the last decades, but one should be careful to formulate the critique so as to avoid replacing the valorization of mourning with a valorization of melancholia. First of all, one should note that Freud him-self indicates that his notion of successful mourning is insufficient to ac-count for the phenomena it is supposed to explain. In "Mourning and Melancholia" he concedes that it is "not at all easy to explain" why it is "so extraordinarily painful" (14:245/10:430) to let go of the lost object, and in "On Transience" he confirms that he in fact has no explanation: "why it is that the detachment of libido from its objects should be such a painful process is a mystery to us and we have not hitherto been able to frame any hypothesis to account for it. We only see that libido clings to its objects and will not renounce those that are lost even when a substitute lies ready to hand. Such then is mourning" (14:306–07/10:360).

The reason why Freud fails to explain the pain involved in letting go is because his notion of successful mourning assumes that there is a self who precedes the bond to the other and who can return "free and uninhibited again" after having traversed the ordeal of loss. If this were the case, to sever the bond to the other would simply be a matter of withdrawing an investment made by a self who remains essentially the same and who can substitute the object of attachment for another object with equal value or effect. Freud himself undermines this assumption, however, when he makes clear that the incorporation of the other is at work not only in mel-ancholia but also in mourning and indeed in the very formation of the self.[7] To sever the bond to a significant other is not merely to relinquish something external but *to relinquish one self*—to betray what one has been and to become someone who is irreducibly altered—which accounts for the intensification of pain and the internal conflict in the experience of mourning. By the same token, there can never be a self who emerges "free and uninhibited" from the process of mourning, since there is always a memory and anticipation of loss with which one has to reckon. Indeed, no matter how much one may seek to "kill off" the past, one may always be haunted by it in ways that exceed one's control and find oneself overtaken by it when one least expects it.

Let me emphasize, however, that the constitutive bond to the other does *not* entail that there is an inherent obligation to cultivate the bond to a given other or that one should resist the violence of mourning in the name of an "ethical" melancholia. On the contrary, it is because alterity is irreducible that neither mourning nor melancholia can be exempt from violence. Moreover, there is no given way to negotiate the violence of mourning. To be sure, mourning necessarily involves a "betrayal" of the other who is left behind. But to assume that this betrayal by default is unethical is a fallacy, since there is no intrinsic value in being faithful to the other. There are innumerable situations where "mourning" the other consists in coming to terms with abuse inflicted by the other. To betray or kill the attachment to the other can therefore be better and to keep it can be worse. Depending on the content and the situation, one may want to welcome or resist, embrace or lament, the loss of the past. The point, however, is that one always has to *reckon* with it. Whatever one does, one is haunted by a past that is repressed or commemorated, and often repressed precisely by being commemorated or vice versa. The temporal condition of survival is the reason why there is a problem of repression in the first place and why one must always respond to the past by "burying" the dead, either in the sense of forgetting or remembering.

My argument here can be seen to develop the logic of Derrida's claim that "to mourn and not to mourn are two forms of fidelity and two forms of infidelity," so that there is always a "terrible fatality of mourning: semimourning or double mourning. The psychoanalytic discourse, despite its subtlety and necessity, does not go into this fatality, this necessity: the double constraint of mourning."[8] Yet when Derrida takes issue with Freud's conception of mourning he tends to employ the latter's terminology in a misleading way, which compromises the articulation of his argument. Derrida regularly criticizes the notion of "normal" or "successful" mourning by aligning it with incorporation: "In successful mourning, I incorporate the one who has died, I assimilate him to myself, I reconcile myself with death, and consequently I deny death and the alterity of the dead other and of death as other. I am therefore unfaithful."[9] Since the other is "effectively, presently, undeniably dead," it follows that "if I take him into me as part of me, and if, consequently, I 'narcissize' this death of the other by a successful work of mourning, I annihilate the other, I reduce or mitigate his death. Infidelity begins here" (160/258). At the same time, Derrida recognizes that there can be no fidelity to the other without incorporation. He underlines that "*I must* (and this is ethics itself) carry the other in me in order to be faithful to him," but nevertheless emphasizes that "a certain melancholy must still protest against normal mourning" since the latter is "the good conscience of amnesia. It allows us to *forget* that to keep the other within the self, *as oneself,* is already to *forget* the other. Forgetting begins there. Melancholy is therefore *necessary* [Il faut *donc la mélancolie*]."[10] The exact status of this argument is unclear. Derrida certainly provides a powerful argument against those (e.g., Elisabeth Roudinesco) who think that mourning can be deemed "successful" if it incorporates the love for the lost other in subsequent relations. As Derrida emphasizes in *For What Tomorrow,* when one perpetuates the love for a lost other through the love of another, "the loved object is perpetuated in being betrayed, in being forgotten" (160/258). However, by confusing Freud's own terminology of mourning and melancholia, Derrida blurs the stakes of his argument and invites the misreading that deconstruction advocates an "ethics" of melancholia. As we have seen, Freud's notion of successful mourning does *not* hinge on incorporating the other in oneself but on severing the attachment to the other. To take issue with Freud's notion of successful mourning it is therefore insufficient to problematize the idea of incorporation. Inversely, Freud's notion of melancholia cannot be mobilized against the idea of incorporating the other as oneself in oneself, since melancholia consists in precisely such incorporation.

Rather than promoting the "fidelity" of melancholia against the "infidelity" of mourning, Derrida's logic of the double bind should lead one to articulate the constitutive violence of both mourning and melancholia, both the letting go and the incorporation of the other. Indeed, the logic of Derrida's arguments allows one to see the internal contradictions of the very idea of a faithful melancholia or mourning. There can be no fidelity to the dead other without incorporation, but this fidelity is at the same time marked by infidelity, since it denies the death of the other. Conversely, to be faithful to the fact that the other is dead is to be unfaithful, since it entails that one leaves the other behind. Fidelity is therefore a form of infidelity and infidelity is a form of fidelity. Furthermore, as I argue, nothing ensures that one should be more rather than less faithful to the other. The other who is "mourned" can be someone who has inflicted severely violent trauma just as well as someone who has given deeply positive love, not to mention that both of these aspects can be part of the legacy of the "same" other. Consequently, there is nothing that can determine a priori whether more or less fidelity to the other who is mourned is preferable in a given case. Successful mourning is strictly impossible—in the sense that one is always bound to an other and never emerges unscathed from loss—but it does not follow that it is better to embrace rather than to resist the failure of mourning.

For the same reason, the problem of survival and mourning is operative not only in the relation to others but also in the most immediate self-relation. Of course, the loss that is inherent in the experience of survival is made much more palpable in the actual mourning of someone's death, but it is operative on a minimal level in every experience, since the movement of survival necessarily entails the eradication of what does *not* survive. If one survived wholly intact—unscathed by the alteration of time—one would not be surviving; one would be reposing in absolute presence. The violation of integrity is therefore inscribed in the movement of survival as such. When one lives on it is always at the expense of what does not live on, of those past selves that are obliterated or eradicated in the movement of survival.

The temporality of survival is thus the condition both for preservation and violation, fidelity and infidelity. The temporality of survival opens the possibility of maintaining libidinal bonds, but it also opens the possibility of betraying, manipulating, or terminating libidinal bonds. This is why the theory of chronolibido seeks to rethink the constitution of the libidinal economy on the basis of the temporal process of *binding*. On Freud's own account, there is no libidinal life without the tension of excitation, which can be experienced only by being "bound." This binding is not an external restriction but indispensable for the being of libido as such: without binding there would be no pathways and no possible flow of desire. The bonds may always be broken, however, and thus call forth the economic capacity to redistribute resources or withdraw investments. This economization is a response to being bound to the mutable and losable, which is a condition for libidinal being in general. Even the most immediate auto-affection presupposes a temporal difference, without which one could never affect or be affected by oneself. This temporal difference constitutes both the possibility of binding and the impossibility of any final bonding.

The decisive question, then, is how the process of binding should be understood. It is a chief insight of Freud's discourse that the libidinal bonds that bind us to others are marked by a fundamental ambivalence of love and hate. Given that we are never self-sufficient—that we depend on others for our survival from the moment we are born—we are structurally bound to a life that exceeds our control. This dependency is the source of love, since only a being that is not self-sufficient can be invested in something other than itself. But the same dependency is also the source of hate, since only a being that is not self-sufficient can feel adversity to something other than itself. The same bond that inspires love can therefore inspire hate, since it is predicated on the relation to an undecidable other.

For Freud, however, the drama of libidinal bonding is *secondary* in relation to a state of being that precedes it. As he puts it in *Group Psychology and the Analysis of the Ego:*

> By being born we have made the step from an absolutely self-sufficient narcissism to the perception of a changing external world and the beginnings of the discovery of objects. And with this is associated the fact that we cannot endure the new state of things for long, that we periodically revert from it, in our sleep, to our former condition of absence of stimulation and avoidance of objects. (18:130/13:146)

The very fact of being bound to life—of being dependent on others—is here described as the loss of a primordial state of being ("an absolutely self-sufficient narcissism") that did not have to reckon with the problem of binding excitation. The reason one may be unable to bear libidinal bonds—the reason one may dream of escaping or terminating them—is thus not explained on the basis of an investment in the undecidable fate of survival. Rather, the ambivalence of libidinal bonds is explained on the basis of a longing to return to a state of being that precedes the condition of survival, what Freud here describes as "our former condition of absence of stimulation." In psychoanalytic theory, this state is typically ascribed to the perpetual fulfilment that is assumed to have existed in the womb and is regarded as the ontogenetic source of metaphysical fantasies of paradise or eternity. Yet it is not hard to see that the supposed state of absolute bliss is inseparable from a state of absolute death. As Freud himself makes clear, there is no life without the stimulation of excitation, so if there is an "absence of stimulation" there is no life whatsoever.

The latter conclusion is made explicit in *Beyond the Pleasure Principle,* where the ontogenetic myth of an absolute self-sufficiency to which we long to return is supplemented by the phylogenetic myth of an absolute death to which we are driven to return. In both cases, our aim would be to attain an absence of stimulation. The binding of excitation is thus understood as an intermediary function in the service of what Freud calls the death drive. The function of binding would be to find pathways for relieving excitation, with the ultimate purpose of discharging all excitation from the organism. The very advent of life—in introducing the tension of excitation—is thereby taken to be a traumatic event that gives rise to the death drive. "The attributes of life were at some time evoked in inanimate matter," Freud speculates, and "the tension which then arose in what had hitherto been an inanimate substance endeavored to cancel itself out. In this way the first drive came into being: the drive to return to the inanimate state" (18:38/13:40).

The excitation of life is thus assumed to be experienced as a violation of the quietude that supposedly precedes life and to give rise to the drive to return to this state by seeking to eliminate all tension, all excitation. Following this logic, Freud proposes that the death drive is the ultimate explanation for sadism and masochism, as well as negative affects in general. Sadism is explained as an externalization of the drive to quietude, which feels hatred toward objects because they give rise to excitation. Furthermore, given that the tension of excitation is internal to the living organism itself, there is a "primary masochism" where the self turns against itself and seeks to extinguish itself as the source of unpleasurable tension. Both our aggression toward others and toward ourselves are thus understood as an effect of the drive to rest in peace, to die one's "proper" death by eliminating the excitation of life that is internal to one.

The death drive has often been regarded as a radical element in Freud's thought, which calls into question the pleasure principle and accounts for how the psyche can be driven toward trauma and destruction. While Freud claims that the death drive is "beyond the pleasure principle," however, his own reasoning shows that they are based on the same axiom. For Freud, to be bound to life is by definition an experience of "unpleasure," since life is driven by an excitation that prevents the organism from coming to rest and compels it to survive in a state of tension. In contrast, the aim of the pleasure principle is to discharge the tension of life in favor of a complete release. The aim of the pleasure principle is thus inseparable from the aim of the death drive. The death drive seeks to restore the living organism to a supposed primordial state of total equilibrium, which is exactly the aim of the pleasure principle. As Freud himself points out, the pleasure principle operates in accordance with "the most universal striving *[Streben]* of all living substance—namely to return to the quiescence *[Ruhe]* of the inorganic world" (18:62/13:68), which is to say that it operates in accordance with the death drive.

If the pleasure principle and the death drive are based on the same axiom, however, the death drive cannot account for what is "beyond the pleasure principle." This logical fact undermines the reason for introducing the death drive in the first place, since the latter is supposed to account for the phenomena that contradict the pleasure principle. These phenomena comprise the compulsion to repeat traumatic events, as well as masochistic self-destruction and sadistic aggression. Their common denominator is that they contradict the pleasure principle by not seeking to reduce tension. On the contrary, the experience of pain (whether traumatic, masochistic, or sadistic) *increases* tension, so the compulsion to repeat or provoke painful experiences cannot be explained by a principle that dictates that we seek to eliminate tension. Consequently, it cannot be explained by the death drive. If the compulsion to repeat or provoke pain calls into question the pleasure principle, it necessarily calls into question the death drive, since the latter two are based on the same axiom.

Freud's main example of the repetition compulsion is the nightmares suffered by survivors of trauma. These nightmares call into question the pleasure principle by compulsively repeating experiences that are charged with *unpleasure*. If this repetition was ruled by the death drive, its goal would be to eliminate the bonds to the traumatic event and to extinguish the organism that has to endure unpleasure. As is clear from Freud's own account, however, the compulsion to repeat trauma is rather a matter of *binding*. In Freud's economical model for the psyche, a trauma is defined by being *too much*. In the traumatic event, it is impossible to bind the stimulus that breaches the psyche, in the sense that one cannot assimilate what happens to oneself. The return to the event in nightmares or flashbacks is an attempt to make up for this temporal lag: to "bind" the stimulus of the traumatic event into an experience that can be processed and understood.

Rather than being driven by a desire for death, the attempt to bind trauma presupposes an investment in living on. It is indeed true that the excitation of life marks an originary alterity that can come to be experienced as intolerable and precipitate a violent response toward the internal source of tension that persists as long as one is alive. Yet while the *response* to the excitation of life may always be destructive, one cannot have any relation to it at all without binding it, without being bound to it, and thereby minimally invested in it. It is thus because one is invested in survival—because one cannot be indifferent to what happens, because one is bound to it—that one may come to experience the exigencies of survival as unbearable and be driven to terminate survival. The investment in survival is not *sufficient* to determine a given affective response (it may lead to a desire for destruction as well as preservation), but without being invested one would not even respond to what happens and seek to renew, destroy, or maintain libidinal bonds.

The investment in survival can also be seen to inform the repetition compulsion in Freud's second example. Freud recounts the story of a child who does not cry or complain when his mother leaves him, despite his great attachment to her. The child's feelings before the experience of abandonment are rather displaced to a game he plays with his toys. The child deliberately throws them away while uttering a "long-drawn-out 'o-o-o-o,' accompanied by an expression of interest and satisfaction" (18:14/13:12). In Freud's interpretation, the *o-o-o-o* is an abbreviation of the German word *fort,* so the game consists in playing "gone" with the toys. The experience of the mother's disappearance is thus re-enacted through the game. Sometimes a toy that has been *fort* is pulled back and greeted with a joyful *da* ("there"), but Freud emphasizes that the act of playing *fort* is often "staged as a game in itself and far more frequently than the episode in its entirety" (18:16/13:13). The question, then, is why the child is driven to repeat the distressing experience of the mother's disappearance. Freud's answer is that the game allows the child to transform his *passive* exposure to the departure of the mother into an *active* choice. Rather than being powerless to prevent a loss that he fears, the child posits himself as willing the disappearance of the mother. When throwing away the toy, he in effect says: "All right, then, go away! I don't need you. I'm sending you away myself" (18:16/13:14).

The repetition compulsion here reveals a drive toward aggression and vengeance, but once again we can note that it has nothing to do with a death drive. Freud's examples show that the psyche can be driven to repeat destructive experiences, but they do not show that the drive is oriented toward the absolute quietude of death. On the contrary, both the traumatic nightmares and the child's game testify to an investment in survival. Through the nightmares, the psyche attempts to process what has happened to it by establishing a bond to the traumatic event, and through his game the child attempts to come to terms with the experience of being dependent on an other who is mutable and may be lost. However adequate or inadequate, successful or unsuccessful, these strategies arise in response to the experience of temporal finitude and are precipitated by an investment in survival. Even when the desire for a finite being is negated (as when the child stages a negation of the mutable mother), the negation itself testifies to a prior attachment and is performed *to enable the child to survive* beyond the loss of the mother.

To be clear, I am not arguing that self-destruction, aggression, or other negative phenomena are derivative in relation to a positive affirmation of life. On the contrary, the investment in survival accounts for both the impetus to preserve and the impetus to destroy, so any dualistic opposition between a life drive and a death drive is untenable. Consequently, I am not arguing that it is impossible to desire death, but that the desire for death presupposes the investment in survival. Even the most suicidal desire to end all survival presupposes such an investment, for at least two reasons.

First, without the investment in survival, one would not experience any suffering that could motivate suicide, since one would not care about what *has happened* or *is happening* to one. Second, without the investment in survival, one would not care to end all survival, since one would not care about what *will happen* to one. The investment in survival is not only the source of all joy in life but also the source of all suffering in life and can thus turn against itself. It is an essential possibility of the condition of survival that it can become unbearable. The response to the condition of survival can therefore not be given in advance and may call forth the most positive as well as the most negative affective responses. Indeed, the value of survival itself is undecidable: it opens the chance for pleasure *and* pain, satisfaction *and* suffering, preservation *and* destruction in the same stroke.[11]

In challenging Freud's notion of the death drive, then, I do not seek to replace it with another drive that would play the same constitutive role, e.g., a drive for survival that would compel us to live on at all costs and in every situation. Rather, I argue that there is no drive that precedes or provides the purpose of binding. Contra Freud, the excitation of life is not traumatic because we have lost or seek to attain the absolute peace of death. Rather, the excitation of life is traumatic because we *cannot experience it as such* and must bind it to something other than itself to have any relation to it at all. If this seems like an enigmatic formulation, we can clarify it through Freud's own account. As he emphasizes, in being alive we always have to reckon with external and internal stimuli that exceed what we can comprehend at any given moment. The primary problem of psychic life is therefore the same as the one that is intensified in the experience of trauma, namely, "the problem of mastering the amounts of stimulus that have broken in and of binding them" (18:30). Even in relation to myself, I cannot have any experience without binding excitation, and this bond is necessarily a double bind. On the one hand, the bond makes it possible to master stimuli: to manage, calculate, and negotiate what happens. On the other hand, the bond makes it impossible to master stimuli, since it is bound to an existence that can upset any calculation and undermine any negotiation. It is this process of binding, rather than the death drive, that calls into question the pleasure principle. Again, my point is not to deny the *phenomena* that Freud seeks to explain with the notion of the death drive, but to argue that these phenomena require a different explanation and that Freud's own text provides us with the resources for an alternative account through the notion of binding. As Freud himself underlines, the function of binding "must be accomplished before the dominance of the pleasure principle can even begin" (18:32/13:32), since it is "more originary than the purpose of gaining pleasure and avoiding unpleasure" (18:32/13:32).

It follows that binding precedes the constitution of any drive, desire, or will, since it precedes the constitution of any possible purpose for psychic life. For the affective self who comes into being through the bond, the binding of excitation is therefore undecidable: it is the source of both pleasure and unpleasure, chance and threat, love and hate. As an *effect* of this double bind, one can certainly be driven to seek the termination of life and libidinal bonds, since the excitation and tension of life may become too overwhelming or unbearable. But this explanation of suicidal or destructive behavior as an effect of the double bind must be strictly distinguished from an explanation that posits a death drive as the cause of such behavior. In responding affectively to the loss or gain of a given bond, we are necessarily invested in survival and can come to engage in all sorts of purposeful activity when establishing, maintaining, or terminating libidinal bonds. But the investment in survival—and whatever purposeful activity it may precipitate—derives from a binding that itself cannot be described in terms of a purpose. Indeed, to speak of a purpose of binding itself is to misconstrue the constitutive status of binding. Binding itself cannot have a purpose, since being bound is the condition for having a purpose.

The most important reference point for my argument here is Derrida's analysis of Freud in *The Post Card*. Through a close reading of *Beyond the Pleasure Principle,* Derrida argues that the libidinal economy should be understood as a "bindinal economy" that operates in accordance with the logic of "stricture."[12] The logic of stricture entails that any given X always already is bound to its other. Any apparent opposition between a "positive" and a "negative" principle is an internal limitation within the positive principle itself. Accordingly, Derrida argues that there can be no opposition between the pleasure principle and what Freud calls the reality principle. The reality principle binds and restricts the possibility of pleasure in an economy of loss and gain. Due to the reality principle, desire can never simply abandon itself to a free flow but has to bind itself to something other than itself and calculate with latent threats. This restriction, however, is not preceded by anything else. As Freud admits in the last chapter of *Beyond the Pleasure Principle:* "binding is a preparatory act which introduces and assures the dominance of the pleasure principle *[die Herrschaft des Lustprinzips]*" (18:62/13:67). Derrida places considerable stress on this admission, since it reveals an originary stricture of pleasure. Without the binding of excitation, there could be no pleasure in the first place. But the binding that makes pleasure possible at the same time limits it and charges it with unpleasure. To be sure, Freud thinks the stricture within a teleological horizon, where binding is "a preliminary function designed to prepare the excitation for its final elimination in the pleasure of discharge" (18:62/13:68). But since there is no libidinal life without a more or less pressing charge, a more or less tense excitation, the teleological schema is untenable. There cannot be any pleasure that is not bound to its other: no pleasure without unpleasure. *Pure* pleasure—if such a thing were possible—would be pure death.

The apparent opposition between pleasure and unpleasure is thus an internal limitation within pleasure itself. As Derrida emphasizes: "there is only pleasure which itself limits itself, only pain which itself limits itself, with all the differences of force, intensity, and quality that a set, a corpus, a 'body' can bear or give 'itself,' let itself be given."[13] For the same reason, one cannot know in advance which relations will give rise to pleasure or pain, suffering or satisfaction. In contrast to Freud's axiom, an increase of tension cannot be equated with unpleasure and a decrease of tension cannot be equated with pleasure. Pleasure is not an autonomous quality or quantity; it is generated by being bound to other qualities and quantities. In this heteronomous relation, an increase of tension just as well as a decrease of tension may be experienced as pleasurable, depending on what happens. What cannot happen, however, is that one is liberated from the stricture of pleasure. The stricture may be more or less tight, but it cannot be removed. On the contrary, all possible affects play themselves out in the bindinal economy of stricture. The bindinal economy is always more or less perforated by its own finitude, more or less traversed by pleasure and pain, so that even "the most normal step has to bear disequilibrium"

(406/433). This is ultimately because pleasure *must* bind itself to something other than itself in order to be what it is. If pleasure were to absolve itself from differential binding—to detach itself from all mortal bonds—it would cancel itself out in the same gesture.

Freud's own work here provides the resources to call into question his axiom that an increase of tension is unpleasurable and a decrease of tension is pleasurable. As Freud points out in "The Economic Problem of Masochism," *if* we adopt the former axiom, the pleasure principle "would be entirely in the service of the death drives, whose aim is to conduct the restlessness of life into the stability of the inorganic state" (19:160/13:372). However, Freud himself goes on to argue that "such a view cannot be correct" since "it cannot be doubted that there are pleasurable tensions and unpleasurable relaxations of tension" (19:160/13:372). Pleasure and unpleasure are therefore not a matter of quantitative relations whose ideal point would be the elimination of tension in complete equilibrium. Rather, Freud speculates that pleasure is a matter of "the *rhythm,* the temporal sequence of changes, rises and falls in the quantity of stimulus" (19:160/13:372). The same line of thought can be found in *Beyond the Pleasure Principle,* where Freud suggests that the experience of pleasure depends on "the amount of increase or diminution in the quantity of excitation *in a given period of time*" (18:8/13:4, see also 18:63/13:69). Following these remarks, one can develop a chronolibidinal conception of pleasure, where pleasure is not oriented toward a *telos* of absolute repose. If pleasure is a matter of rhythm and periodicity, it depends on temporal succession, which divides the very experience of presence from its inception and entails that unpleasure is intrinsic to pleasure as such.

In accordance with the logic of lack, however, Freud assumes that we seek to transcend the double bind of pleasure/unpleasure. The fact that absolute pleasure would be absolute death does not lead Freud to call into question this logic of lack. On the contrary, he maintains that death itself is the proper destination of pleasure. According to Freud, only "external influences" force the primordial death drive "to diverge ever more widely from its original course of life and to make ever more complicated *detours* before reaching its aim of death" (18:38–39/13:40–41). Even the reality principle would thus be motivated by a death drive that seeks to ensure that the organism will die "in its own fashion" (18:39/13:41). The proper drive is the drive for a "proper" death, which answers to Freud's definition of pure pleasure by being liberated from all tension. Far from being radical, then, the death drive is based on the same logic of lack as the pleasure principle. Both the notion of the pleasure principle and the death drive adhere to the traditional assumption that the aim of desire is to *not* desire. The movement of desire would thereby have a proper—albeit unattainable—destination: to rest in peace.

In contrast, Derrida argues that the principle of desire is a *postal principle* that has no proper destination. The postal principle may seem like an enigmatic term, but we will see how it provides a congenial way to describe the temporal constitution of libidinal bonds. In sending a letter one binds oneself both to the material support of the letter and to the other who receives it. Hence, one is bound to something that is inherently divided between past and future. On the one hand, the letter establishes a relation to what has been: the Latin word *post* means *after* and reminds us that a letter never arrives without delay. On the other hand, the letter is by definition written for a reader to come. Both the sender and the addressee must, from the beginning, calculate with an interval of time that separates them from each other. When writing a letter, one knows that the message will belong to the past when it is read. In this transition from one time to another, there is both a chance and a threat. By corresponding, one can establish connections across spatial and temporal distance, but at the same time one is dependent on a sending that cannot finally be controlled. The letter may be destroyed or end up in the wrong hands. And even if it arrives safely, the interval between sender and addressee is a source of disquietude in itself. When the letter arrives, the sender may already be dead or no longer subscribe to the meaning of the letter. This is a *necessary possibility,* which is latent even when the correspondence apparently works smoothly. To send a letter is by definition to inscribe a trace of the past that is addressed to a future that may erase it.

The postal principle does not, however, supervene on an immediate presence that is *first* given in itself and *then* sent forward/backward in time. The postal principle is rather the condition for anything to be given to itself, namely, the condition for auto-affection in general. Due to the constitutive negativity of time, every moment is stamped with the postal mark of being delayed *(no longer)* and deferred *(not yet)* in its very event.

Even the most immediate moment ceases to be as soon as it comes to be and must therefore be inscribed as a trace of the past, which by the same token is sent forward in time. Such postal sending is the minimal condition of survival. The trace of the past is the condition for anything to live on in time, but in living on it is exposed to erasure, since it is delivered to a future that may transform, corrupt, or delete it.

The postal principle is thus the principle of survival, which allows us to account for Derrida's apparently paradoxical statements about the relation between destination and death. On the one hand, Derrida maintains that the letter *cannot* arrive at its destination: "the condition for the letter to arrive is that it ends up and even that it begins by not arriving" (29/34). The reason why the letter cannot arrive is not because it has been cut off from an origin or end; it is due to the essence of the letter itself. Even ideally speaking the letter *must not* arrive at its destination—it "must bear within itself a force and a structure, a straying of the destination, such that it *must* also not arrive in any way" (123/135)—since if it were to arrive it would cancel itself out. The destination of the letter is thus understood as the final destination of death. On the other hand—but for the same reason—Derrida maintains that the destination of the letter is not the final destination of death. Death is *not* our destination in the sense that "we would be destined to die, no, not in the sense in which to arrive at our destination, for us mortals, is to end by dying."[14] Contra Freud's notion of the death drive, death is neither a past state of being from which we have departed nor a future state of being at which we could arrive. No one has ever been and no one will ever be dead, since death is not a state of being. Rather, we can only have a relation to death through the deferral of death that is the movement of survival. The point is not that life is deferred but that life *is* deferral and cannot overcome the movement of deferral without ceasing to be alive.

Nevertheless, while I argue that the postal principle provides powerful resources to call into question the logic of the death drive, Derrida himself sometimes invokes the notion of the death drive with apparent approval. Thus, in his essay "Différance," Derrida glosses the death drive "as expenditure without reserve, as the irreparable loss of presence, the irreversible usage of energy" and "as the relationship to the entirely other [*rapport au tout-autre*] that apparently interrupts every economy."[15] Derrida qualifies his statement by saying "apparently inter-rupts," since he wants to think the economical and the aneconomical as co-implicated. Yet it is misleading to align the death drive with the an-economical that is at work within the economical. Contrary to what Derrida implies in "Différance," the idea of the death drive is the idea of *the most economical,* since it aims at restoring a state of absolute full-ness/emptiness where nothing can be lost. Far from being compatible with the idea of the death drive, the co-implication of the economical and the aneconomical that Derrida seeks to articulate follows from the deferral of death in the movement of survival that neither has an origin nor an end. As Derrida himself rightly underlines in "Freud and the Scene of Writing": "there is no life present *at first* which would *then* come to protect, postpone, or reserve itself"; rather, "life can defend itself against death only through an *economy* of death, through defer-ment, repetition, reserve."[16]

The key to articulating this economy of death in Freud is the deferral *(Aufschub)* of the reality principle rather than the death drive. Indeed, the passage from *Beyond the Pleasure Principle* that Derrida himself most often refers to as his resource (and quotes at length in "Différance") is one where Freud maintains that the pleasure principle must submit itself to the *Aufschub* of the reality principle. Derrida radicalizes this argument by emphasizing that "the difference between the pleasure principle and the reality principle is not uniquely, nor primarily, a distinction, an exteriority, but rather the original possibility, within life, of the detour, of *différance (Aufschub)* and the economy of death" ("Freud and the Scene of Writing," 198/295, trans. mod.). The glossing of *Aufschub* as *différance* also recurs in "Différance" (18–19/19–20) and in *The Post Card* (282/301). The point is that *différance*—as the tracing of time—designates an originary deferral that is not preceded by anything else and not oriented toward anything beyond itself. The logic of this argument is incompatible with the logic of the death drive. The latter does not articulate an originary deferral but rather assumes that there is a teleological end (absolute stasis) that is de-ferred and in relation to which the movement of survival is a provisional detour away from the lost origin (absolute stasis) to which we supposedly long to return. As Derrida himself points out in *The Post Card,* the logic of the death drive follows "the law of the proper *(oikos, oikonomia)* which governs the detour and indefatigably seeks the proper event, its own, proper propriation" (359/381), which Derrida goes on to link to "the poetics of the proper as reconciliation, consolation, serenity" (363/386). In contrast, the postal principle undermines precisely the notion of a proper death, since it elucidates a co-implication of life and death that "consists not only in compromising oneself *[s'auto-entamer]* but in compromising the self, the *autos*—and thus ipseity. It consists not only in committing suicide but in compromising *sui-* or *self-*referentiality, the *self* or *sui-* of suicide itself."[17] The logic of deconstruction is thus incompatible with the logic of the death drive, since the latter depends on the idea of a proper death, a proper *sui-* of suicide. To think the postal principle as constitutive is rather to think the inherently violent condition of survival, which entails that one can live and die only by compromising one's own integrity, without archeological origin or teleological end.

Now, Derrida's own articulation of the postal principle is pursued through a critique of Lacan. The point of departure is Lacan's seminar on Edgar Allan Poe's short story "The Purloined Letter," where a stolen letter circulates among the characters and precipitates their actions. The content of the stolen letter is never revealed; its significance hinges instead on its position in relation to the characters of the drama. Lacan draws on this plot to exemplify his linguistically oriented version of psychoanalysis, in which the *signifier* and not the signified constitutes the subject. Lacan thereby rejects the notion of a self-identical subject and maintains that we are subjected to the symbolical order of language, where the process of signification cannot be stable or brought under the control of an autonomous will. Nevertheless, Lacan claims that "a letter always arrives at its destination" and ultimately is indivisible ("cut a letter into little pieces, and it remains the letter it is").[18] These remarks are at the center of Derrida's critique. A number of readers have defended Lacan by emphasizing that the remarks in question do not express a notion of absolute identity. The letter in Lacan's analysis does not have an inherent meaning, but marks an ever-possible displacement of determinations and definitions. The principle of the letter is precisely that meaning is *never* given and always may be retroactively altered by the one who receives the message.

It should be noted that such a defense of Lacan does deflate a number of the theses that Derrida criticizes. Derrida often seems to assume that

Lacan actually believes that there is an indivisible integrity or given meaning of the letter—namely, that the letter does arrive at its destination—and the latter assumption compromises the force of his critique.[19] The argument that needs to be developed is rather the deconstruction of the logic of lack that underpins Lacan's account. Indeed, we can say that for Lacan the letter of desire *never* arrives at its destination, since the proper destination is an absent fullness. But it is precisely the notion of an absent fullness that allows Lacan to assert that a letter *always* arrives at its destination, since the failure of the letter to arrive at an absolute fullness verifies the truth of ontological lack. Or as Derrida puts it in *The Post Card:* "[for Lacan] the letter will always refind its proper place, a circumvented lack (certainly not an empirical one, but a transcendental one, which is better yet, and more certain)" (425/453).

To deconstruct Lacan's account, one must therefore (beyond the limitations of Derrida's critique) take issue with the notion of the death drive that informs it. While Lacan revises Freud's theory of the death drive in a number of important ways, he nonetheless retains a version of the logic of lack. For Lacan, the death drive is *not* a biological tendency that pertains to living organisms in general. The death drive is proper only to human beings, who articulate their desire along a signifying chain and seek to understand the cause of their suffering. Human desire is then, according to Lacan, not primarily oriented in relation to the natural world but in relation to a transcendent Thing *(das Ding, la Chose)* that is supposed to have been lost and whose return would relieve suffering in satisfying desire completely. As Lacan explains in *Seminar VII,* the Thing "will be there when in the end all conditions have been fulfilled" but by the same token it is "clear that what is supposed to be found cannot be found again. It is in its nature that the object as such is lost."[20] Lacan goes on to explain that "it is this object, *das Ding,* as the absolute Other of the subject, that one is supposed to find again" (52/65), which entails that the "goal of the specific action which aims for the experience of satisfaction is to reproduce the initial state, to find *das Ding*" (53/66–67).

As we will see, both Lacan and his commentators equivocate regarding the question of whether there ever was an initial state of satisfaction. On the one hand, they often ascribe the experience of the Thing to a state of fulfilment that is assumed to have existed in the womb or in the unity with the mother's breast. On the other hand, Lacan can also be seen to recognize that there never was such an experience of unity or fulfilment and that the Thing is nothing but a retrospective projection, which creates the illusion of an absolute satisfaction that was lost. Regardless of whether it is conceived as a lost reality or as a retrospective fantasy, however, the idea of absolute satisfaction turns out to be inseparable from the idea of absolute termination, the idea of pure fullness turns out to be inseparable from pure emptiness, and the idea of pure life turns out to be inseparable from pure death. This is why Lacan employs the death drive as a metapsychological model for both the register of the drive and the register of desire.

In the register of desire, Lacan makes clear that there can be no satisfaction because of the absence of the Thing. What is desired under the heading of the Thing is a state of absolute fullness to which no object can ever be adequate. Any given object of desire thus fails to provide the satisfaction of the Thing and propels the subject to search for new objects that in turn fail to satisfy its desire, in a chain of metonymic displacements that for Lacan testifies to the subject's fundamental lack of being. In his late work, however, Lacan introduces the register of the drive to explain how there can be satisfaction despite the fundamental lack of being.[21] "It is clear," he points out in *Seminar XI,* "that those with whom we deal, the patients, are not satisfied, as one says, with what they are. And yet, we know that everything they are, everything they experience, even their symptoms, involves satisfaction" (166/151). On Lacan's account, it is the register of the drive that accounts for this satisfaction: "the function of the drive has for me no other purpose than to put in question what is meant by satisfaction" (166/151). In the register of the drive, there is satisfaction in the movement of circling around the object rather than in the possession of the object itself, and pleasure is derived from the process of attaining the object rather than from the attainment itself. As Lacan puts it, "even when you stuff the mouth—the mouth that opens in the register of the drive—it is not the food that satisfies it, it is, as one says, the pleasure of the mouth" (167/153).

If every drive is a death drive—as Lacan maintains—it can therefore operate only by "inhibiting" its own aim and "braking" its own drive toward death. As Joan Copjec has argued, "the drive inhibits, as part of its very activity, the achievement of its aim. Some inherent obstacle—the object of the drive—simultaneously *brakes* the drive and *breaks it up,* curbs it, thus preventing it from reaching its aim" (34). While this establishes a distinction between desire and drive, the founding assumption in both cases is that the *aim* of libidinal being is the complete satisfaction that is inseparable from death. The difference is that desire rejects all objects as inadequate in comparison to the Thing that would satisfy it once and for all, whereas the drive satisfies itself with a substitute. As is clear from this schema, however, the lack of fullness is not called into question but is located at the root of both desire and drive.[22] Consequently, Copjec maintains that the object of the drive "emerges *out of the lack,* the void, opened by the loss of the original plenum or *das Ding.* In place of the mythical satisfaction derived from being at one with the maternal Thing, the subject now experiences satisfaction in this partial object" (60).

Like other Lacan scholars, Copjec vacillates when determining the status of the original plenum. On the one hand, she maintains that the idea of a lost plenum is a "retrospective illusion" (33). On the other hand, she subscribes to the idea of a maternal Thing that has been lost. "The problem is not simply that I cannot think the primordial mother," Copjec asserts, "but that her loss opens up a hole in being . . . the *jouissance* that attached me to her has been lost and this loss depletes the whole of my being" (35–36).[23] Similarly, Bruce Fink argues that the idea of a lost object is "essentially phantasmatic in nature, not corresponding to a *remembered* experience of satisfaction," while nevertheless maintaining that there is a "first experience of satisfaction" in which the mother's breast is not constituted as an object at all. This primordial satisfaction precedes the experience of the desired object as "separate from and not controlled by the child." Given the latter experience of alterity, "the child can never again refind the breast as experienced the first time around: as *not separate* from his or her lips, tongue, and mouth, or from his or her self. Once the object is constituted, the 'primal state' wherein there is no distinction between infant and breast, or between subject and object . . . can never be re-experienced, and thus the satisfaction provided the first time can never be repeated. A kind of innocence is lost forever, and the actual breasts found thereafter are never quite *it.*"[24] According to this narrative, there once was a primordial satisfaction in the experience of the breast, which the subject seeks to recreate in all subsequent relations.

Every attempt to do so will prove to be vain, since no object can measure up to the ideal of perfect unity. The idea that an object can ever fill our lack or complete our being is thus regarded as a phantasmatic illusion. But what is not regarded as a phantasmatic illusion is the idea that there indeed was a primary experience of unity with the breast, before the separation between subject and object.

The most powerful elaboration of such a Lacanian theory can be found in Adrian Johnston's *Time Driven: Metapsychology and the Splitting of the Drive.* Systematizing the implications of Slavoj Zizek's groundbreaking reading of Lacan, Johnston describes the drive as split between an axis of iteration and an axis of alteration. The axis of iteration demands the repetition of a primordial satisfaction, which Johnston ascribes to an experience in early infancy when "the breast is not registered as being a separate/separable object belonging to another subject."[25] According to Johnston, the drive originates in this experience of primary unity—the experience of the Thing—and the axis of iteration constitutes the endlessly repeated attempt to recover what has been lost. The experience of the Thing can never be restored, however, since no actual object of desire can yield an experience of unity. Rather, every actual object of desire is temporal and can only be given along an axis of alteration, where nothing is ever repeated as the same.

Consequently, there is a fundamental conflict between the demand for atemporal unity that is articulated along the axis of iteration and the temporal objects of desire that are given along the axis of alteration. Johnston's main argument is that nothing can resolve this conflict, since it is inherent to the constitution of the drive itself. The Lacanian notion of "castration" should therefore *not* be understood as an external prohibition—a socially induced repression or symbolic Law—that if removed would give the subject access to full enjoyment. Rather, castration should be understood as the irrevocable loss of the Thing, which gives rise to the drive but at the same time dooms it to strive for something that never can be retrieved. The reason why the drive cannot attain the full enjoyment of the Thing is not because of an empirical-historical barrier, but because of a deadlock that is intrinsic to the drive itself.

Now, Johnston insightfully demonstrates that this Lacanian notion of the drive amounts to a rethinking of the death drive. Johnston is well aware of many inconsistencies in Freud's notion of the death drive, but he seeks to rectify them by regarding the death drive not as a drive in itself but as characteristic of all drives. For Johnston, Freud's main mistake is that he literally conceives of death as the origin and goal of the drive. Given that death is not a state of being, there cannot have been an experience of death to which the organism longs to return. Drawing on Lacan's reading of the death drive in *Seminar XVII,* Johnston argues that the origin to which the drive strives to return is not the literal state of death but the lost experience of the Thing.[26] The death drive does not aim at a return to the inorganic but rather articulates "the insistent demand for an absolute enjoyment" (238).

We can thus understand why Johnston, following Lacan, regards the death drive as characteristic of all drives. On the one hand, the death drive exemplifies his assumption that we are driven to repeat a primordial experience of the Thing. On the other hand, the death drive exemplifies how the constitution of the drive itself makes it impossible to (re)experience the Thing. In order to achieve full satisfaction—that is, in order to experience the Thing—the drive would have to evacuate all tension from the organism. Yet the drive itself is an internal generator of tension, so the drive to eliminate tension comes to generate tension in its turn. Johnston therefore concludes that the drive is "inherently self-defeating, since it aims at eliminating tension while, at the same time, being itself responsible for generating tension" (237).

For the same reason, however, there cannot ever have been an experience of full satisfaction in early infancy or at any other stage. Johnston cogently argues that "Freud fails to respect the limits imposed by finite, ontogenetic experience" (181) by locating the origin of the drive in a state of death to which there cannot ever have been access. But the same critique can be launched against Johnston's own conception of a lost fullness at the origin of the drive, since fullness is incompatible with finite, ontogenetic experience. Given Johnston's own admission that "full satisfaction implies a kind of psychical death, an evacuation of the tension of dissatisfaction that perpetually drives the libidinal economy" (239), the child in early infancy must be dead in order to experience full satisfaction.

Hence, Freud's inability to separate the idea of full satisfaction from the idea of complete death is not a speculative mistake. Rather, the idea of full satisfaction is strictly inseparable from the idea of complete death. While Lacan explicitly recognizes this logical equivalence of absolute fullness/absolute emptiness, it does not lead him to call into question that the death drive is an adequate metapsychological model for understanding the libidinal economy. On the contrary, Lacan maintains that we are constitutionally driven toward an unattainable absolute life/absolute death.

The fundamental experience of survival—of the life that lives on by *not* being absolute—is therefore assumed to be a fundamental experience of lack. A striking example of this logic can be found in *Seminar XI,* where Lacan describes how "two lacks overlap" in the constitution of the subject. We are thus treated to a clear account of what Lacan understands as the ontological lack of being, which is worth quoting at length:

> Two lacks overlap here. The first emerges from the central defect around which the dialectic of the advent of the subject to his own being in relation to the Other turns—by the fact that the subject depends on the signifier and that the signifier is first of all in the field of the Other. This lack takes up the other lack, which is the real, earlier lack, to be situated at the advent of the living being, that is to say, at sexed reproduction. The real lack is what the living being loses, that part of himself *qua* living being, in reproducing himself through the way of sex. This lack is real because it relates to something real, namely, that the living being, by being subject to sex, has fallen under the blow of individual death.
>
> Aristophanes' myth pictures the pursuit of the complement for us in a moving, and misleading, way, by articulating that it is the other, one's sexual other half, that the living being seeks in love. To this mythical representation of the mystery of love, analytic experience substitutes the search by the subject, not of the sexual complement, but of the part of himself, lost forever, that is constituted by the fact that he is only a sexed living being, and that he is no longer immortal. (204–05/186–87)

Lacan begins by rehearsing his doctrine that our dependency on language answers to an alienation; here described as the "central defect" of being dependent on a signifier that cannot be controlled by the subject. This

notion of language presupposes that the necessity of mediation—the necessity of relating to ourselves via the alterity of time and language—is
experienced as a lack of being. Lacan goes on to say that the ultimate
source of this lack is that the subject is *no longer immortal*. This may appear to be a startling statement, but Lacan has anticipated his point a
couple of pages earlier, when arguing that all objects of desire are "representatives" of "immortal life, or irrepressible life, life that has need of no
organ, simplified, indestructible life. It is precisely what is subtracted
from the living being by virtue of the fact that it is subject to the cycle of
sexed reproduction" (198/180). The temporal process of survival—here
exemplified by sexual reproduction—is thus opposed to a proper immortality. As living beings subjected to generation and corruption, we can
never be immortal: we can only *live on* through reproduction—whether
this reproduction is sexual, linguistic, or dependent on some other form
of mediation. This movement of survival will never yield a proper immortality, since whatever lives on through reproduction is itself subject to corruption and death. If one assumes that we seek a proper immortality—an
absolute self-sufficiency—one must therefore conclude that the experience of survival is one of ontological lack, since the movement of survival
compromises any self-sufficiency from its first inception. The aim of what
Lacan here calls "analytic experience" is to make us recognize this fundamental lack at the core of our libidinal being. In contrast to the experience
of love, which makes us believe that the relation to another can fulfill us,
analytic experience would make us recognize that what we are *really* seeking in seeking love is an absolute self-sufficiency that is forever lost and
inaccessible to us as mortal beings.

Again, whether there ever was a state of self-sufficiency is equivocal
both in Lacan's text and in the established commentaries. According to
Copjec's detailed interpretation, libidinal objects are "representatives"
of an immortal life that has been lost (52), but the status of the lost immortality is unclear. On the one hand, Copjec asserts that "immortal,
indestructible life has been subtracted from us" (52) and that "the body
and satisfaction have lost the support of the organic body and the noumenal Thing" (37), which implies that there once was an immortal life
or a noumenal Thing. On the other hand, she asserts that the self-
sufficiency of immortal life is a myth of something that never existed.

Copjec's contradictory assertions culminate when she writes that "pure and total self-sufficiency does not now and never did exist (or: there is no original plenum), yet something nevertheless remains of that never-existing, mythical time and self-sufficiency" (52). One is thus left to wonder how something can remain from what never existed.

A defender of Lacan could certainly avoid the inconsistency by strictly maintaining that the supposed loss of immortality is nothing but a retrospective projection and that Lacan only analyzes it as the fundamental fantasy of the subject. Yet this qualification does not affect the premise with which I take issue, namely, that the "truth" of desire is the lack of immortality. In Lacan's terms, there is a constitutive difference between the *jouissance* expected (full enjoyment) and the *jouissance* obtained (temporal enjoyment), since no object of experience can answer to the desired Thing. As he puts it in *Seminar XX:* " 'That's not it' is the very cry by which the *jouissance* obtained is distinguished from the *jouissance* expected."[27] For Lacan, the *jouissance* expected is not inaccessible for contingent reasons that can be overcome. On the contrary, it is inaccessible due to the ontological lack of being. Following *Seminar XI,* this ontological lack should ultimately be understood in terms of the fact that we are mortal. The absent Thing is proper immortality, and the impossibility of ever attaining such an absolute self-sufficiency—the impossibility of ever transcending the temporal finitude of survival—is the repressed "truth" of desire that Lacan aims to elucidate.

Furthermore, the very desire for the Thing is, according to Lacan, marked by a fundamental ambivalence. As Adrian Johnston recalls: "desire à la Lacan is not simply a matter of attraction to the impossible-to-attain, forever-absent, always-already missing Thing; it also consists of a simultaneous repulsion from the Real of *das Ding.*"[28] Specifying this logic of ambivalence, Johnston maintains that the Thing is an "absent presence" that is "both alluring and horrifying" as well as a "present absence" that is "both painful and energizing" (167). It follows that the Thing "both is and is not desired at the same time, functioning as a center of libidinal gravity that the desiring subject neither can live with nor can live without" (167). This is certainly a compelling presentation of the ambivalence of Lacanian desire, but it does not answer my chronolibidinal critique. What I am calling into question is precisely the notion of an absent Thing that functions as the "center of libidinal gravity." According to this model, the Thing is "alluring" since it promises the state of absolute fullness that we desire, but at the same time it is "horrifying" since such an absolute fullness would in fact be absolute emptiness and eliminate ourselves along with our desire. Following the same logic, the absence of the Thing is "painful" since it prevents us from attaining the aim of our desire, but at the same time it is "energizing" since it is only because we do not attain the aim of our desire that we are driven to do or to desire anything at all.

The Lacanian model thus reads the ambivalence of desire as a response to the investment in the absent Thing. The ambivalence of the Thing does not call into question its organizing role in the libidinal economy but rather allows it to explain both repulsion and attraction, both the pain of loss and the energy of aspiration. This assumed "truth" of desire has two major consequences. First, the fantasy of the absolute is diagnosed as the cause of our inability to come to terms with reality. The reason we develop neuroses, phobias, and resentful aggression is ultimately because we sustain the fantasy of an absolute enjoyment (the transcendent Thing) that no actual object or real human being ever can provide. Second, this diagnosis assumes that *if* we were able to let go of the fantasy of absolute enjoyment, we would be able to come to terms with reality. Lacanian analysis therefore sets out to dispel the idea that there is a Thing out there that can be obtained by the subject. The moment of "authenticity" in Lacanian analysis is the moment when one recognizes the lack of being that nothing can fill and assumes the "symbolic castration" that constitutes one's subjectivity. By "traversing the fantasy" of absolute enjoyment, the analysand is supposed to arrive at the insight that nothing can satisfy his or her desire—that nothing can be *it*—and learn to live with this absence of the Thing.

In contrast, the theory of chronolibido reads the ambivalence of desire as a response to the investment in the undecidable fate of survival: in temporal finitude as the source of both the desirable and the undesirable. The reason desire is ambivalent is ultimately *not* because we are driven toward the absolute but because we are invested in survival—an investment that gives rise to acknowledgment *and* denial, compassion *and* aggression, vital change *and* deadening repetition. At stake in the difference between these two accounts of ambivalence are two different models for reading the drama of desire. On Lacan's account, the drama of desire stems from the conflict between the primordial aim of transcending libidinal bonds (the death drive toward the state of absolute self-sufficiency that is represented by the Thing) and the self-defeating nature of the attempt to achieve such transcendence, which serves to explain the ambivalence, reversals, and tragic fates of desire. On the chronolibidinal account, however, the drama of desire—with its ambivalence, reversals, and tragic fates—stems from a double bind that is internal to the temporal process of binding itself. Rather than being derived from a primordial aim of eliminating or transcending libidinal bonds, the drama of desire derives from an economy of binding that has no given aim.

Chronolibidinal reading thereby seeks to show that the ontological lack of being is not the repressed truth of desire. On the contrary, the idea of an ontological lack *is itself a repression* of the constitutive investment in survival that derives from the necessity of binding. Following my analysis of Freud's "On Transience," the supposed experience of ontological lack—the lament over the absence of a timeless being—dissimulates the preceding investment in the survival of a temporal being. The experience of loss does not stem from the mourning of a Thing we never had but from the mourning of a temporal being who is ceasing to be from the beginning. The fundamental problem of desire is not that mortal life cannot answer to the immortality we desire, in accordance with Lacan's formula *That's not it.* Rather, the fundamental problem of desire is that *This is it:* the bond to mortal life is the condition for everything we desire and everything we fear.

Conclusion

Binding Desire

T HE MUSIC HAS stopped. During the performance of the sonata, the little phrase they cherished as the national anthem of their love has held him spellbound. With the violin rising to a series of high notes— "holding on to them in a prolonged expectancy, in the exaltation of already seeing the object of its expectation approaching, and with a desperate effort to try to endure until it arrived, to welcome it before expiring, to keep the way open for it another moment" (1:358/1:339)—it was as if she had entered the room. And not only she but also the very texture of the time when they first met and became lovers: "the stormy rains that fell so often that spring, the icy drive home in his victoria, by moonlight, all the meshes formed from habits of thinking, impressions of the seasons, reactions on the surface of his skin, which had laid over a succession of weeks a uniform net in which his body was now recaptured" (1:358–59/1:340). Because of this resuscitation, he can no longer take shelter behind the narrative of the past through which he has tried to domesticate the pain of loss. In and through the repetition of the music, "the abstract expressions *the time when I was happy, the time when I was loved*" (1:358/1:339) have been overtaken by the visceral memory of how it felt to be loved by her. His voluntary protection against the past is thus defeated by an involuntary resurrection. "Deceived by this sudden beam of light from the time of love" his memories of her awake, flying "swiftly back up to sing to him, with no pity for his present misfortune, the forgotten refrains of happiness" (1:358/1:339).

This scene from the first volume of Proust's *Recherche*—when Charles Swann is visited by the memory of his beloved Odette during the performance of a sonata by the composer Vinteuil—belongs to one of Marcel's most intricate accounts of involuntary memory, which will continue to haunt the novel until the end. The repetition of a phenomenon (e.g., the musical phrase) allows a past self to emerge. As we have seen, such involuntary memory depends on the structure of the trace. When Swann first hears the sonata by Vinteuil (in an episode that I discussed in Chapter 1) his very apprehension of the phrase proceeds from the inscription of sound in memory. The inscription of the trace is a condition for the synthesis of the successive melody and even for the perception of the single notes, which depend on retention to be apprehended. This tracing of time marks a minimal *bond* at the heart of experience. Through the structure of the trace one is bound—as a condition of possibility for any experience at all—to a past that precedes one and to a future that exceeds one. This passive bondage, which precedes any act of will, is in turn the condition for any active libidinal binding. Thus, when Swann in the beginning of their relationship actively binds his love for Odette to the little phrase in Vinteuil's sonata (marking it as their "national anthem"), his libidinal investment not only depends on but also is animated by the tracing of time. The phrase is meant to serve "as a token, a memory of his love" (1:227/1:215), and the desire for such a token presupposes a sense of how his love is bound to a future that may take it away; otherwise he would not be seized by the desire to keep it in memory.

From the beginning, Swann can thus read suffering in the smile of the phrase: *il devinait de la souffrance dans son sourire* (1:361/1:342). While witnessing and recording his moments of happiness, the little phrase also "warned him how fragile they were" (1:361/1:342). On the one hand, this sense of suffering and fragility is caused by the capacity of the phrase to be repeated in the future. For Swann in love, this capacity is not only a positive ability to encode the memory of him and Odette but also a negative reminder that the phrase can be repeated without them and ultimately is indifferent to the particularity of their existence. Indeed, Swann in love is "pained by the thought *[souffrant de songer]* that the little phrase, at the moment when it passed so close and yet infinitely far away, did not know them although it was addressed to them," and he even regrets "that the phrase had any meaning, any intrinsic and unalterable beauty, alien to them" rather than being "created exclusively from the essence of a passing love affair and a particular person" (1:227/1:215–16). On the other hand, it is precisely the capacity of the phrase to preserve "the specific, volatile essence of that lost happiness" (1:358/1:340) which will cause Swann "such harrowing pain *[une si déchirante souffrance]*" (1:358/1:339) upon hearing the sonata again when Odette no longer loves him.

The chance of survival through memory, then, is not only inhabited by the threat of forgetting but also by the threat of remembering after the loss of what one wanted to keep. In rendering this double bind, Marcel produces one of his most extraordinary accounts of the temporality of the self. The division between two successive selves is compressed into a scene in which Swann sees "motionless before that relived happiness, a miserable figure who filled him with pity because he did not recognize him right away, and he had to lower his eyes so that no one would see that they were filled with tears. It was himself" (1:360/1:341). The former self who has emerged from the past here sees the present self in mourning and the response is pity. But when he understands that the "miserable figure" is he himself—that this is who he has become—the perspective is reversed. "When he realized this, his pity vanished, but he was jealous of the other self she had loved" (1:360/1:341). As we move from the former self seeing the present self to the present self seeing the former self, pity is thus replaced by jealousy, which further deepens Marcel's account of what it means to be a temporal, chronolibidinal being. The violent passage of time gives rise not only to successive and incompatible selves but also to antagonistic feelings between these selves that are sedimented in the same body. The effect here manifests itself in a pain *(souffrance)* that becomes too vivid *(trop vive)* for Swann to bear it.

Now, it is precisely the susceptibility to such pain that Marcel places at the center of his aesthetic discourse on Vinteuil's sonata. "The field open to the musician," he writes, "is not a miserable scale of seven notes, but an immeasurable keyboard" with "millions of keys of tenderness, of passion, of courage, of serenity which compose it" (1:362/1:343–44). Music thereby has the capacity to open the emotional depths of our lives, "showing us what richness, what variety, is hidden unbeknownst to us within that great unpenetrated and disheartening darkness of our soul which we take for emptiness and nothing" (1:363/1:344). Music can only achieve this effect, however, by resonating in a mortal being. Only a being that can lose something against its will—that is, only a mortal being—can experience the range of emotions that Marcel describes. The precious quality of tenderness, the intensity of passion, the demands of courage, and the relief of serenity would be inconceivable for a being that could not fear or imagine what their absence would mean. Accordingly, the pathos of Vinteuil's sonata stems from the fact that it has "wedded itself to our mortal condition *[épousé notre condition mortelle]*" (1:363/1:344).

By the same token, Swann is gripped by the little phrase because it treats his transient love and "the brief duration of the conditions of the soul" not as "something less serious than the events of everyday life but, on the contrary, something so superior that it alone was worth expressing":

> These charms of an intimate sadness—these were what it sought to imitate, to re-create, and their very essence, even though it is to be incommunicable and to seem frivolous to everyone but the one who is experiencing them, had been captured by the little phrase and made visible. So much so that it caused their value to be acknowledged, and their divine sweetness savored, by all those same people sitting in the audience—if they were at all musical—who would afterward fail to recognize these charms in real life, in every individual love that came into being before their eyes. (1:361–62/1:343)

This is one version of what I have analyzed as Proust's chronolibidinal aesthetics. The affective power of the little phrase resides in making palpable the drama of being invested in what one will lose. Precisely by intensifying the sense of temporal finitude, the little phrase intensifies the sense of the value of the beloved. This effect in turn generates what Marcel in the last volume describes as "the greatness of true art," which grasps hold of and makes us recognize "this reality which we run a real risk of dying without having known, and which is quite simply our life" (6:204/4:474).

The aesthetic and affective implications of the sonata thereby reverberate until the end of the *Recherche*. Throughout the novel, different artworks (mainly linked to the writer Bergotte, the painter Elstir, and the composer Vinteuil) provide occasions for Marcel to reflect on and present the aesthetics of the *Recherche* itself. The common denominator—the central value that is promoted in the sections on aesthetics—is the capacity of art to disclose "another universe" or "another world" that otherwise would be inaccessible. "The only real journey," Marcel emphasizes in a famous passage, "would be to travel not towards new landscapes, but with new eyes, to see the universe through the eyes of another, of a hundred others, to see the hundred universes that each of them can see, or can be; and we can do that with the help of an Elstir, a Vinteuil; with them and their like we can truly fly from star to star" (5:237/3:762). The task of art is thus to reveal "the qualitative difference between what each of us has felt," and this "inexpressible thing" can be expressed only "through art, the art of a Vinteuil or an Elstir, which makes manifest in the colors of the spectrum the intimate make-up of those worlds we call individuals, and which without art we should never know" (5:236/3:762). Following a beautiful chronolibidinal metaphor, the color spectrum through which the states of the soul are refracted is "like a rainbow, whose brilliance weakens, fades, then rises again, and before dying away altogether, flares up a moment more brilliant than ever," thereby generating in the performance of Vinteuil's sonata the sense of a "fragile, exquisite, and supernatural magic that was so close to vanishing" (1:365/1:346). This pathos of finitude cannot, however, be identified with a given affective response. It may inspire compassionate pity or violent jealousy, a sense of precious happiness or devastating loss, and even in the most blissful moments it makes itself felt as a pain in the smile of the phrase.

In making explicit and dramatizing the range of affective responses that follow from being bound to the temporal, the sonata episode illuminates how the expressiveness of art discloses the mortality of the soul. Yet there is a parallel and prominent strain in the *Recherche* that instead links aesthetic revelation to the disclosure of "another world" in a metaphysical sense, invoking a "lost homeland" from which we have been exiled on earth. This latter interpretation comes to the fore when Marcel—many years after Swann was seized by the sonata—hears a performance of Vinteuil's septet and connects this later, more expansive composition to the sonata. As in the sonata, the joyful motif in the septet is co-implicated with "a phrase of sorrowful character *[d'un caractère douloureux]*" which Marcel describes as being "so deep, so formless, so internal, so almost organic and visceral that each time it reappeared one was not sure if what was recurring was a theme or a nerve-pain" (5:239/3:764). Nevertheless, in his analysis of the septet, Marcel maintains that the co-implication of pain and enjoyment is overcome through a teleological movement: "Finally the joyous motif triumphed, it was no longer an almost anxious call from behind an empty sky, it was an inexpressible joy which seemed to come from Paradise" (5:239/3:764–65). He goes on to connect "the ever-true, ever-fertile formula for that unknown joy, that mystic hope of the scarlet angel of morning" to "the promise that something else existed, something perhaps reachable through art, besides the nothingness that I had found in all pleasures, and even in love" (5:241/3:767). This reading adheres to and prefigures the teleological reading of the *Recherche* itself, where the "joy" of involuntary memory is supposed to offer redemption from the destructive effects of time. As in the case of Vinteuil's septet (which Marcel recalls in the last volume), the revelation of involuntary memory is said to consist in a "contemplation of eternity" (6:183/4:454), make "death a matter of indifference" (6:176/ 4:446), and inspire a commitment to art that is essentially distinct from the commitment to temporal, finite life.

We are thus faced with an apparent paradox, which has recurred in different versions throughout my chronolibidinal readings. On the one hand, the pathos of the writing is generated by how life is entangled with death and thus depends on the temporality of survival for its affective and aesthetic effects. On the other hand, moments of supreme affective and aesthetic value are repeatedly linked (by the writer or narrator) to a timeless state of immortality. The question is *why* there is a conflict or contradiction between these two levels. By emphasizing that the desire for immortality dissimulates a desire for survival, it may seem as though I have denied or sought to rationalize the *dream* of immortality and the deep attraction it holds. Psychoanalytic reading—particularly in its most sophisticated Lacanian version—seeks to do justice precisely to the deep and irrational attraction of this dream, while recognizing that it is a *fantasy* to be traversed, an *illusion* to be overcome. Following such a reading,

Marcel's supposed revelations of a pure joy without pain—or a timeless state of being exempt from loss—would be the expression of a fundamental fantasy, which represses the entanglement between enjoyment and pain, desire and loss, that nevertheless keeps coming back to haunt the novel. I do not deny the merits of such a reading and the therapeutic effects it may have. The Lacanian reading stops short, however, of questioning the *structure* of the traditional narrative of desire. The fullness of pure joy or immortality is deemed to be an illusion, but the *desire* for such fullness is itself taken to be self-evident. Even while debunking the promise of fulfillment, the Lacanian account thus conforms to the conception of desire that has been handed down to us from a metaphysical and religious tradition: we are temporal, restless beings but desire to repose in the fullness/emptiness of timeless being.

In contrast, the notion of chronolibido provides the resources to read the internal contradictions of the supposed desire for fullness. Far from rationalizing desire, chronolibidinal reading elucidates a double bind of pleasure and pain that precedes and exceeds any attempt to rationalize desire as a search for transcendent unity. The fundamental trauma of libidinal being is not that we seek a pure joy that is frustrated by pain or a pure repose that is compromised by loss. Rather, the fundamental trauma of libidinal being is that *pain and loss are part of what we desire,* pain and loss being integral to what makes anything desirable in the first place. By the same token, the desire for fullness is not the irrational truth of desire; it is a rationalized repression of the double bind.

To make the difference between these two types of reading concrete, let us return to the conclusion of Proust's novel. On one level, Marcel presents involuntary memory as an experience of transcendent fullness, as a pure joy that obliterates the fear of death and reveals a timeless being. Beyond the mere invocations of eternity, however, there is nothing in Marcel's descriptions of involuntary memory that supports such a reading. Involuntary memory does not transcend but rather—as I argued in Chapter 1—*intensifies* the experience of temporal finitude. Thus, in the final involuntary memory of the *Recherche,* Marcel suffers from the same delayed recognition of himself as Swann does in the sonata episode. Upon opening a copy of *François le Champi,* Marcel is seized by a "painful impression" and feels upset at "the stranger who had just hurt me *[qui venait me faire mal]* " (6:192/4:462–63). He then realizes that the stranger is himself, or rather a self he once was: "This stranger was myself, it was the child I had been, whom the book had just brought back to life within me . . . wanting to be seen only by his eyes, to be loved only by his heart, to speak only to him" (6:192/4:463). As in the case of Swann's recognition that the stranger is himself—expressed through the same formula: *c'était lui-même/c'était moi-même*—Marcel's response is mournful tears. In a dramatic metaphor, he compares his emotional response to what he would feel at his father's funeral, dissolving into tears upon hearing "the band of a regiment which has come to share in his mourning and pay tribute to his father's corpse" (6:191–92/4:462), which is all the more striking since what is at stake is *the resurrection* (rather than the burial) of his former self. The pathos of such resurrection depends on a being who is not dying for timeless repose but *dying for time,* namely, who is animated by a desire to live on in time but also agonized by the loss it entails and who, insofar as he is dying for anything, insofar as he gives his life for anything, it is for someone else or something else to have the time to go on.

As always in Proust, involuntary memory thus turns out to be a painful synthesis of resurrection and death, survival and extinction. Even at the height of his final epiphanic experiences of involuntary memory—when his past days in Venice, Balbec, and Combray are resuscitated—Marcel recalls "the sudden pain *[la douleur subite]* that the little phrase of Vinteuil had caused in Swann by resurrecting those days themselves, such as he once had experienced them" (6:177/4:448).[1] We are thereby reminded—in the midst of ecstasy itself—of the irreconcilable division between past and present self that is at the heart of involuntary memory. Indeed, we are reminded that the temporality of involuntary memory is *traumatic.* On the one hand, involuntary memory happens *too soon.* One is seized by something one is not ready to comprehend, with the memory supervening "brusquely" and at such divergence from one's current state of being that the two selves (past and present) are mutual strangers, "incomprehensible to each other" (6:178/4:449). On the other hand, involuntary memory happens *too late.* When recognizing that the stranger is one's former self, one also recognizes that he or she is irretrievably lost. Precisely because of this traumatic structure, Marcel can experience his former self—returning through involuntary memory—as someone who has come to hurt him, inflicting or recalling a wound that was already there.

Now, a Lacanian reading may grant the traumatic, temporal structure of involuntary memory while still maintaining that the truth of Marcel's desire is expressed by his appeals to an experience of pure joy or timeless being. The latter would then testify to a fundamental fantasy of fullness, which animates desire while being in conflict with the strictures of Marcel's actual experience. The problem with such a reading, however, is that pain and loss are not merely *unavoidable* in the experience of involuntary memory; they are *inextricable* from what makes involuntary memory desirable. Consider here the structural analysis of involuntary memory in the final volume of the *Recherche,* which culminates in an invocation of paradise:

> If the returning memory, thanks to forgetting, can throw no bridge, form no connecting link between itself and the present minute, if it remains in the context of its own place and date, if it keeps its distance, its isolation in the hollow of a valley or upon the highest peak of a mountain summit, it suddenly makes us breathe a new air, an air which is new precisely because we have breathed it in the past, this purer air which the poets have tried in vain to make reign in paradise and which could not provide this profound feeling of renewal if it had not been breathed before, since the true paradises are the paradises that one has lost *[les vrais paradis sont les paradis qu'on a perdus].* (6:178–79/4:449)

The final phrase is one of the most famous Proust ever wrote, but the temporal logic of trauma that informs it has, to my knowledge, never been recognized. The claim is *neither* that paradise once existed and is now lost *nor* that paradise is always inaccessible and unattainable. Rather, paradise is here and now—in the experience of involuntary memory—but it depends on temporal difference. The event that returns through involuntary memory was not experienced as paradise in the past: it happened *too soon* to be apprehended as such. By the same token, it can be enjoyed and appreciated only in retrospect, when it is *too late*. Yet Marcel does not portray such deferral and delay as something that prevents access to a proper paradise of immediate presence. Deferral and delay are rather the condition of possibility for the sense of rejuvenation and joy that follows from involuntary memory. It is "thanks to forgetting *[grâce à l'oubli]*" that involuntary memory can give rise to a sense of renewal. Furthermore, it is the intensified sense of temporal disjunction that reinvigorates Marcel's commitment to life: "now that three times in succession there had been reborn within me a veritable moment of the past, my appetite for life was immense"(6:180/4:450).

The sense of paradisiacal happiness thus depends on the difference that time makes, but for the same reason it is necessarily traversed by the pain of loss. On Marcel's own account, involuntary memory is powerful because it makes one feel "the lost time *[le temps perdu]*" (6:180/4:450), and the joy it generates is therefore internally bound to suffering. Already in one of the first accounts of involuntary memory, Marcel emphasizes that its power resides in being able "to make us cry again" (2:222/2:4). He goes on to link the rejuvenating capacity of involuntary memory to a capacity for suffering, employing the same formulation by which he elsewhere links it to the capacity for joy: "It is thanks to that forgetting *[grâce à cet oubli:* the one intervening between the event and its involuntary recollection] that we can from time to time rediscover the being that we were, can place ourselves in relation to things as that being was placed, can suffer anew *[souffrir à nouveau]*" (2:222/2:4).

Beneath the traditional narrative of lost paradise—where one seeks a pure joy that is inaccessible due to temporal finitude—we can thus discern a more disconcerting story of desire and loss. Rather than being the victim of time as an external trauma, one must be traumatized by temporal finitude to experience anything as valuable and desirable. This is the story that the notion of chronolibido allows one to read. The deepest problem of desire is not that pure joy is unattainable (as the rationalized conception of the double bind would have it) but that enjoyment itself is bound to pain and loss to be what it is. The notion of chronolibido thereby seeks to capture both the terror and the beauty of being a *temporal* being, namely, a being who can suffer, can lose things, and can die, but for that very reason also has a sense of what it means for something to be precious, to be valuable, to be worth caring for.

Thus, in Chapter 2 we could see how Woolf's writing allows one to pursue further the traumatic conception of temporality we find in Proust. The deferral and delay that marks involuntary memory characterizes not only the resurgence of the past but also the present moment itself. The very epiphany of presence in Woolf is a traumatic event, since it can come into being only by becoming past *(too soon)* and becoming future *(too late)*. Yet it is precisely due to this temporality that anything can be given as a precious "moment of being." The dimension of loss that appears through the temporality of the moment is a condition for the value and significance of experience. A moment of being can therefore be a "negative" just as well as a "positive" trauma, and the latter carries the former within itself. The ecstasy of being alive is inhabited by "the terror, the overwhelming incapacity" and "an awful fear," so that even on a beautifully vital June morning Clarissa Dalloway can suddenly feel herself standing "alone against the appalling night."

Woolf thus explores what it means to be *bound* to temporal life. This is also the question that preoccupies Freud in his *Beyond the Pleasure Principle*, written only a few years before Woolf's *Mrs. Dalloway* and while Proust was finishing his *Recherche*. Freud's treatise has a central place in my argument, since it provides the theoretical resources to think the problem of binding. In postulating the pleasure principle, Freud had assumed a version of the traditional narrative of desire. What we seek *in principle* is pure pleasure (defined by Freud as the complete release of tension), which *in fact* is unattainable since there is no life without the tension of excitation that is generated by internal and external stimuli. The same narrative is supported by Freud's notion of the death drive, which holds that we are inherently driven to seek an absolute repose (death) that we fail to attain because it would require the elimination of excitation (life). According to this narrative, the binding of excitation is *secondary:* an intermediary function that is motivated by a principle or drive that precedes it and seeks to discharge excitation in favor of repose. Yet what Freud ends up showing through his exploration of trauma is that binding is *primary:* one cannot have any relation to excitation without binding and being bound to it. Freud's real discovery, then, is not a death drive *beyond* but rather a binding *before* the pleasure principle. One is bound before having any kind of purpose—including any kind of principle or drive—since being bound is the condition for having a purpose.

The structural necessity of binding entails that the experience of pleasure is bound internally to unpleasure. The reason why pleasure is entangled with pain is not because it falls short of an ideal repose, but because one is bound to an excitation that perforates pleasure in advance and opens the dimension of exhaustion or loss within the experience of fulfillment itself. The structural necessity of binding thus allows one to read a different narrative of desire. Rather than beginning with a drive or desire for fullness, one begins from a bond to temporal life. This bond—as I have argued in detail—entails a minimal investment, in the sense that one cannot be indifferent to what happens. Because one is bound to a temporal life (as a condition for experiencing anything at all), one is invested in what happens to it, even in denying or rejecting it. This investment in survival—namely, the impossibility of being indifferent to what happens—is a condition for every affective response. The investment itself, however, does not have any teleological direction: it can lead one to seek preservation or destruction, maintenance or termination. Furthermore, due to the death of life in the movement of survival, the apparent binaries are co-implicated even when one unilaterally affirms survival as a positive value. If I am invested in survival, I am invested not only in persistence but also in the destruction that is the condition of persistence. In maintaining my life I am also killing it off.

Nevertheless, as we have seen throughout this book, there is a powerful and deeply influential narrative that insists on a constitutive desire to transcend the temporality of survival in favor of the timeless state of immortality. Chronolibidinal reading does not dismiss this narrative but allows one to differentiate between its manifestations and engage its specific articulations. It is here helpful to distinguish between two different versions of the narrative, both of which we could read already in Plato's *Symposium*. The first version links the desire for immortality to the desire of a mortal being to *live on* in time. Diotima thus invokes the desire for reproduction (through children, books, memory) as paradigmatic of the desire for immortality. Yet reproduction does not make one immortal; it only gives one the chance to live on in time despite ceasing to be. Chronolibidinal reading elucidates how this temporal finitude animates the desire for reproduction itself and thereby generates an internal conflict in the supposed desire for immortality. The desire for reproduction presupposes a chronophilic investment in temporal life—otherwise one would not seek to ensure its persistence—but by the same token it is bound to a chronophobic fear of losing life. Indeed, it is because one is susceptible to the experience of loss—and seeks to preempt it—that one takes care to reproduce or retain anything at all. This does not mean that the fear of and resistance to loss is a *sufficient* motivational factor for care, but it is a *necessary* one. Temporal finitude is not only a negative condition of care but also a positive condition for its inspiration.

The second version of immortality therefore seeks to eliminate the very condition of care, following a logic that receives its most consistent articulation in ascetic philosophies. Albeit in the form of denial, this logic also acknowledges the double bind of survival. Precisely because every bond to pleasure exposes one to pain—and every attachment to life exposes one to death—ascetic sages preach *detachment.* Detachment is the condition for one to achieve final peace, since *attachment* always can lead to negative affective responses—jealousy, resentment, violence—due to the threat of loss. For the same reason, detachment is the condition for one to embrace proper immortality. The latter is a state where one "neither comes into being nor passes away" (as Diotima puts it) and cannot be attained as long as one is attached to a temporal life that passes away.

The desire for the fullness of immortality is thus inseparable from a desire for death. Far from being compatible with a desire to live on, proper immortality would eliminate the condition of survival. Ascetic philosophers are certainly right that the investment in survival is the source of all destructive responses to life, but it is also the condition for all constructive responses, and one cannot eliminate this double bind except at the price of extinction. Again, chronolibidinal reading does not deny that one can come to embrace such a desire for death, but it seeks to show that it is an *effect of* and a *response to* the investment in survival, thereby enabling one to read how the ideal of detachment dissimulates a preceding attachment.

The ultimate cause of chronophobia—with its fear of death, fantasies of survival, and denials of loss—is therefore not a metaphysical ideal of immortality. While such an ideal may aggravate the symptoms, chronophobia precedes and exceeds the ideal of immortality, since it is an effect of the chronophilic investment in temporal life. For example, the emphatic chronophilia of Nabokov's protagonists in *Ada*—who celebrate "our marvelous mortality"—does not reconcile them with the finitude of their lives. On the contrary, they are all the more assaulted by the threat of time because they are so invested in persisting as temporal beings. As we saw in Chapter 3, even the story of fulfilled happiness thus turns out to be a story of chronolibidinal trauma. The threat of time is not only unavoidable but also part of what animates the experience of fulfilled desire. By the same token, chronophobia cannot be cured by a therapeutic chronophilia, which would teach one to affirm finitude or embrace transience. Such a therapy may certainly be beneficial, but chronophobia will remain both before and after it has been accomplished, continuing to aggravate even the one who has renounced all ideals of an existence beyond time.

We can thus return to the question of the constitutive difference of desire with which I began this book. As Socrates argues in the *Symposium,* the existence of desire is incompatible with absolute fulfillment. The existence of desire rather depends on a constitutive difference, since one can only desire to have what one does *not* have and only desire to be what one is *not.* As I outlined in the Introduction, this constitutive difference of desire has traditionally supported the inference that desire testifies to an ontological lack. Because desire depends on the fact that it is not fulfilled, it is understood as the *lack* of fulfillment. This logic of lack persists, as we have seen, from Socrates to Freud and Lacan. While neither Freud nor Lacan thinks that desire can be fulfilled, they assume that the aim of desire is absolute fulfillment and that the lack of such fulfillment accounts for the relentless movement of desire, namely, the impossibility of desire coming to an end in the experience of fulfillment. As Freud puts it in *Beyond the Pleasure Principle*—in an argument that anticipates the Lacanian notion of "That's not it" as the law of desire—it is the difference "between the pleasure of satisfaction that is *demanded* and that which is actually *achieved* that provides the driving factor which will permit of no halting at any position attained" (18:42/13:44–45). The reason we keep going, the reason we never come to rest, is thus because we never arrive at the desired destination.

In contrast, the notion of chronolibido allows us to give a different account of the constitutive difference of desire. The reason desire persists even in the most ideal fulfillment is *not* because it fails to arrive at the desired destination but because the arrival at the destination—the experience of fulfillment—is temporal in itself. Even at the moment one *is* fulfilled the moment is passing away. This immediate passing away opens the difference that sustains desire and accounts for why the double bind of chronolibido is irreducible. On the one hand, the experience of fulfillment is *chronophobic,* since it bears the threat of loss within itself. On the other hand, the experience of fulfillment is *chronophilic,* since it is because the fulfillment can be lost—because it is in the process of being lost in the very moment of fulfillment—that one cares about and is affected by it in the first place.

The principle of desire is therefore a *postal principle:* one can only arrive at the destination of fulfillment by inscribing it as a trace of the past and sending it to the future. Indeed, all forms of enjoyment are "posted in their very instance" *(postées à l'instant même)*, as Derrida puts it.[2] In Chapter 4 I analyzed this postal principle in theoretical terms, but by considering the performativity of Derrida's literary writing in *The Post Card* we can press home its implications. In addition to the analysis of binding in Freud and the critical essay on Lacan, the book opens with almost three hundred pages that are written as postcards to the beloved. These postal sendings *(Envois)* enact the drama of survival and—through the notion of chronolibido—we can see how they perform an implicit deconstruction of the logic of lack that is more powerful than the explicit one formulated in the essay on Lacan.[3]

The drama of desire in the *Envois* is staged as a matter of destination, but the destination in question is not an absent fullness. Rather, the drama of desire is a matter of the temporal process of binding that has no given destination. Derrida plays considerably with gender and identity throughout the *Envois,* but it is instructive to first consider them as love letters written by Derrida to a feminine addressee. The letters are dated from June 3, 1977, to August 30, 1979, recording events in Derrida's life alongside philosophical arguments and notes for the book that will become *The Post Card.* There are indications that the lovers meet from time to time, but in the period traced by the *Envois* their relation mainly relies on letters, postcards, telegrams, and phone calls. The drama of the relation thus revolves around the act of addressing the other and waiting for a response, with all the anxious concern, excited anticipation, and neurotic speculation that follows from the postal principle. The gap in time—which entails that a given address cannot coincide with a given response, that the posted questions cannot coincide with the posted answers—opens the possibility for all sorts of misunderstandings, manipulations, and fatal accidents. Indeed, the postal principle of the *Envois* leads not only to attraction and intimate correspondence but also to jealousy, blackmail, and destruction.

The same condition is operative even when the lovers do not have to rely on an empirical postal system. Their neurotic speculations regarding what has happened or what may happen to the letters they send to one another—along with their fascination with teletechnological possibilities of transmission—answer to how desire always operates in space and time, at different frequencies and according to different degrees of distance. Even face to face with the other, neither thoughts nor feelings, neither words nor gestures, can be synchronized. Rather, they depend on a diachronic process that exceeds any final control. The one cannot know whether it will be possible to go on living with the other, and the connection may always be broken. In being bound to one another, then, there is always "the discord, the drama between us: not to know whether we are to continue living together (think of the innumerable times of our separation, of each auto-da-fé), whether we can live *with* or *without* the other, which has always passed outside our decision, but at what distance, according to what mode of distancing" (47/53-54). Promises and assurances between lovers are made precisely because of this undecidability that may break any promise or shatter any assurance. The bond to the other is the condition for *any* affective response, which means that there is no given way to negotiate the bond: one may be led to burn the binding letters or seek to preserve them, to maintain the relation with a given other or seek to do without it.

The same problem of binding is operative even if we limit ourselves to auto-affection. As Derrida emphasizes, "every being-together" (whether with oneself or with another) "begins by *binding-itself,* by a binding-itself in a differential relation to itself. It thereby sends and posts itself" (402/429). While apparently being a collection of love letters, Derrida's *Envois* can thus also be read as a diary in which he writes to himself. The address to an other is not only a turn to the beloved but also stages the temporality of auto-affection, where the self is both the sender and the addressee of its own experience. Indeed, the very givenness of one's own experience—the way in which one is affected by oneself—is dependent on the material support of a trace that retains the past for the future. Before being given to oneself, then, one is bound and posted. The inherent temporal difference of this postal principle is the source of the most positive *and* the most negative affective responses. As Derrida puts it: "the time difference *[le décalage horaire]* is in me, it is me. It blocks, inhibits, dissociates, arrests—but it also releases, makes me fly" (108/119). And again: "this discrepancy is killing me, and it is also making me live, it is enjoyment itself" (111/122).

Accordingly, Derrida emphasizes that the postal principle opens the chance of everything that is desired *and* the threat of everything that is feared. His postal sendings pursue "the demonstration that a letter can always—and therefore must—never arrive at its destination. And that this is not negative, it's good, and is the condition (the tragic condition, certainly, and we know something about that) that something does arrive— and that I love you" (121/133). Rather than being marked by a lack of being, the letter of desire is destined to have no final destination: "it begins with a destination without address, the direction cannot be situated in the end" (29/34). The direction cannot be situated in the end because all fulfillments of desire are "deferred as soon as obtained, posted in their very instance" (397/424). Thus, even when the letter arrives it "takes itself away *from the arrival at arrival.* . . . The letter demands this, right here, and you too, you demand it" (123–24/135). The key word here is the French verb *arriver,* which means to come, to happen, and to arrive. Derrida plays on these multiple meanings in order to underline that the fulfillment of desire—the arrival at the destination—cannot be given in the form of presence but is divided by the trace of time. Every event is both superseded *(no longer)* and to come *(not yet)* in its very event. Wherever we arrive, the destination is therefore transgressed by the future and becomes past. Due to this postal principle, not only the potential movement but also the actual fulfillment of desire is subjected to what Derrida calls *destinerrance:* the possibility of errancy that is inscribed in every destiny and every destination.

The postal principle is thus neither something to be celebrated nor something to be lamented as such. It is rather the general principle of survival that enables both attraction and rejection, preservation and destruction, the most faithful correspondences and the most violent betrayals. In one of his letters from June 10, 1977, Derrida articulates this condition of survival in a remarkably disconcerting address:

> Murder is everywhere, my unique and immense one. We are the worst criminals in history. And right here I kill you, save, save, you, save yourself *[sauve-toi],* the unique, the living one over there whom I love. Understand me, when I write, right here, on these innumerable post cards, I annihilate not only what I am saying but also the unique addressee that

I constitute, and therefore every possible addressee, and every destination. I kill you, I annul you at my fingertips, wrapped around my finger. To do so it suffices only that I be legible—and I become illegible to you, you are dead. If I say that I write for dead addressees, not dead in the future but already dead at the moment when I get to the end of a sentence, it is not in order to play. Genet said that his theater was addressed to the dead and I take it like that on the train in which I am going writing you without end. The addressees are dead, the destination is death: no, not in the sense of S. or p.'s predication, according to which we would be destined to die, no, not in the sense in which to arrive at our destination, for us mortals, is to end by dying. No, the very idea of destination includes analytically the idea of death, like a predicate (p) included in the subject (S) of destination, the addressee or the addressor. And you are, my love unique

the proof, the living proof precisely, that a letter can always not arrive at its destination, and that therefore it never arrives. And this is really how it is, it is not a misfortune, it is life, living life, beaten down, tragedy, by the still surviving life. For this, for life I must lose you, for life, and make myself illegible for you. (33–34/38–39)

As always in the *Envois,* the question of who is addressed as "you" makes a decisive difference for the reading. At the same time we need to bear in mind that the claim made here concerns the general condition of addressing anyone at all: whoever "you" are will be subject to the law of survival that Derrida articulates in such striking and violent—strikingly violent—terms. The apparently hyperbolic claim is that the mere act of addressing someone amounts to "killing" or "murdering" the unique addressee. I can never address "you" as an absolute singularity, since the word "you" can operate only by detaching itself from any given life, by inscribing itself as a dead letter that in principle can be taken up at any number of destinations. "Even in arriving," Derrida writes, "it arrives elsewhere, always several times. You can no longer take hold of it" (123/135). To describe this necessity of mediation as a "murder" may seem to presuppose a metaphysics of immediacy, where existence is an absolute singularity that is "killed" by the generality of language, a wholly unique and ineffable other who is betrayed by the repeatability of linguistic signs. The logic of Derrida's writing, however, undermines such a metaphysics of immediacy. There is no one and no thing that exists immediately in itself. Rather, because the singular is temporal in itself, it begins to pass away as soon as it comes to be and must rely on mediation to live on—to survive—in the first place.

The postal principle of mediation is thus "not a misfortune, it is life, living life, beaten down, tragedy, by the still surviving life." On the one hand, the postal principle enables one to counteract the violent passage of time that is already at work, to retain the past for the future, thereby enabling something to survive long enough to be sent from—or addressed to—"you." On the other hand, while the postal principle makes it possible for something to be transmitted, it also makes it impossible for anything to be shielded from interception and destruction. In the interval between sending and receiving—however minimal the interval may be—there is in principle the possibility of the letter going astray, being misunderstood, or co-opted for other purposes. Furthermore, even in the most faithful address, what is transmitted is "already dead at the moment when I get to the end of a sentence" since it can only come to be by ceasing to be. Even if we take the address to "you" as a matter of auto-affection, the violence of time is at work, since "the still surviving life" must reckon with the loss of time and the loss of life that is intrinsic to its own movement. In living on, the succeeding self must leave the preceding self behind, and the one is ultimately "illegible" for the other, since neither the past nor the future can be read in advance. "For this, for life, I must lose you, for life, and make myself illegible for you."

Nevertheless, it would be a mistake to read the block quote above merely in terms of the structural condition of survival. The latter is a necessary but not sufficient condition for assessing the dramas of desire that are enacted in the *Envois*. As David Wills has suggested, the *Envois* can be read as organized around the deflection and avoidance of a message that already has been received from the addressee, namely, her announced "determination" to end their relationship, to never come back to him again.[4] The reference to this determination is a haunting refrain throughout the letters: "you won't come back again, neither on your decision (sorry, on your 'determination,' as you always say!), you won't want to come to rejoin me again, and it's my fault" (32/37); "Every day you give yourself one more day, and I really have the impression that you no longer want to come back" (53/61); "You are coming back with your 'decision,' your 'determination,' and I prepare myself for it without knowing, like a condemned man in his cell" (101–02/112). The postal principle—the possibility that a letter may not arrive at its destination, that one may not receive the message sent by the other—is thus employed to buy him time, to question her decision, to postpone their parting. What he objects to and refuses to accept, he tells her, "is not the possibility of your 'determination' (I have been thinking it and preparing for it from the first day, I love you on the basis of this thought itself), it is the date. Yes, the 'moment' that you choose and which seems to have no relation to anything significant (the argument of the September letter has no value and I will never take it into account). Why not years ago or in years? Why this time? How are you counting it?" (125/137). Of course, for the one who is being abandoned and whose love is sentenced to death, the timing will always appear "untimely," so the plea for a stay of the execution is an understandable response. It becomes increasingly clear, however, that his refusal to get the message (e.g., of "the September letter") is based on an aggressive disavowal. Even in seemingly innocent statements one can begin to read the traces of a stalker: "it doesn't matter if you can't come for me, I'll call you from the airport" (32/37), "When are you coming back? I will call Sunday at the latest" (42/48), and occasionally we learn of her responses: "On the telephone, you screamed again, just now. But no, I did not 'drive you crazy,' not so crazy" (49/56).

If he did drive her crazy, we could certainly understand why. Rather than listening to her, he claims that her "determination" comes from another in her whom he refuses to acknowledge. "Without her," he writes, "not one of all your good 'reasons,' which, once more, I understand perfectly, would hold for a second. It would suffice that we look at each other, that you turn toward me, and pff . . . we would be alone together, no force in the world could unjoin us" (125/137). Thus, while allegedly "understanding, justifying, accepting all your 'reasons,'" he clings to "a feeling that another decides for you, destines you to this 'determination' without your really knowing yourself what is going on. There is an other in you, who from behind dictates this terrible thing to you, and she is not my ally. I have certainly never had anything to do with her, we (yes, we) do not know her" (125/137). The addresses to her can thus turn into downright accusations—"you also showed me absolute horror, hatred, injustice, the worst concentration of evil" (43/49) —which in turn leads to a disavowal of her: "You expedite me in a way that I previously would have accepted from no one—but I no longer cry when you depart, I walk, I walk" (43/49).

Returning to the block quote above, we can thus read the emphasis on "murder" and "killing" in a more disconcerting light. By writing her ("you"), he transforms "the living one over there whom I love" into a dead letter that he can manipulate at will: "I kill you, I annul you at my finger-tips, wrapped around my finger." He thus capitalizes on the discrepancy between address and destination to take command of her identity, to define who she is and who she is not, precisely to kill her resistance to him. This reading is further supported by the idea he introduces right before the passage I quoted, namely, "the idea that one is killing by burning a letter or a sign, a metro ticket that the other has held in her hand, a movie ticket, the wrapper of a sugar cube" (33/38). Yet the impotence of these acts of violence—of this aggressive game of *fort-da*—is more than evident. He may fantasize about rejecting her in the most violent ways—of burning, killing, murdering—but she has preceded him, she has already rejected him. The violence directed at "you" may thus be read not only as an externalized sadism directed against the other but also as an internalized masochism directed against the self. In mourning her, he must not only attack the bond that binds him to her but also the self who is defined by this bond and who cannot be allowed to survive as such if he shall be able to go on living. "For this, for life I must lose you, for life, and make myself illegible for you."

The logic of binding that emerges in Derrida's *Envois* thus allows us to think both the violence directed toward others and toward oneself as an effect of the investment in survival rather than a death drive.[5] The drama of libidinal being here proceeds from an investment that has always already taken place, but the investment has no given aim or destination and can motivate the destruction as well as the protection of a given legacy. Already on the first page we are told that the letters are "the remainders of a recently destroyed correspondence," which has been "destroyed by fire or by that which figuratively takes its place" (3/7). The destruction in question has not only eliminated some of the letters that are referred to; it has also eradicated a number of passages in the preserved letters, which display blank spaces and incomplete sentences. However this destruction may have taken place, the possibility of burning the letters recurs throughout as a matter of passion and anxiety, blackmail and seduction, possibility and threat. On the one hand, there is an almost obsessive desire to record everything, to guard against death. On the other hand, it becomes clear that the inverse movement is also at work and that there is no intrinsic value in keeping memories or preventing erasure. Even in view of a given survival, one may want to burn the archive rather than preserve it. "Our only chance for *survival,* now," he writes toward the end, "would be to burn everything, in order to come back to our initial desire. Whatever 'survival' it might be a question of, this is our only chance, I mean common chance. I want to start over" (171/185). Furthermore, even the value of survival itself is thoroughly equivocal and may be the object of fear as well as desire. "Afraid of dying, yes, but that is nothing next to the other terror, I know no worse: to survive, to survive my love, to survive you *[survivre, à mon amour, à toi]*" (199/214).

Derrida, then, stages the double bind of survival in his own text and thereby pursues a version of the literary writing of chronolibido.[6] For all their internal differences, the texts examined in this book converge in the exploration of how the drama of libidinal being—its mourning, trauma, and bliss—derives from and depends on the double bind. Indeed, *the same bond* that binds one to pleasure binds one to pain and the same bond that binds one to life binds one to death. To be invested in living on is therefore not only to desire but also to fear survival, since survival entails that one may be left to mourn or to suffer an unbearable fate. This condition of chronolibido cannot be cured; it is rather the source of both hope and despair, compassion and aggression, protection and exposure. It follows that there is chronophobia at the heart of every chronophilia and chronophilia at the heart of every chronophobia. The notion of chronolibido provides the framework for thinking this double bind and thereby opens a new way of reading the dramas of desire as they are staged in philosophy and literature.

Notes

1. To speak of "literature" with regard to the Platonic dialogues is of course anachronistic, since there is no equivalent term or category for literature in ancient Greece. I use the term as shorthand for what Plato criticizes in terms of poetry, tragedy, and *mimesis* more generally, to underline the relevance of the debate for modern understandings of the relation between philosophy and literature. For incisive analyses of the stakes of the Platonic critique of poetry and tragedy, see Martha Nussbaum's *The Fragility of Goodness: Luck and Ethics in Greek Tragedy and Philosophy* (Cambridge: Cambridge University Press, 1986) and Henry Staten's *Eros in Mourning: Homer to Lacan* (Baltimore: Johns Hopkins University Press, 1995).

2. Plato, *Republic,* 605d, trans. P. Shorey, in *The Collected Dialogues of Plato,* ed. E. Hamilton and H. Cairns (Princeton: Princeton University Press, 1961). Subsequent page references are given in the text.

3. Plato, *Symposium,* 211a, trans. M. Joyce, modified, in *The Collected Dialogues of Plato.* Subsequent page references are given in the text.

4. Lacan, *The Seminar of Jacques Lacan, Book II: The Ego in Freud's Theory and in the Technique of Psychoanalysis,* ed. J-A. Miller, trans. S. Tomaselli (New York: W. W. Norton, 1988), 223, trans. mod.; *Le Séminaire de Jacques Lacan, Livre II: Le moi dans la théorie de Freud et dans la technique de la psychanalyse, 1954-1955,* ed. J-A. Miller (Paris: Seuil, 1978), 261.

5. This locution is repeated twice in 200d.

6. Although my argument does not depend on it, one may here note that the "device" *(mêchanê)* through which the mortal perpetuates itself is a term that Plato employs for the Greek gods as well. As Stanley Rosen has observed, the term *mêchanê* (which he translates as "contrivance") "appears in various key passages throughout the dialogue; it is used to describe the cunning of Orpheus, Zeus, Eros, and now of the mortal generally. One may wonder whether Plato thereby links the Olympian gods to the daimonic

poetry of mortals. They may be alike because they are bound by genesis, in contrast to the truly divine." Rosen, *Plato's Symposium,* 2nd ed. (New Haven: Yale University Press, 1987), 255.

7. See Plato, *Phaedo,* 68b–c, trans. H. Tredennick, in *The Collected Dialogues of Plato.*

8. Epicurus, *Letter to Menoeceus,* 124, in *The Epicurus Reader,* ed. and trans. B. Inwood, L. P. Gerson and D. S. Hutchinson (New York: Hackett, 1994).

9. Epicurus, *Letter to Menoeceus,* 126.

10. For an immanent critique of Epicurus and Lucretius, which establishes the intrinsic link between care and the fear of death with exemplary rigor, see Martha Nussbaum, *The Therapy of Desire: Theory and Practice in Hellenistic Ethics* (Princeton: Princeton University Press, 1996), chap. 6.

11. Plato, *Apology,* 40d, trans. H. Tredennick, in *The Collected Dialogues of Plato.* Subsequent page references are given in the text.

12. The most consistent version of this logic can be found in the tradition of negative theology. In negative theology, the absolute fullness of God is inseparable from absolute emptiness. God is Nothing since everything that is finite—which is to say, everything—must be eliminated in God. Thus, for the negative theologian Meister Eckhart, the way to unity with God (the *via negativa*) is achieved through an inner "destruction" of all bonds to finite beings. The logic of Eckhart's argument is epitomized in his definition of God as the negation of negation. Finite being is necessarily inhabited by negation, since its being entails that it may *not* be. God is the negation of negation, since finite being is negated in the infinite fullness/emptiness of God. The same logic applies to the question of desire. Man must negate the desire for finite beings in order to become one with God, which amounts to a consummating annihilation. See the analysis of Eckhart's logic of desire in Hägglund, *Radical Atheism: Derrida and the Time of Life* (Stanford, CA: Stanford University Press, 2008), 117–19.

13. This is a significant shift in terminology with regard to earlier versions of my argument. In both *Radical Atheism* and the essay "Chronolibidinal Reading" (in *CR: The New Centennial Review,* 9.1 (2009): 1–44), I invoked a constitutive "drive" for survival. While I made clear that this drive does not compel one to live on at all costs, but rather can always turn against itself, I now hold this qualification to be insufficient. Moreover, it begs the question of the legitimacy of postulating a given drive of any kind at the basis of libidinal being. What is at stake is not a constitutive *drive* but rather a constitutive *investment,* which does not need to be postulated but can be derived from the necessity of binding. In developing my thinking on this point, I have benefited from the incisive responses to my work by William Egginton, Adrian Johnston, Ernesto Laclau, and Michael Naas. See Laclau, "Is Radical Atheism a Good Name for Deconstruction," *Diacritics,* 38.1–2 (2008): 180–89, and Naas, "An Atheism that *(Dieu merci!)* Still Leaves Something to be Desired," *CR: The New Centennial Review,* 9.1 (2009): 45–68, as well as the two essays by Egginton and Johnston that I address in Chapter 4.

14. Lacan, *The Seminar of Jacques Lacan, Book XI: The Four Fundamental Concepts of Psychoanalysis, 1964,* ed. J-A. Miller, trans. A. Sheridan (New York: W. W. Norton, 1977), 198, see also 204–05; *Le Séminaire de Jacques Lacan, Livre XI: Les quatre concepts fondamentaux de la psychanalyse, 1964,* ed. J-A. Miller (Paris: Seuil, 1973), 180, see also 186–87. I discuss these passages in Chapter 4.

15. As Derrida points out, "this locution [*at the same time* or *hama* in Aristotle's articulation of the problem of time] is first neither spatial nor temporal" bur rather articulates "the complicity, the common origin of time and space." Derrida, *Margins of Philosophy,* trans. A. Bass (Chicago: University of Chicago Press, 1982), 56/*Marges— de la philosophie* (Paris: Minuit, 1972), 64–65. For my elaboration of this argument, see Hägglund, "Radical Atheist Materialism: A Critique of Meillassoux," in *The Speculative Turn,* ed. L. Bryant, G. Harman, N. Srnicek (Melbourne: Re-press, 2011), 114–129.

16. For a detailed analysis of the trace structure of time, see also Hägglund, *Radical Atheism,* chaps. 1 and 2.

17. See, for example, Elisabeth Ladenson, *Proust's Lesbianism* (Ithaca, NY: Cornell University Press, 1999) and Sara Danius, *The Senses of Modernism: Technology, Perception, and Aesthetics* (Ithaca, NY: Cornell University Press, 2002). Two recent studies that do revive basic metaphysical and philosophical questions in reading Proust are Joshua Landy's *Philosophy as Fiction: Self, Deception, and Knowledge in Proust* (Oxford: Oxford University Press, 2004) and Miguel de Beistegui's *Jouissance de Proust: Pour une esthétique de la métaphore* (Fougères: Encre Marine, 2007). As we will see in Chapter 1, however, both Landy and de Beistegui hold on to different versions of the idea that the decisive aesthetic revelation of the *Recherche* is the revelation of a timeless essence.

1. MEMORY: PROUST

1. References to Proust refer to the volume number followed by the page number, with the reference to the English translation given first, followed by reference to the French Pléiade edition of *À la recherche du temps perdu,* ed. J-Y. Tadié (Paris: Gallimard, 1987–88). References to the English translation are to *In Search of Lost Time,* 6 volumes, ed. C. Prendergast: vol. 1 *Swann's Way,* trans. L. Davis (New York: Viking, 2003); vol. 2 *In the Shadow of Young Girls in Flower,* trans. J. Grieve (New York: Viking, 2004); vol. 3 *The Guermantes Way,* trans. M. Treharne (New York: Viking 2004); vol. 4 *Sodom and Gomorrah,* trans. J. Sturrock (New York: Viking, 2004); vol. 5 *The Captive and The Fugitive,* trans. C. Clark and P. Collier (London: Penguin, 2003); vol. 6 *Finding Time Again,* trans. I. Patterson (London: Penguin, 2003). In some cases, translations have been modified.

2. Following convention, I refer to Proust's narrator and protagonist as "Marcel," even though the name is employed only twice in the entire *Recherche* (see 5:64/3:583 and 5:140/3:663). Famously, the first passage does *not* identify the name of the narrator/ protagonist, but rather presents it in a conditional mode, recounting how Albertine addressed him as " 'My' or 'My darling,' followed by my Christian name, which, if we give the narrator the same name as the author of this book, would be: 'My Marcel,' 'My darling Marcel' " (5:64/3:583). Furthermore, given that the second, unqualified use of the name "Marcel" belongs to a section of the novel that Proust did not have time to revise before his death, having eliminated the name in other places, it is understandable that one may decide not to use the name Marcel and instead simply refer to "the Narrator" and "the Protagonist." This is, for example, the decision made by Richard Bales,

editor of *The Cambridge Companion to Proust* (Cambridge: Cambridge University Press, 2001). I have, however, chosen to follow the more standard critical practice.

3. This is the central question even if one accepts Joshua Landy's argument that Marcel is speaking of *two* different books at the end of the *Recherche,* one being the memoir he has almost completed and the other a novel he has barely begun (see Landy, *Philosophy as Fiction,* 38–43). Indeed, Landy himself treats involuntary memory as the key to what enables Marcel "to begin writing his masterpiece" and "the future book" (111).

4. Beckett, *Proust* (London: John Calder, 1999 [1931]), 75.

5. Poulet, *Studies in Human Time,* trans. E. Coleman (Baltimore: Johns Hopkins University Press, 1956), 314–15. Subsequent page references are given in the text.

6. Ricoeur, *Time and Narrative,* vol. 2, trans. K. McLaughlin and D. Pellauer (Chicago: University of Chicago Press, 1986), 147.

7. Genette, *Narrative Discourse: An Essay in Method,* trans. J. E. Lewin (Ithaca, NY: Cornell University Press, 1980), 253.

8. Girard, "Introduction," in *Proust: A Collection of Critical Essays* (Westport: Greenwood Press, 1977), 11. Subsequent page references are given in the text.

9. Deleuze, *Proust and Signs,* trans. R. Howard (Minneapolis: University of Minnesota Press, 2000), 19. Subsequent page references are given in the text.

10. See here also the reflections on the possibility of "resurrection" through literature, which occur in the narration of the death of the writer Bergotte. In a famous passage, Marcel writes: "They buried him, but all through the night of the funeral, in the lighted shop-windows, his books, arranged three by three, kept watch like angels with outspread wings and seemed, for him who has no more, the symbol of his resurrection" (5:170/3:693). Yet in an extraordinary passage that is (symptomatically) never quoted in the secondary literature, Marcel makes clear that the "resurrection" in question has nothing to do with immortality. Rather, the possibility of resurrection is the possibility of *survivance* through the generation of traces that remain exposed to destruction, vividly described by Marcel in terms of the destruction of life on Earth (the condition of possibility for generations) and the short-circuiting of the transmission of language (the condition of possibility for literature). A propos the death of Bergotte, one can thus read: "he grew colder and colder, a little planet offering a foretaste of what the last days of the big one will be, when first warmth and then life recede from the Earth. Then resurrection will have come to an end *[la résurrection aura pris fin],* for however far into the world of future generations the works of men may have cast their light, still they will need human beings to see them. Even if certain animal species stand up better than men to the encroaching cold, and even supposing Bergotte's glory to have survived for so long, at this moment it will suddenly be extinguished for ever *[brusquement elle s'éteindra à tout jamais].* The last surviving animals will not read him, for it is hardly likely that, like the apostles at Pentecost, they will be able to understand the language of the various human peoples without having learned it" (5:166–67/3:689).

11. Bowie, *Proust Among the Stars* (New York: Columbia University Press, 1998), 31. Subsequent page references are given in the text.

12. My argument here resonates with a memorable claim made by Michael Wood in his book on Nabokov: "paradise and its loss are integral to each other. Not only that the true paradises are lost paradises, as Proust suggests, but that there is no paradise without

loss, it isn't paradise if you can't lose it" (Wood, *The Magician's Doubts,* London: Chatto & Windus, 1994, 219). The context of this claim is Wood's insightful reading of Nabokov's *Ada,* which I address in Chapter 3. Curiously, when Wood in another context discusses the notion of paradise in Proust, he does not unearth the same insight in the *Recherche.* Wood provides a rich and perspicacious reading of the motif of paradise in Proust, but he does not draw on the passage from the fourth volume of the *Recherche* that I have just quoted. See Wood, "The Death of Paradise," *Philosophy and Literature* vol. 21, no. 2 (1997): 245–261.

13. For a further reading of this scene, see also the Conclusion.

14. In a remarkable essay, Richard Moran has provided important resources for such a reading of the experience of the beautiful in the *Recherche* (see "Kant, Proust, and the Appeal of Beauty," *Critical Inquiry* vol. 39, no. 1, 2012). Moran proceeds from Kant's argument that what distinguishes the beautiful from the merely pleasant or agreeable is "a sense of *requirement* or obligation in connection with the experience of the beautiful" (2). To say that something is beautiful is to make the judgment that one *ought* to respond to it with pleasure and admiration, which for Kant entails an at least implicit appeal to universal agreement, namely, that everyone ought to agree that the object of judgment is beautiful. Moran argues, however, that "Kant's emphasis on the demand for universal agreement to distinguish the judgment of the beautiful from the judgment of the agreeable is not in fact primary, but is derived from a prior sense of necessity or demand that characterizes the experience of the beautiful itself. In short, universal agreement does not always matter (because aesthetics and ethics are *not* one), but the sense of the beautiful making a claim upon us does" (5). Proust allows one to explore the latter claim, since he eliminates the appeal to universal agreement but nevertheless insists on a sense of being obligated or bound by the experience of the beautiful. Thus, when the young Marcel experiences the beauty of the hawthorns, he places himself "under an obligation, something like the vow: 'May I never cease to be responsive to this beauty! May it continue to define me!'" (29). What I want to underline here is that the sense of bindingness—of being bound by the experience of the beautiful—is inextricable from the sense of temporal finitude. As Moran observes, Marcel attempts to bind himself to the value of the hawthorns "because he feels that the appeal of the hawthorns, however intense, is nonetheless something fragile and that were he to lose the responsiveness to this appeal it would count as a loss of the self he presently is and cares about. By contrast, the experience of the agreeable does not carry with it a similar threat. With respect to something agreeable, to lose the desire for it is simply to find something else more agreeable or equally so. There is no experience of the loss of some part of oneself, and hence nothing to mourn or regret in this change of tastes. Marcel does not measure himself against his responsiveness to the agreeable, and he does not make vows to their objects because the possibility of ceasing to find them a source of pleasure is not something he needs to *preserve* himself against, because that possibility is not experienced as any kind of failure on his part. . . . Binding oneself against loss or lapse is not called for, and therefore there is no sense to a vow of any kind" (29–30). Inversely, the sense of a vow, promise, or commitment to the beautiful only makes sense given the possibility of betrayal, just as the value of the beloved is measured by what it would mean to lose it. "It is regarding the beautiful, or an object of love, that there is

room for the idea of betrayal in the possibility of the abandonment or replacement of one's desire, the prospect of which is experienced as a threat to the self" (30). I hope to return to this argument in a different context.

15. See, for example, 6:188/4:458–59, 6:354/4:621, and 6:345/4:612.

16. For an elaboration of this argument with regard to the phenomenology of temporal experience, see Hägglund, "Arche-Writing: Derrida and Husserl," in *Radical Atheism,* 50–75.

17. Bergson, *L'évolution créatrice* (Paris: Presses Universitaires de France, 2008), 2.

18. Bergson, "La perception du changement," in *La pensée et le mouvant* (Paris: Presses Universitaires de France, 1941), 170, 177.

19. See Bergson, "De la nature du temps," in *Durée et simultanéité* (Paris: Presses Universitaires de France, 2007), 41–42. Subsequent page references are given in the text.

20. De Beistegui, *Jouissance de Proust,* 110n.1. Subsequent page references are given in the text.

21. Bergson, *L'évolution créatrice,* 2.

22. Bergson, "La perception du changement," 169–170.

23. Poulet, *Proustian Space,* trans. E. Coleman (Baltimore: Johns Hopkins University Press, 1977), 4. Subsequent page references are given in the text.

24. Landy, *Philosophy as Fiction,* 101. Subsequent page references are given in the text.

25. Landy is thus committed to the view (which he ascribes to Proust) that there must be a coherent and unique "essence" of the self that is exempt from the radical alterability of the successive, temporal selves. Such a reading can helpfully be contrasted to Robert Pippin's analysis of the problem of selfhood in Proust (see "On 'Becoming Who One Is' (and Failing): Proust's Problematic Selves," in *The Persistence of Subjectivity: On the Kantian Aftermath,* Cambridge: Cambridge University Press, 2005). Pippin explicitly argues against the idea of an essence of the self that would be "revealed in a moment of epiphanic insight" (311, 334) and emphasizes that "the novel does nothing to establish that there is or even can be any point of view 'outside' the narrative flux and instability described, that Marcel's quasi-religious discovery of 'real time past' in the last novel is anything other than *yet another* moment in a temporal story" (317). While recognizing the need for a perspective that provides coherence and unity to the self ("we need to achieve some such coherent connections among deeds—to be able to understand why someone who did *that* would do *this*—or we will not be able to recover the deeds as *ours,* to recognize ourselves in them" (310)), Pippin cogently argues that the condition of possibility for such unity should not be located in an atemporal essence, in "something one just substantially 'is' over time" (308–09). Self-knowledge should not be understood in terms of "introspecting an inner essence, on the model of *being S* or *not being S,* but is more like the expression of a commitment, usually a provisional commitment, which one can sustain or fail to sustain, and so is something one can always *only* 'be becoming' (or failing to become)" (309). Moreover, the measure of such success or failure is "not fidelity to an inner essence but is ultimately a matter of action, what we actually do, a matter of engagement in the world, as well as, in a way, a kind of negotiation with others about what, exactly, it *was* that one did" (309). The coherence or unity of the self is thus not a given but a *claim,* and as such it is subject to contestation or repudiation both by others and by the self one will have become through the actions

undertaken. The trace structure of time that I elucidate is compatible with Pippin's insightful argument, while operating at a different level, making explicit the temporal logic that is implicit in his account of the social constitution of subjectivity. As Pippin himself points out, the constitution of the self through a claim rather than an essence has the structure of a *promise* and this promise can always *not* be kept, since it must be kept across time and in relation to others. The necessary tracing of time accounts for why this structure of the promise is a general structure of experience. On the one hand, to promise is to commit oneself to the future, since one can only promise something that is to come. On the other hand, to promise is to commit oneself to the past, since it entails a promise to remember the promise. Whatever I promise, I implicitly promise to remember the promise. There is thus an interval of time that divides the promise within itself, which answers to the interval that divides every temporal present from the beginning. Even the most immediate experience must be inscribed as a memory for the future and thus promise to remember itself. Because of this necessary interval, there is always time for the promise to be broken. Indeed, even the most ideal fulfillment of the promise must be haunted by the possibility of nonfulfillment, since the temporal must remain open to its own alteration. For the same reason, it is misleading to say that the promise cannot be fulfilled. Rather, the promise *does not promise fulfillment* insofar as fulfillment is understood as the consummation of time. The promise does not promise a future that will be present in itself, but rather an experience that in its turn will have the structure of the promise. See also the analysis of the temporality of the promise in Hägglund, *Radical Atheism*, 136–38.

26. Beckett, *Proust*, 75.

27. See Proust, 6:239, 240/4:508–9, 510.

28. My argument here can be compared to the one suggested by Walter Benjamin in his essay "On the Image of Proust" (see Benjamin, *Selected Writings 1927–1930*, vol. 2, part 1, ed. M.W. Jennings, H. Eiland, G. Smith, trans. R. Livingstone, Cambridge, MA: Harvard University Press, 1996). While Benjamin does not explicitly address the relation between the revelation in the Guermantes's library and the revelation at the Guermantes's party, he highlights the structural similarity between the experience of involuntary memory and the experience of aging: "The eternity which Proust opens to view is intertwined time, not boundless time. His true interest is in the passage of time in its most real—that is, intertwined—form, and this passage nowhere holds sway more openly than in remembrance within and aging without. To follow the counterpoint of aging and remembering means to penetrate to the heart of Proust's world, to the universe of intertwining" (244). Benjamin also notes that while there are gestures toward an eternity à la Plato or Spinoza in Proust, "it is not these elements that determine the greatness of his work" (244). Rather, Benjamin links the "rejuvenation" of involuntary memory to "the monstrous feat of letting the whole world age a lifetime in an instant" (244). Benjamin does not develop these observations further through a reading of the textual articulations of involuntary memory in the *Recherche,* but his remarks are nevertheless suggestive of the argument that I am pursuing.

29. For the most powerful example of the latter type of reading, see Vincent Descombes's *Proust: Philosophy of the Novel,* trans. C. C. Macksey (Stanford, CA: Stanford University Press, 1992). Descombes rightly argues that the explicit theories or "philosophical"

propositions of the *Recherche* are much weaker than, and in many cases refuted by, the insights of the novel in which they are situated. As Descombes puts it: "The Proustian novel is bolder than Proust the *theorist*. By this I mean that the novel is philosophically bolder; that it pursues further the task Proust identifies as the writer's work: the elucidation of life, the elucidation of what was experienced in obscurity and confusion" (6, see also Descombes's succinct formulation that "the thoughts reported in the narrative do not coincide with thoughts that may be communicated by the narrative" (30)). Yet when Descombes addresses the status of involuntary memory and its relation to the declarations of the last volume (see 284–85, 290–92), he does not pursue a reading of the narrative articulations of involuntary memory. Rather, Descombes limits himself to brief accounts of one episode of involuntary memory and links it to Marcel's invocations of eternity and immortality, which Descombes dismisses as having "no other sense than that of underlining the epiphanic *aura* of the whole episode" (285). Descombes thereby disregards how the claims to eternity or immortality are undermined by the very passages on involuntary memory in which they occur.

30. For an overview of the tendency to dismiss the philosophical claims made in the *Recherche,* see Landy's *Philosophy as Fiction,* 3–49. In contrast, Landy pursues the most ambitious attempt to defend the cogency of Proust's aesthetic-philosophical program.

31. Bersani, *The Culture of Redemption* (Cambridge, MA: Harvard University Press, 1990), 1. Subsequent page references are given in the text.

32. See volume IV of the Pléiade edition, 1268–69.

2. TRAUMA: WOOLF

1. Ann Banfield, "Time Passes: Virginia Woolf, Post-Impressionism, and Cambridge Time," *Poetics Today* vol. 24, no. 3 (2003): 471–516, 486. See also Banfield's book *The Phantom Table: Woolf, Fry, Russell and the Epistemology of Modernism* (Cambridge: Cambridge University Press, 2000) and her essay "Tragic Time: The Problem of the Future in Cambridge Philosophy and *To the Lighthouse,*" *Modernism/modernity,* vol. 7, no. 1 (2000): 43–75.

2. See Banfield, "Time Passes," 492, 495.

3. Banfield, "Time Passes," 486.

4. For all their differences, the problem of living on is central to Mr. Ramsay as well as to Mrs. Ramsay. Mr. Ramsay dreams of achieving lasting fame through his work as a philosopher, but he is plagued by the thought that even those who are remembered for thousands of years are not immune from oblivion. "What are two thousand years? (asked Mr. Ramsay ironically, staring at the hedge). What, indeed, if you look from a mountain top down the long wastes of the ages? The very stone one kicks with one's boots will outlast Shakespeare" (35). While Mr. Ramsay's concern for philosophical fame is much more solipsistic and self-centered than Mrs. Ramsay's concern for the maintenance of intimate bonds, the structural care for survival is highlighted in both cases and vividly exemplified by their investment in their children. This investment can be read as an expression of the desire to live on, but by the same token it exemplifies the precarious nature of survival, since every offspring that serves as a resistance to death is

itself mortal. Mr. Ramsay reflects on how he has managed to "stem the flood a bit" (69) through his eight children, but nothing can finally stave off the flood of time that sweeps everything away.

5. See Derrida, "Typewriter Ribbon," trans. P. Kamuf, in *Without Alibi* (Stanford, CA: Stanford University Press, 2002), 159–60; *Papier Machine* (Paris: Galilée, 2001), 146.

6. The temporal structure of such trauma can be read in the very affirmation that opens and closes *To the Lighthouse*. As Hermione Lee has observed in an insightful reading, "this dark book of loss and grief begins and ends with sentences starting 'Yes': yes, and a tentative conditional future ('if it's fine tomorrow'); yes, and an immediately vanished past ('I have had my vision'). The 'yes' of narrative—something shaped, but liable always to shapelessness—keeps having to be reaffirmed." Lee, "To the Lighthouse," in *Virginia Woolf: Introductions to the Major Works*, ed. J. Briggs (London: Virago Press, 1994), 183–84.

7. Ricoeur, *Time and Narrative*, vol. 2, 9.

8. See Christine Froula, *Virginia Woolf and the Bloomsbury Avant-Garde: War, Civilization, Modernity* (New York: Columbia University Press, 2007), 96–101.

9. Froula, *Virginia Woolf and the Bloomsbury Avant-Garde*, 99, 100.

10. Miller, *Fiction and Repetition* (Cambridge, MA: Harvard University Press, 1985), 202. Subsequent page references are given in the text.

11. See Woolf, "An Introduction to *Mrs. Dalloway*," in *The Mrs. Dalloway Reader*, ed. F. Prose (Orlando: Harcourt, 2003), 11.

12. See DeMeester, "Trauma and Recovery in Virginia Woolf's *Mrs. Dalloway*," *Modern Fiction Studies*, vol. 44, no. 3 (1998): 649–673.

13. Clewell, "Consolation Refused: Virginia Woolf, The Great War, and Modernist Mourning," *Modern Fiction Studies*, vol. 50, no. 1 (2004), 198–99. Subsequent page references are given in the text. For contributions to the debate, see also Mark Spilka, *Virginia Woolf's Quarrel With Grieving* (Lincoln: University of Nebraska Press, 1980), Thomas Caramagno, *The Flight of the Mind: Virginia Woolf's Art and Manic-Depressive Illness* (Berkeley: University of California Press, 1992), John Mepham, "Mourning and Modernism," in *Virginia Woolf: New Critical Essays*, ed. P. Clements and I. Grundy (London: Vision Press Limited, 1983), Susan Bennett Smith, "Reinventing Grief Work: Virginia Woolf's Feminist Representations of Mourning in *Mrs. Dalloway* and *To the Lighthouse*," *Twentieth-Century Literature*, vol. 41, no. 4 (1995): 310–327, Karen L. Levenback, *Virginia Woolf and the Great War* (Syracuse: Syracuse University Press, 1999), DeMeester, "Trauma and Recovery in Virginia Woolf's *Mrs. Dalloway*," and Froula, *Virginia Woolf and the Bloomsbury Avant-Garde*.

14. Froula, *Virginia Woolf and the Bloomsbury Avant-Garde*, 87. Subsequent page references are given in the text.

15. See Froula, *Virginia Woolf and the Bloomsbury Avant-Garde*, 118.

16. See Froula, *Virginia Woolf and the Bloomsbury Avant-Garde*, 123.

17. My argument here can be related to the wider political implications of Woolf's style of writing, which have been analyzed insightfully by Rebecca L. Walkowitz. As Walkowitz observes, Woolf demonstrates that "to critique euphemism, which translates intense experiences into language that is habitual and therefore invisible, one must also critique literalism, which proposes that there is only one objective experience to present.

She demonstrates also, however, that the critique of euphemism and literalism will have to involve gestures that are in some ways both euphemistic and literal because writing a novel or making an argument or maintaining a friendship requires moments of purposeful blindness as well as moments of direct attention." Walkowitz, *Cosmopolitan Style: Modernism Beyond the Nation,* New York: Columbia University Press, 1996, 88.

18. John Graham, "Time in the Novels of Virginia Woolf," in *Critics on Virginia Woolf,* ed. J. E. M. Latham (Coral Gables: University of Miami Press, 1970), 33, 30, 31.

19. Virginia Woolf, "A Sketch of the Past," in *Moments of Being,* ed. J. Schulkind (London: Hogarth Press, 1985), 79, 72.

20. Schulkind, "Introduction," in *Moments of Being,* 17. Subsequent page references are given in the text.

21. Bohrer, *Suddenness: On the Moment of Aesthetic Appearance,* trans. R. Cowley (New York: Columbia University Press, 1994), 59.

22. Woolf, "A Sketch of the Past," 72. Subsequent page references are given in the text.

23. Woolf, "Modern Fiction," in *The Common Reader: First Series* (Orlando: Harcourt, 1984), 150. See also the argument in Woolf's essay "Mr. Bennett and Mrs. Brown": "In the course of your daily life this past week you have had far stranger and more interesting experiences than the one I have tried to describe. You have overheard scraps of talk that filled you with amazement. You have gone to bed at night bewildered by the complexity of your feelings. In one day thousands of ideas have coursed through your brain; thousands of emotions have met, collided, and disappeared in astonishing disorder. Nevertheless, you allow the writers to palm off upon you a version of all this, an image of Mrs. Brown, which has no likeness to that surprising apparition whatsoever. . . . You should insist that she is an old lady of unlimited capacity and infinite variety; capable of appearing in any place; wearing any dress; saying anything and doing heaven knows what. But the things she says and the things she does and her eyes and her nose and her speech and her silence have an overwhelming fascination, for she is, of course, the spirit we live by, life itself." ("Mr. Bennett and Mrs. Brown," in *The Virginia Woolf Reader,* ed. M. A. Leaska, San Diego: Harcourt, 1984, 335–36). For an analysis of this ambition to render "life" in relation to the aesthetics of the art of cinema, see Laura Marcus's excellent *The Tenth Muse* (Oxford: Oxford University Press, 2008), chapter 2.

3. WRITING: NABOKOV

1. Nabokov, *Ada or Ardor: A Family Chronicle* (New York: Penguin, 1971), 433. Subsequent page references are given in the text.

2. For important discussions of how Nabokov attempts to preserve the particular through the powers of his prose, which nonetheless is marked by an irrevocable temporal finitude, see Robert Alter, "Nabokov and Memory," *Partisan Review* vol. 54, no. 4 (1991): 620–29, and Michael Wood, *The Magician's Doubts,* 83–102. For an excellent account of Nabokov's notion of memory in relation to the problem of nostalgia, see also Svetlana Boym, *The Future of Nostalgia* (New York: Basic Books, 2001).

3. The same chronophobic awareness leads Van Veen "to sleep on one side only, so as not to hear his heart; he had made the mistake one night in 1920 of calculating the maximal number of its remaining beats (allowing for another half-century), and now the preposterous hurry of the countdown irritated him and increased the rate at which he could hear himself dying" (*Ada*, 446).

4. Boyd, *Nabokov's Ada: The Place of Consciousness* (Ann Arbor, MI: Ardis Publishing, 1985), 65. The idea that Nabokov seeks to transcend time and finitude is a guiding thread in all of Boyd's studies, which in addition to the book on *Ada* include *Vladimir Nabokov: The Russian Years* (Princeton: Princeton University Press, 1990), *Vladimir Nabokov: The American Years* (Princeton: Princeton University Press, 1991), and *Nabokov's Pale Fire: The Magic of Artistic Discovery* (Princeton: Princeton University Press, 1999). Another major and influential study that maintains Nabokov's visions of a life beyond death is Vladimir Alexandrov's *Nabokov's Otherworld* (Princeton: Princeton University Press, 1991). See also Alex de Jonge's early essay "Nabokov's Uses of Pattern," which prefigures Boyd's and Alexandrov's understanding of Nabokov's metaphysics. De Jonge holds that for Nabokov "time must be denied or overcome in order to establish the truth," namely "that nothing is ever lost, and that apparent loss is an illusion, the creation of a partial and blinkered consciousness." De Jonge, "Nabokov's Uses of Pattern," in *Vladimir Nabokov: A Tribute*, ed. P. Quenell (London: Morrow & Co., 1972), 72.

5. Boyd, *Vladimir Nabokov: The Russian Years*, 10.

6. See, for example, *Vladimir Nabokov: The Russian Years*, 283, and *Nabokov's Ada*, 73.

7. Boyd, *Nabokov's Ada*, 65.

8. See also Martin Hägglund, "Nabokov's Afterlife: A Reply to Brian Boyd," *New Literary History*, vol. 37, no. 2 (2006): 479–481.

9. Boyd, *Nabokov's Ada*, 65.

10. Boyd, *Nabokov's Ada*, 72.

11. Boyd, *Nabokov's Ada*, 74, and *Nabokov's Pale Fire*, 258.

12. Boyd, *Nabokov's Ada*, 73.

13. Michael Wood, *The Magician's Doubts*, 220. The theme of incest in *Ada* further underlines this point and can helpfully be elucidate through a comparison with the treatment of the same theme in the Romantic tradition. As Peter Brooks has argued, "throughout the Romantic tradition, it is perhaps most notably the image of incest (of the fraternal-sororal variety) that hovers as the sign of a passion interdicted because its fulfillment would be too perfect, a discharge indistinguishable from death, the very cessation of narrative movement. Narrative is in a state of temptation to oversameness, and where we have no literal threat of incest (as in Chateaubriand, or Faulkner) lovers choose to turn the beloved into a soul sister so that possession will be either impossible or mortal: Goethe's Werther and Lotte, for instance; or Rousseau's *La Nouvelle Héloïse*." Brooks, *Reading for the Plot: Design and Intention in Narrative* (Cambridge, MA: Harvard University Press, 1984), 109. In contrast, *Ada* takes up the incest motif and frees it of guilt and anxiety, insisting on the happy consummation of Van and Ada's love. The tragic drama of desire is thus shown to reside not in a barred access or a taboo that makes the object of desire unattainable, but rather in the temporal finitude that animates and agonizes the very fulfillment of love. *Ada* here abounds with references to

Chateaubriand's *René* in particular. While René and his sister Amélie die unhappy, consumed by guilt and having never consummated their love, Van and Ada live happily ever after, while being haunted by the shadow of loss and death that is intrinsic to happiness itself.

14. Genette, *Narrative Discourse,* 222. Subsequent page references are given in the text.

15. See here also Michael Wood's analysis of the narration of Lucette's suicide and his eloquent description of the pathos of the scene of writing: "the sight of this old man dictating a death he can scarcely bear to think about thickens and darkens the story without reducing its impact in the least . . . Lucette's death is not described, and he can't really imagine it. What we see is his attempt to write it, with its combination of uncertain tone, distraction, a deep regret that is not quite guilt, and patches of spectacular verbal success" (*The Magician's Doubts,* 223).

16. Robert Alter, "*Ada,* or the Perils of Paradise," in *Vladimir Nabokov: A Tribute,* 118.

17. Note that Ronald Oranger can be read as Ronald Or Anger, which underlines the character trait that can be discerned from his notes.

18. To be clear, I regard the difference between Proust and Nabokov on this score as a difference of degree rather than of essence. Thus, I do not agree with Genette's assessment that "Marcel's act of narrating bears no mark of duration, or of division; it is instantaneous . . . a single moment without progression" (*Narrative Discourse,* 223). Rather, as Landy has argued in detail, "the apparently homogeneous narrative of the *Recherche* in fact comprises several superimposed layers, each one deposited by a separate narrating instance, a separate diachronic *moi.* . . . Subtle shifts in tone are detectable across the main body of the novel, from the bright, extroverted shades of the first third to the dark insularity of the last; in addition, its narrator gradually countenances a greater degree of complexity in the world, acknowledging for example that societies and individuals change in and of themselves, as well as in relation to the observer. . . . Proust, in other words, is using the temporal aspect of his narrative to convey an inner tridimensionality, to make powerfully palpable an existence that not only incorporates a multiplicity of minor selves but also—even when one is merely narrating one's life, and thus barely living it—changes across time" (Landy, *Philosophy as Fiction,* 133). While I fully agree with this incisive analysis, I seek to highlight how Nabokov takes the staging of the act of narration one step further, precisely in order to make the temporality of narration even more "powerfully palpable."

19. For an insightful reading of the telephone in Proust with regard to the question of technological mediation, see Danius, *The Senses of Modernism,* 12–17.

4. READING: FREUD, LACAN, DERRIDA

1. Freud, "On Transience," 14:305/10:358. References to Freud refer to the English translation first, followed by reference to the German *Gesammelte Werke,* 18 volumes, ed. A. Freud (Frankfurt am Main: S. Fischer, 1968–1978), with volume number followed by page number. References to the English tradition are to the *Standard Edition,* 24 volumes, ed. J. Strachey (London: Hogarth Press, 1953–1974), except in the case of "Timely Reflections on War and Death," where I refer to Shaun Whiteside's

new translation in Freud, *On Murder, Mourning and Melancholia* (London: Penguin, 2005). In some cases translations have been modified and throughout I have changed the standard translation of *Trieb* from "instinct" to "drive."

2. My thinking of libidinal economics is indebted to Henry Staten's exceptional books *Nietzsche's Voice* (Ithaca, NY: Cornell University Press, 1990) and *Eros in Mourning*. Staten argues that the libidinal economy should be understood in terms of a "dialectic of mourning" which "begins with the process of attachment to, or cathexis of, an object, without which mourning would never arise, and includes all the moments of libidinal relation in general (the moments of libidinal approach, attachment, and loss), as well as the strategies of deferral, avoidance, or transcendence that arise in the response to the threat of loss—strategies by which the self is 'economized' against the libidinal expenditure involved in mourning. . . . As soon as desire is something felt by a mortal being for a mortal being, eros (as desire-in-general) will always be to some degree agitated by the anticipation of loss—an anticipation that operates even with regard to what is not yet possessed. This anticipation calls forth the strategies of libidinal economization" (*Eros in Mourning*, xi–xii). Staten goes on to trace the dialectic of mourning in masterful readings of a number of canonical texts in the Western tradition. Similarly, in *Nietzsche's Voice* Staten pursues a very powerful "psychodialectical reading" of the strategies of libidinal economization in Nietzsche's texts.

3. Freud, *Beyond the Pleasure Principle*, 18:28/13:28. Subsequent page references are given in the text.

4. Freud, "Timely Reflections on War and Death," 192/10:353. Subsequent page references given in the text.

5. Letter to Jones on October 27, 1928, in *The Complete Correspondence of Sigmund Freud and Ernest Jones*, ed. R. A. Paskauskas (Cambridge, MA: Belknap Press of Harvard University Press, 1993), 652–53.

6. Freud, "Mourning and Melancholia," 14:257/10:445. Subsequent page references are given in the text.

7. See in particular Freud's *The Ego and the Id*. For a perspicacious analysis of the shift in Freud's conception of mourning from "Mourning and Melancholia" to *The Ego and the Id*, see Judith Butler, *The Psychic Life of Power* (Stanford, CA: Stanford University Press, 1997), chapters 5 and 6. I want to underline, however, that the shift in Freud's conception of mourning should not lead one to deny the necessity of a violent severing from the other in the experience of mourning. Butler herself does not make this mistake, but it is a move that her analysis has been taken to support. An instructive example is Tammy Clewell's influential and in many ways thoughtful and nuanced essay "Mourning Beyond Melancholia" (in *Journal of American Psychoanalytical Association* vol. 52, no. 1, 2004: 43–67). Clewell reads Freud's insistence on the necessity of "killing off" the attachment to the other in mourning as an effect of the assumption that there is "a subject who might exist without its losses, a subject capable of repudiating attachments to lost others" (60), whereas "all this changes" (60) in the later period beginning with *The Ego and the Id* (1923). On Clewell's account, Freud's later work would allow us to "reconceive the unresolved grief in melancholic mourning as a foundation for an affirmative theory of endless mourning" (56) and thus lead us "toward an affirmation of enduring attachments that no work of mourning can sever" (56, see also

64–65). It suffices, however, to consider *Inhibitions, Symptoms and Anxiety* (1926) to see that this is not the case. Freud here reiterates his early analysis of the necessity of a violent severing from the lost other, where the task of the work of mourning is "to carry out this withdrawal from the object in all those situations where the object was the focus of intense cathexis. The painful nature of this separation fully accords with our explanation, given the intense cathexis—caused by unassuageable longing—that occurs during the reproduction of the various situations in which the subject has to undo the ties that bound him to his object" (20:172/14:205). In contrast, Clewell asserts that for the later Freud "mourning no longer entails abandoning the object and reinvesting the free libido in a new one; it no longer entails accepting consolation in the form of an external substitute for the loss. . . . Rather, working through depends on taking the lost other into the structure of one's own identity, a form of preserving the lost object in and as the self" (61). One should here wonder why Clewell thinks that substitution and incorporation are mutually exclusive alternatives. Furthermore, one should ask how she imagines that one could ever survive the loss of the other without reinvesting libido in something else and finding some sort of substitute for what has been lost. The fact that there is no sovereign subject who can survive intact through this process of substitution and reinvestment does not make the violence of mourning any less necessary. On the contrary, it means that the subject itself—as constituted by the attachment—suffers from and is violently altered by the process of severing, substituting, and reinvesting.

8. Derrida, "Dialanguages," trans. P. Kamuf, in *Points . . .* , ed. E. Weber (Stanford, CA: Stanford University Press, 1995), 152; *Points de Suspension,* ed. E. Weber (Paris: Galilée, 1992), 161.

9. Derrida, *For What Tomorrow,* trans. J. Fort (Stanford, CA: Stanford University Press, 2004), 159; *De Quoi Demain* (Paris: Fayard and Galilée, 2001), 257. Subsequent page references are given in the text.

10. Derrida, "Rams," trans. T. Dutoit and P. Romanski, in *Sovereignties in Question,* ed. T. Dutoit and O. Pasanen (New York: Fordham University Press, 2005), 160; *Béliers* (Paris: Galilée, 2003), 74.

11. My argument here can helpfully be compared to Schopenhauer's argument against suicide in *The World as Will and Representation,* vol. 1, trans. E. F. J. Payne (New York: Dover, 1969). Schopenhauer's notion of desire is the full-blown metaphysical version of the model that Freud adopts with his notion of the death drive. For Schopenhauer, the will (which he understands as the structure of human desire) aims to achieve a "permanent fulfillment which completely and forever satisfies its craving," a "contentment that cannot again be disturbed" (362), an "unshakable peace" that would entail a "deliverance from life and suffering" (398, 397). The problem, however, is that the very activity of willing generates unrest and thereby prevents the will from achieving its aim. Furthermore, in willing something, we expose ourselves both to the possible frustration of not attaining what we want and to the possible agony of losing it, just as in desiring something we can never come to rest completely but rather bound to go "from joy to sorrow" (411) due to the temporality of every attained fulfillment. As Schopenhauer puts it, "so long as our consciousness is filled by our will, so long as we are given up to the throng of desires with its constant hopes and fears, so long as we are the subject of willing, we never obtain lasting happiness or peace" (196). The proper

aim of the will is therefore *not* to will and the proper aim of desire is *not* to desire. To achieve such an aim it is vain to commit suicide, according to Schopenhauer, since the one who commits suicide is still motivated by the will-to-live. "The suicide wills life, and is dissatisfied merely with the conditions on which it has come to him. Therefore he by no means gives up the will-to-live, but merely life, since he destroys the individual phenomenon. He wills life, wills the unchecked existence and affirmation of the body; but the combination of circumstances does not allow of these, and the result for him is great suffering. . . . Just because the suicide cannot cease willing, he ceases to live; and the will affirms itself here even through the cessation of its own phenomenon, because it can no longer affirm itself otherwise" (398–99). In contrast, the negation of the will-to-live that Schopenhauer advocates does not lead to suicide, since it makes one completely indifferent to suffering, in favor of "that peace that is higher than all reason, that ocean-like calmness of the spirit, that deep tranquility," which Schopenhauer links to the ascetics "who have overcome the world, in whom the will, having reached complete self-knowledge, has found itself again in everything, and then freely denied itself, and who then merely wait to see the last trace of the will vanish with the body that is animated by that trace" (411). Schopenhauer is thus quite explicit that on his account the aim of the will is the nothingness of death: "we freely acknowledge that what remains after the complete abolition of the will is, for all who are still full of the will, assuredly nothing" (411–12). Yet Schopenhauer can only present such nothingness as a desirable "peace" and "tranquility" by assuming that the will precedes the bond to life and can remain after its self-negation to experience nothingness as "peace" and "tranquility." As soon as we recognize, however, that the bond to the affectivity of life is the condition of possibility of the will—rather than an effect of willing—Schopenhauer's argument is undermined. The will can never undo its own affectivity, since the very attempt to do so is affected by its own attempt to undo affectivity. Before any act of will, one is *bound* to affectivity, and this bond can never be untied, since without it there could be no experience at all, including any experience of "peace" and "tranquility." While Schopenhauer denigrates actual suicide as a vain attempt to escape suffering, his own argument thereby exhibits the structure of a much more naïve suicide fantasy, in which one imagines that one can do away with oneself and still be there to enjoy the peace afterward.

12. See Derrida, *The Post Card: From Socrates to Freud and Beyond,* trans. A. Bass (Chicago: University of Chicago Press, 1987), 259–409/277–437, in particular 389, 399–402; *La Carte Postale: de Socrate à Freud et au-delà* (Paris: Flammarion, 1980), 415–16, 426–29. See also the trenchant commentary on binding in Geoffrey Bennington's "Derridabase," in *Jacques Derrida* (Chicago: University of Chicago Press, 1993) and the perceptive reading of Freud in Samuel Weber's *The Legend of Freud* (Stanford, CA: Stanford University Press, 2000). Three other insightful readings of *Beyond the Pleasure Principle* can be found in Jonathan Lear's *Happiness, Death, and the Remainder of Life* (Cambridge, MA: Harvard University Press, 2000), Cathy Caruth's *Unclaimed Experience: Trauma, Narrative, History* (Baltimore: Johns Hopkins University Press, 1996), and Jean Laplanche's *Life and Death in Psychoanalysis,* trans. J. Mehlman (Baltimore: Johns Hopkins University Press, 1976). Lear pursues a critique of the teleological assumptions that inform Freud's notion of the death drive and declares, in a memorable phrase, that "the very activity of taking the death drive seriously

is a resistance. It is a resistance to seeing a trauma at the core of psychoanalytic theory. In short, there is no such thing as the death drive" (62). Caruth's reading of *Beyond the Pleasure Principle* links the temporality of trauma to the problem of survival in an illuminating way, but her important analysis does not lead her to take issue with the notion of the death drive, although I think that her observations can be employed to that end. Laplanche identifies a "major contradiction" in Freud's notion of the death drive, which "consists in attributing to a single 'drive' the tendency towards the radical elimination of all tension, the supreme form of the pleasure principle, and the masochistic search for unpleasure, which, in all logic, can only be interpreted as an increase of tension" (108); yet Laplanche nevertheless maintains that "the death drive is the very soul, the constitutive principle, of libidinal circulation" (124). The latter conclusion is challenged by Judith Butler's incisive essay "The Pleasures of Repetition" (in *Pleasure Beyond the Pleasure Principle*, ed. R. A. Glick and S. Bone, New Haven: Yale University Press, 1990), which calls into question the idea that the death drive provides adequate conceptual resources for understanding the phenomena of sadism and masochism that Freud seeks to explain.

13. Derrida, *The Post Card*, 401; *La Carte Postale*, 428. Subsequent page references are given in the text.

14. Derrida, *The Post Card*, 33; *La Carte Postale*, 38. I return to the context of this quote in the Conclusion.

15. Derrida, "Différance," in *Margins of Philosophy*, trans. A. Bass (Chicago: University of Chicago Press, 1982), 19, trans. mod.; *Marges—de la philosophie* (Paris: Minuit, 1972), 20. Subsequent page references are given in the text.

16. Derrida, "Freud and the Scene of Writing," in *Writing and Difference*, trans. A. Bass (London: Routledge, 1978), 203, 202; *L'écriture et la différence* (Paris: Seuil, 1967), 302, 300–01. Subsequent page references given in the text.

17. Derrida, *Rogues: Two Essays on Reason*, trans. P.-A. Brault and M. Naas (Stanford, CA: Stanford University Press, 2005), 45; *Voyous. Deux essais sur la raison* (Paris: Galilée, 2003), 71.

18. Lacan, "Seminar on 'The Purloined Letter,'" in *The Purloined Poe*, ed. J. P. Muller and W. J. Richardson (Baltimore: Johns Hopkins University Press, 1988), 53, 39.

19. The most influential argument against Derrida's critique of Lacan is the one presented by Barbara Johnson in her essay "The Frame of Reference: Poe, Lacan, Derrida" (reprinted in *The Purloined Poe*, 213–251), which is brilliant in its own right but does not assess Derrida's thinking of desire. In the Conclusion to this book, I return to the latter through a reading of Derrida's "Envois" in *The Post Card*, showing that they perform an implicit, chronilibidinal critique of Lacan that is more powerful than the explicit one formulated in the essay on Lacan in the same book. Drawing on Johnson's account, Andrea Hurst has recently sought to "undo the axial argument of Derrida's criticism" of Lacan in *The Post Card*. See her *Derrida Vis-à-vis Lacan* (New York: Fordham University Press, 2008), 376. It is striking, however, that Hurst does not take into account Derrida's reading of *Beyond the Pleasure Principle* in *The Post Card* and assimilates the logic of deconstruction to the logic of the death drive without even addressing Derrida's notion of bindinal economy. According to Hurst, "'originary finitude'" is "the Derridean equivalent of Lacan's notion of 'lack'" (161), which is exactly the thesis

that I contest. A lucid and challenging critique of Derrida's reading of Lacan, which also draws on Johnson, can be found in William Egginton's *The Philosopher's Desire: Psychoanalysis, Interpretation, and Truth* (Stanford, CA: Stanford University Press, 2007). Egginton cogently demonstrates that Lacan's notion of truth cannot be assimilated to the classical form of truth as *adaequatio intellectus et rei* or to a simple schema of veiling/unveiling. The "truth" of the letter is rather its endless referral and the impossibility of a full identity (91–92, 96). This point is well taken, but it does not address the difference between the psychoanalytic and the deconstructive conception of desire, which I seek to elaborate here. Egginton reduces Derrida's critique of Lacan to the assumption that "psychoanalysis believes that [the lost object] actually exists out there in the world somewhere or in the past" (95, see also 107). While Egginton rightly maintains that psychoanalysis does not have to subscribe to such a belief, but rather analyzes it as phantasmatic, he does not take into account the logic of survival that on my account is at the heart of the deconstructive and chronolibidinal challenge to the Lacanian logic of lack. In a subsequent response to my work, Egginton has argued that the notion of chronolibido is indeed compatible with Lacan's thinking, provided that we take into account the register of the drive in Lacan; see Egginton, "On Radical Atheism, Chronolibidinal Reading, and Impossible Desires," *CR: The New Centennial Review* 9.1 (2009): 191–208. As in the case of Adrian Johnston's Lacanian response to my work (which I address at the end of this chapter), Egginton's rich and thoughtful response has pushed me to make my arguments more precise.

20. Lacan, *The Seminar of Jacques Lacan, Book VII: The Ethics of Psychoanalysis, 1959–1960,* ed. J-A. Miller, trans. D. Porter (New York: W. W. Norton, 1992), 52; *Le Séminaire de Jacques Lacan, Livre VII: L'éthique de la psychanalyse* (Paris: Seuil, 1986), 65. Subsequent page references are given in the text.

21. For Lacan's remarks on the drive, see in particular *Seminar XI* and *Seminar XX*. For instructive commentary on Lacan's notion of the drive, see Alenka Zupancic, *Ethics of the Real* (London: Verso, 2000), and Joan Copjec, *Imagine There's No Woman: Ethics and Sublimation* (Cambridge, MA: MIT Press, 2003).

22. See also Zupancic, who points out that the ontological lack of being is the common denominator for both desire and the drive in Lacan (*Ethics of the Real,* 242).

23. See also Copjec's formulation that "The jouissance of the drive, of the organ of the libido, *replaces* the jouissance attributed to the primordial union, the blissful state of the body without organs" (*Imagine There's No Woman,* 64, my emphasis).

24. Bruce Fink, *The Lacanian Subject: Between Language and Jouissance* (Princeton: Princeton University Press, 1995), 94.

25. Adrian Johnston, *Time Driven: Metapsychology and the Splitting of the Drive* (Evanston: Northwestern University Press, 2005), 151, see also 375. Subsequent page references are given in the text.

26. See Lacan, *Le Séminaire de Jacques Lacan, Livre XVII: L'envers de la psychanalyse,* ed. J-A. Miller (Paris: Seuil, 1991), 51, and Johnston's commentary in *Time Driven,* 237–38. For Johnston's critique of Freud's notion of the death drive, see *Time Driven,* 127, 176–181.

27. Lacan, *The Seminar of Jacques Lacan, Book XX: Encore, On Feminine Sexuality, The Limits of Love and Knowledge, 1972–1973,* ed. J-A. Miller, trans. B. Fink (New York:

W. W. Norton, 1998), 111. The French original reads: "*Ce n'est pas ça*—voilà le cri par où se distingue la jouissance obtenue, de celle attendue." *Le Séminaire de Jacques Lacan, Livre XX: Encore, 1972–1973,* ed. J-A. Miller (Paris: Seuil, 1975), 101.

28. Johnston, "Life Terminable and Interminable: The Undead and the Afterlife of the Afterlife—A Friendly Disagreement with Martin Hägglund," *CR: The New Centennial Review* 9.1 (2009): 147–189, 166.

CONCLUSION

1. For incisive accounts of how Swann in mourning haunts the final volume of the *Recherche,* see also Richard Terdiman's *Present Past: Modernity and the Memory Crisis* (Ithaca, NY: Cornell University Press, 1993), chapter 6, and Wood, "The Death of Paradise."

2. Derrida, *The Post Card,* 397; *La Carte Postale,* 424. Subsequent page references are given in the text.

3. Derrida himself points out that his argument with Lacan is first of all inscribed in the *Envois,* but he does not elaborate a reading of the latter. See Derrida, *Resistance of Psychoanalysis,* trans. P-A. Brault and M. Naas (Stanford, CA: Stanford University Press, 1998), 63; *Résistances de la psychanalyse* (Paris: Galilée, 1996), 81–82.

4. See David Wills, *Matchbook: Essays in Deconstruction* (Stanford, CA: Stanford University Press, 2005), 65.

5. Nevertheless, as we saw in Chapter 4, Derrida himself sometimes invokes the notion of the death drive with apparent approval. To inherit his work in chronolibidinal terms one must therefore distinguish between those aspects that allow us to think the logic of survival and those aspects that do not follow through on this logic. For example, in *Archive Fever* Derrida provides compelling resources for a chronolibidinal reading of how the desire to archive presupposes the threat of a radical destruction that may eradicate what one is trying to preserve. As Derrida emphasizes, there would be "no archive desire without the radical finitude, without the possibility of a forgetfulness which does not limit itself to repression," namely, the possibility of a "radical destruction without which no archive desire or fever would happen." Derrida, *Archive Fever: A Freudian Impression,* trans. E. Prenowitz (Chicago: University of Chicago Press, 1998), 19, 94/ *Mal d'archive: Une impression freudienne* (Paris: Galilée, 1995), 38, 146. The desire to archive is thus an effect of the chronolibidinal investment in living on. Without the chronophobic apprehension of the threat of destruction there would be chronophilic desire to preserve anything in the archive. Derrida's misleading move, however, is to align the threat of radical destruction with the death drive. For example, he writes that there is "a death drive without which there would not in effect be any desire or any possibility for the archive" (29/52). Contrary to Derrida's claim here, radical destructibility does not stem from a death drive, for at least two reasons. First, radical destructibility is inherent to finitude in general, so the archive would be threatened by destruction even if there were no drive to destroy it: any number of random events can destroy it. Second, insofar as there is a drive to destroy the archive it does not stem from a death drive but from the investment in survival,

which accounts *both* for acts of preservation *and* acts of destruction. The investment in survival gives rise to the desire to institute or maintain archives, but it also gives rise to the desire to destroy archives. Indeed, as we have seen, the eradication of what does *not* survive is intrinsic to the movement of survival itself. To institute and maintain a certain archive is necessarily to violate other archives: whether the violence consists in ignoring, subordinating, or destroying those archives. And even if one comes to be driven to destroy the archive without in turn wanting to archive anything, wanting to leave no traces, this response to finitude still derives from an investment in survival. Archive fever—as the co-implication of being passionate for and being sick of the archive—should be understood in terms of the double bind of survival rather than in terms of the death drive.

6. Another striking example of such literary writing in Derrida's oeuvre is his *Circumfession,* which I have elsewhere analyzed in detail; see Hägglund, *Radical Atheism,* 146–61.

Acknowledgments

I have worked on the ideas presented in this book throughout my adult life, from the first book I wrote and published in Swedish to the dissertation I defended at Cornell University and beyond. To those whose confidence sustained me during some difficult years in Sweden I will always be grateful: Anders Lundberg and Niklas Brismar Pålsson were my first intellectual friends, Mikael van Reis my first, inspiring editor, and Horace Engdahl the one who made me dream of writing on literature in the first place. At Cornell, Jonathan Culler's outstanding intellectual example and personal dedication taught me how an academic life should be led, while his feedback made my work better. Richard Klein believed in me with a strength and generosity that always carried me further, along with his insightful comments on my writings. I am also very grateful to Walter Cohen for his careful readings of my work and his acute sense of the demands of literary criticism.

At Harvard, I was fortunate to complete this book in the most wonderful institutional setting I can imagine: the Society of Fellows, run by Diana Morse and Kelly Katz with irreplaceable care and wisdom. As Senior Fellows, Elaine Scarry and Bill Todd were always ready to offer guidance and intellectual insight and their support of my work has been invaluable. Noah Feldman in turn offered a combination of brilliance, enthusiasm, and critical vigilance that inspired me to think harder and write better, while Amartya Sen asked exactly the right question about "survival," which led me to a deeper articulation of my argument.

Numerous friends helped along the way. Rocío Zambrana's philosophical insight, our many formative conversations, and her feedback on drafts were important for the book on every level. David E. Johnson helpfully and generously commented on several versions of the manuscript, which also benefited from comments by Joshua Andresen, Samir Haddad, Richard Moran, Siobhan Phillips, and Jessica Smith. Nathan Brown not only proved to be a most lucid interlocutor but also invited me to speak at both UC Davis and in Zagreb, where we had illuminating discussions. With gracious collegiality, Jason Aftosmis shared his expertise in Greek with me as we read the *Symposium* together on a memorable afternoon. And incisive as always, Corina Tarnita studied the entire manuscript with a mathematician's sense of precision, pinpointing details that needed adjustment while encouraging me with her deep understanding of the stakes of the book.

I owe a special debt to the many careful and demanding respondents to my previous book in English, *Radical Atheism*. I here especially want to thank the philosophers who challenged me on the question of desire: William Egginton, Adrian Johnston, Ernesto Laclau, and Michael Naas. Their trenchant, written responses to *Radical Atheism* have directly pushed me to refine my thinking and develop my arguments in this book, so I hope they can read it as a belated response to the important questions they raised. I also want to thank Derek Attridge and the two anonymous readers for Harvard University Press, whose clear-sighted criticisms led to significant revisions of the manuscript and inspired me to write the Conclusion in response to their concerns. As I indicate in the book, Henry Staten's work has been a great inspiration for my own and his comments on the final draft led to valuable additions. Throughout this process, Lindsay Waters has been an exemplary editor and I would like to express my profound gratitude to him.

Thanks to kind invitations, I was able to present material from the book at various universities, where I learned a lot from engaged audiences and interlocutors. I especially want to thank Bruce Robbins for organizing a seminar on chronolibido at Columbia (with Mark Sanders as an insightful respondent) and John Hamilton for doing the same at Harvard.

For their generous hospitality and critical engagement, I also thank the Department of Philosophy at the American University of Beirut, the Department of English and Comparative Literature at Columbia University, the Department of Comparative Literature at Harvard University, the Departments of Philosophy and Comparative Literature at Northwestern University, the Department of Comparative Literature at SUNY, Buffalo, the Department of English at University of California, Davis, and the Departments of English and French at Wadham College, Oxford University. At different stages, research for the book was supported by scholarships from the Helge Ax:son Johnson Foundation and the Birgit and Gad Rausing Foundation, as well as by fellowships from the Charlotte W. Newcombe Foundation, the Thanks to Scandinavia Fund, the American Scandinavian Foundation, Cornell University's Sage Fund, and the Fulbright Commission. I want to express my deep gratitude to all these organizations and institutions for the path they made possible for me and their commitment to higher education.

Finally, I am happy to concede that my mother came up with the title for this book, which owes more than I can say to my family. I thank my sisters, Karin and Maria, for always being there and for continuing to teach me about life in their distinctive ways. And I thank my parents, Hans-Lennart and Margareta, for giving me more than I ever can return. From day one, they have sustained me with a love and support that is beyond measure, while offering in their own marriage the most inspiring example of partnership that I can imagine. This book is dedicated to them.

Index